Burgess | A Clockwork Orange

Fremdsprachentexte | Englisch

Anthony Burgess
A Clockwork Orange

Herausgegeben von Claus Melchior

Reclam

RECLAMS UNIVERSAL-BIBLIOTHEK Nr. 19897
Alle Rechte vorbehalten
Copyright für diese Ausgabe
© 1992, 2014 Philipp Reclam jun. GmbH & Co. KG, Stuttgart
Durchgesehene Ausgabe 2014 (s. dazu Editorische Notiz, S. 235)
Copyright für den englischen Text
© 2012 by the Estate of Anthony Burgess
A CLOCKWORK ORANGE. The Restored Edition.
Edited with an Introduction and Notes by Andrew Biswell
Foreword by Martin Amis
published by William Heinemann, London, 2012
Umschlagfoto: Malcolm McDowell als Alex im Film
A Clockwork Orange von Stanley Kubrick, 1971
(Filmarchiv Austria, Wien)
Gestaltung: Friedrich Forssman, Cornelia Feyll
Gesamtherstellung: Reclam, Ditzingen. Printed in Germany 2014
RECLAM, UNIVERSAL-BIBLIOTHEK und
RECLAMS UNIVERSAL-BIBLIOTHEK sind eingetragene Marken
der Philipp Reclam jun. GmbH & Co. KG, Stuttgart
ISBN 978-3-15-019897-1
www.reclam.de

A Clockwork Orange

SHEPHERD. I would that there were no age between ten and three-and-twenty, or that youth would sleep out the rest; for there is nothing in the between but getting wenches with child, wronging the ancientry, stealing, fighting –

(Shakespeare, *The Winter's Tale*, Act III, Scene 3)

[Titel] **clockwork:** Uhrwerk. | 4 **wench:** Mädchen. | **ancientry** (arch.): alte Leute.

Part One

One

"What's it going to be then, eh?"

There was me, that is Alex, and my three droogs, that is Pete, Georgie, and Dim, Dim being really dim, and we sat is the Korova Milkbar making up our rassoodocks what to do with the evening, a flip dark chill winter bastard though dry. The Korova Milkbar was a milk-plus mesto, and you may, O my brothers, have forgotten what these mestos were like, things changing so skorry these days and everybody very quick to forget, newspapers not being much read neither. Well, what they sold there was milk plus something else. They had no licence for selling liquor, but there was no law yet against prodding some of the new veshches which they used to put into the old moloko, so you could peet it with vellocet or synthemesc or drencrom or one or two other veshches which would give you a nice quiet horrorshow fifteen minutes admiring Bog And All His Holy Angels And Saints in your left shoe with lights bursting all

3 **eh?** (coll.): hä?, he? | 4 **droog** (auch: *droogie*; N.): Freund, Kumpel. | 5 **dim** (coll., fig.): schwer von Begriff. | 6 **korova** (Russ.): Kuh. | **to make up one's rassoodock** (N.): sich entschließen. | 7 **flip** (coll.): frech; hier: Bedeutung unklar. | **chill**: frostig, eisig. | 8 **milk-plus** (N.): mit Drogen angereicherte Milch. | **mesto** (N.): Ort, ‚Laden‘. | 10 **skorry** (N.): schnell. | 13 **liquor**: alkoholisches Getränk. | 14 **to prod** (N.): Kurzform von *to produce.* | **veshch** (N.): Ding. | 15 **moloko** (N.): Milch. | 16 **to peet** (N.): trinken. | **vellocet / synthemesc / drencrom** (N.): Drogen. Verbindet man das »1« aus *vellocet* mit den Initialen der beiden anderen Wörter, so ergibt sich LSD. | 17 f. **horrorshow** (N.): gut, toll. | 18 **Bog** (N.): Gott; Wortspiel mit (slang) *bog* ›Lokus‹ und *bog(e)y* ›Teufel‹.

over your mozg. Or you could peet milk with knives in it, as we used to say, and this would sharpen you up and make you ready for a bit of dirty twenty-to-one, and that was what we were peeting this evening I'm starting off the story with. 5

Our pockets were full of deng, so there was no real need from the point of view of crasting any more pretty polly to tolchock some old veck in an alley and viddy him swim in his blood while we counted the takings and divided by four, nor to do the ultra-violent on some shivering starry 10 grey-haired ptitsa in a shop and go smecking off with the till's guts. But, as they say, money isn't everything.

The four of us were dressed in the heighth of fashion, which in those days was a pair of black very tight tights with the old jelly mould, as we called it, fitting on the 15 crutch underneath the tights, this being to protect and also a sort of a design you could viddy clear enough in a certain light, so that I had one in the shape of a spider, Pete had a rooker (a hand, that is), Georgie had a very fancy one of a flower, and poor old Dim had a very hound-and-horny one 20

1 **mozg** (N.): Gehirn. | 2 **to sharpen s.o. up:** jdn. anregen, ‚anmachen‘. | 3 **twenty-to-one** (N.): wörtl.: Zwanzig gegen einen; Gewalt; auch: Rhyming Slang für *fun*. | 6 **deng** (N.): Geld. | 7 **to crast** (N.): stehlen. | **pretty polly** (N.): Geld. | 8 **to tolchock** (N.): schlagen. | **veck** (N.): Person, Mann, Kerl. | **alley:** (schmale) Gasse. | **to viddy** (N.): sehen. | 9 **takings:** Einnahmen. | 10 **to do the ultra-violent** (N.): vergewaltigen. | **starry** (N.): alt. | 11 **ptitsa** (N.): Frau (von russ. *ptitsa* ›Vogel‹). | **to smeck** (N.): lachen. | 12 **till:** Ladenkasse. | **guts:** Eingeweide; (fig.) Inneres, Inhalt. | 13 **in the heighth of fashion:** nach der neuesten Mode (*heighth* [dial., arch.]: *height*). | 15 **jelly mould:** Puddingform. | 16 **crutch:** *crotch*: Zwickel, Schritt. | 19 **rooker** (auch: *rook*; N.): Hand, Arm. | **fancy:** phantastisch, bunt, ausgefallen. | 20 **hound-and-horny** (N.): gewöhnlich.

of a clown's litso (face, that is), Dim not ever having much of an idea of things and being, beyond all shadow of a doubting thomas, the dimmest of we four. Then we wore waisty jackets without lapels but with these very big built-up shoulders ("pletchoes" we called them) which were a kind of mockery of having real shoulders like that. Then, my brothers, we had these off-white cravats which looked like whipped-up kartoffel or spud with a sort of a design made on it with a fork. We wore our hair not too long and we had flip horrorshow boots for kicking.

"What's it going to be then, eh?"

There were three devotchkas sitting at the counter all together, but there were four of us malchicks and it was usually like one for all and all for one. These sharps were dressed in the heighth of fashion too, with purple and green and orange wigs on their gullivers, each one costing not less than three or four weeks of those sharps' wages, I should reckon, and make-up to match (rainbows round the glazzies, that is, and the rot painted very wide). Then they had long black very straight dresses, and on the groody part

1 **litso** (N.): Gesicht. | 2 f. **beyond all shadow of a doubting thomas** (N.): ohne jeden Zweifel; Anspielung auf den »ungläubigen Thomas«, den an der Auferstehung zweifelnden Jünger Jesu Christi (vgl. Joh. 20,24–29). | 4 **waisty** (N.): *waisted:* tailliert. | **lapel:** (Jacken-)Aufschlag, Revers. | 5 **pletcho** (N.): Schulter. | 6 **mockery:** Spott, Hohn, Nachäffung. | 7 **off-white:** grauweiß, nicht ganz weiß. | **cravat:** Krawatte, breite Halsbinde. | 8 **to whip up:** schlagen, rühren. | **spud** (slang, dial.): Kartoffel. | 12 **devotchka** (N.): Mädchen. | 13 **malchick** (N.): Junge. | 14 **sharp** (N.): Frau; viell. abgeleitet von *sharp and blunt* ›Fotze‹ (Cockney Rhyming Slang für *cunt*). | 16 **gulliver** (N.): Kopf; Anspielung auf den satirischen Roman *Gulliver's Travels* (1726) von Jonathan Swift (1667–1745). | 19 **glazzy** (auch: *glaz*; N.): Auge. | **rot** (N.): Mund. | 20 **groody** (N.): Brust.

of them they had little badges of like silver with different malchicks' names on them – Joe and Mile and suchlike. These were supposed to be the names of the different malchicks they'd spatted with before they were fourteen. They kept looking our way and I nearly felt like saying the three of us (out of the corner of my rot, that is) should go off for a bit of pol and leave poor old Dim behind, because it would be just a matter of kupetting Dim a demi-litre of white but this time with a dollop of synthemesc in it, but that wouldn't really have been playing like the game. Dim was very very ugly and like his name, but he was a horrorshow filthy fighter and very handy with the boot.

"What's it going to be then, eh?"

The chelloveck sitting next to me, there being this long big plushy seat that ran round three walls, was well away with his glazzies glazed and sort of burbling slovos like "Aristotle wishy washy works outing cyclamen get forficulate smartish." He was in the land all right, well away, in orbit, and I knew what it was like, having tried it like everybody

---

1 **badge:** Abzeichen, Kennzeichen, Marke. | 4 **to spat** (N.): (mit jdm.) schlafen. | 7 **pol** (N.): Sex. | 8 **to kupet:** kaufen. | **demi-litre:** halber Liter. | **white** (slang): Weißwein. | 9 **dollop:** Klumpen, Brocken, Happen. | 10 **to play the game** (coll.): sich fair, korrekt verhalten. | 12 **filthy:** schmutzig, dreckig. | **handy:** geschickt, gewandt. | 14 **chell-oveck** (N.): Person, Mann, Kerl. | 15 **plushy:** plüschig, plüschartig; vornehm. | **to be well away** (N.): ‚hinüber', berauscht sein. | 16 **glazed:** glasig (Blick). | **to burble:** plappern. | **slovo** (N.): Wort. | 16 f. **Aristotle:** Aristoteles (384–322 v. Chr.), griechischer Philosoph. | 17 **wishy washy:** labberig, saft- und kraftlos. | **outing:** Ausflug. | **cyclamen:** Alpenveilchen. | **forficulate:** Nonsens-Wort. | 18 **smartish:** gerissen, raffiniert, geistreich. | **in the land** (N.): berauscht, auf einem (Drogen-)Trip. | **orbit:** (Planeten-)Bahn.

else had done, but at this time I'd got to thinking it was a cowardly sort of a veshch, O my brothers. You'd lay there after you'd drunk the old moloko and then you got the messel that everything all round you was sort of in the past. You could viddy it all right, all of it, very clear – tables, the stereo, the lights, the sharps and the malchicks – but it was like some veshch that used to be there but was not there no more. And you were sort of hypnotised by your boot or shoe or a finger-nail as it might be, and at the same time you were sort of picked up by the old scruff and shook like it might be a cat. You got shook and shook till there was nothing left. You lost your name and your body and your self and you just didn't care, and you waited till your boot or your finger-nail got yellow, then yellower and yellower all the time. Then the lights started cracking like atomics and the boot or finger-nail or, as it might be, a bit of dirt on your trouser-bottom turned into a big big big mesto, bigger than the whole world, and you were just going to get introduced to old Bog or God when it was all over. You came back to here and now whimpering sort of, with your rot all squaring up for a boohoohoo. Now, that's very nice but very cowardly. You were not put on this earth just to get in touch with God. That sort of thing could sap all the strength and the goodness out of a chelloveck.

4 **messel** (N.): Gedanke, Idee. | 6 **stereo:** Stereo-Anlage. | 10 **scruff:** Nacken, Genick, ‚Kragen'. | 11 **shook:** *shaken.* | 15 **atomics:** Kurzform von *atomic bombs.* | 20 **to whimper:** wimmern, winseln. | 21 **to square up:** in Position gehen (Boxer). | **boohoohoo:** *boohoo:* lautes Weinen. | 22f. **to get in touch with s. o.:** mit jdm. Kontakt aufnehmen, in Verbindung treten. | 23 **to sap s.th. out of s.o.:** jdm. etwas austreiben (*to sap:* [Kräfte] untergraben, erschöpfen).

"What's it going to be then, eh?"

The stereo was on and you got the idea that the singer's goloss was moving from one part of the bar to another, flying up to the ceiling and then swooping down again and whizzing from wall to wall. It was Berti Laski rasping a real starry oldie called "You Blister My Paint." One of the three ptitsas at the counter, the one with the green wig, kept pushing her belly out and pulling it in in time to what they called the music. I could feel the knives in the old moloko starting to prick, and now I was ready for a bit of twenty-to-one. So I yelped, "Out out out out!" like a doggie, and then I cracked this veck who was sitting next to me and well away and burbling a horrorshow crack on the ooko or earhole, but he didn't feel it and went on with his "Telephonic hardware and when the farfarculule gets rubadubdub." He'd feel it all right when he came to, out of the land.

"Where out?" said Georgie.

"Oh, just to keep walking," I said, "and viddy what turns up, O my little brothers."

So we scatted out into the big winter nochy and walked

---

3 **goloss** (N.): Stimme. | 4 **to swoop down:** herabstoßen, -stürzen. | 5 **whizz:** zischen, schwirren, sausen. | **Laski:** Alle Namen von Sängern und Titel von Pop-Songs sind fiktiv, beinhalten jedoch häufig Anspielungen auf reale Personen; die englische Schriftstellerin Marghanita Laski (1915–1988) verfasste 1961 einen Verriss von Burgess' Roman *The Right to an Answer*. | **to rasp:** krächzen, mit krächzender, kratziger Stimme singen. | 6 **You blister my paint:** Du ziehst Blasen auf meiner Farbe. | 8 **in time:** im Rhythmus. | 10 **to prick:** stechen, pieken. | 11 **to yelp:** kläffen, jaulen. | **doggie:** Hündchen. | 12 **to crack:** schlagen. | 13 **ooko** (N.): Ohr. | 15 **hardware:** Eisen-, Metallwaren. | **farfarculule:** Nonsens-Wort. | **rubadub-dub:** *rubadub:* Taramtamtam (lautmalerisch für: Trommelwirbel). | 20 **to scat** (slang): eilen, eilig aufbrechen. | **nochy** (N.): Nacht.

down Marghanita Boulevard and then turned into Boothby Avenue, and there we found what we were pretty well looking for, a malenky jest to start off the evening with. There was a doddery starry schoolmaster type veck, glasses on and his rot open to the cold nochy air. He had books under his arm and a crappy umbrella and was coming round the corner from the Public Biblio, which not many lewdies used those days. You never really saw many of the older boorjoyce type out after nightfall those days, what with the shortage of police and we fine young malchickiwicks about, and this prof type chelloveck was the only one walking in the whole of the street. So we goolied up to him, very polite, and I said, "Pardon me, brother."

He looked a malenky bit poogly when he viddied the four of us like that, coming up so quiet and polite and smiling, but he said, "Yes? What is it?" in a very loud teacher-type goloss, as if he was trying to show us he wasn't poogly. I said:

"I see you have them books under your arm, brother. It is indeed a rare pleasure these days to come across somebody that still reads, brother."

"Oh," he said, all shaky. "Is it? Oh, I see." And he kept looking from one to the other of we four, finding

1 f. **Marghanita Boulevard / Boothby Avenue:** fiktive Straßennamen; vgl. aber S. 12, Z. 5. | 3 **malenky** (N.): klein, ein bisschen, ein wenig. | 4 **doddery:** schwankend, zittrig; senil, tatterig, vertrottelt. | 6 **crappy** (slang): schäbig. | 7 **public biblio:** öffentliche Bibliothek. | **lewdies** (N.): Leute. | 9 **boorjoyce** (N.): bürgerlich; Bürger; Bürgertum. | **nightfall:** Einbruch der Nacht. | **what with:** infolge, durch; in Anbetracht. | 10 **shortage:** Mangel, Knappheit. | 12 **to gooly** (N.): gehen. | 14 **poogly** (N.): erschrocken, ängstlich.

himself now in the middle of a very smiling and polite square.

"Yes," I said. "It would interest me greatly, brother, if you would kindly allow me to see what books those are that you have under your arm. I like nothing better in this world than a good clean book, brother."

"Clean," he said. "Clean, eh?" And then Pete skvatted these three books from him and handed them round real skorry. Being three, we all had one each to viddy at except for Dim. The one I had was called *Elementary Crystallography*, so I opened it up and said, "Excellent, really first-class," keeping turning the pages. Then I said in a very shocked type goloss, "But what is this here? What is this filthy slovo? I blush to look at this word. You disappoint me, brother, you do really."

"But," he tried, "but, but."

"Now," said Georgie, "here is what I should call real dirt. There's one slovo beginning with an f and another with a c." He had a book called *The Miracle of the Snowflake*.

"Oh," said poor olf Dim, smotting over Peter's shoulder and going too far, like he always did, "it says here what he done to her, and there's a picture and all. Why," he said, "you're nothing but a filthy-minded old skitebird."

---

7 **to skvat** (N.): wegnehmen, (er)greifen. | 10 f. **"Elementary Crystallography"**: *Einführung in die Kristallographie* (Wissenschaft von den chemischen und physikalischen Eigenschaften der Kristalle). | 11 f. **first-class**: erstklassig. | 18 f. **with an f and another with a c**: Gemeint sind vermutl. die Wörter *fuck* und *cunt*. | 21 **to smot** (N.): sehen. | 22 f. **what he done**: *what he did*. | 24 **skitebird**: hier etwa: Wüstling, Schmutzfink (*to skite* [slang]: ‚angeben').

"An old man of your age, brother," I said, and I started to rip up the book I'd got, and the others did the same with the ones they had, Dim and Pete doing a tug-of-war with *The Rhombohedral System.* The starry prof type began to creech: "But those are not mine, those are the property of the municipality, this is sheer wantonness and vandal work," or some such slovos. And he tried to sort of wrest the books back off of us, which was like pathetic. "You deserve to be taught a lesson, brother," I said, "that you do." This crystal book I had was very tough-bound and hard to razrez to bits, being real starry and made in the days when things were made to last like, but I managed to rip the pages up and chuck them in handfulls of like snowflakes, though big, all over this creeching old veck, and then the others did the same with theirs, old Dim just dancing about like the clown he was. "There you are," said Pete. "There's the mackerel of the cornflake for you, you dirty reader of filth and nastiness."

"You naughty old veck, you," I said, and then we began

---

2 **to rip up:** zerreißen. | 3 **tug-of-war:** Tauziehen. | 4 **"The Rhombohedral System":** *Das System der Rhomboeder (rhombohedral:* Adjektiv zu *rhombohedron* ›Rhomboeder‹, ›von sechs gleichen Rauten begrenzte Kristallform‹). | 5 **to creech** (N.): kreischen, schreien, rufen. | 6 **municipality:** Stadtverwaltung. | **sheer wantonness:** reiner, nackter Mutwille, Übermut, reine Böswilligkeit. | 6 f. **vandal work:** Vandalismus, mutwillige Zerstörung. | 7 f. **to wrest s.th. back:** etwas entreißen, entwinden. | 8 **pathetic:** rührend, ergreifend, bemitleidenswert. | 10 **tough-bound:** fest gebunden, mit festem Einband. | 11 **to razrez** (N.): zerreißen. | 13 **to chuck:** (weg)werfen, schmeißen. | 17 **mackerel of the cornflake:** Wortspiel mit *The Miracle of the Snowflake* (vgl. S. 14, Z. 19 f.; *mackerel:* 1. Makrele; 2. [slang] Zuhälter). | **filth:** Schmutz, Dreck. | 18 **nastiness:** Schmutzigkeit, Bosheit, Gemeinheit.

to filly about with him. Pete held his rookers and Georgie sort of hooked his rot wide open for him and Dim yanked out his false zoobies, upper and lower. He threw these down on the pavement and then I treated them to the old boot-crush, though they were hard bastards like, being made of some horrorshow plastic stuff. The old veck began to make sort of chumbling shooms – "wuf waf wof" – so Georgie let go of holding his goobers apart and just let him have one in the toothless rot with his ringy fist, and that made the old veck start moaning a lot then, then out comes the blood, my brothers, real beautiful. So all we did then was to pull his outer platties off, stripping him down to his vest and long underpants (very starry; Dim smecked his head off near), and then Pete kicks him lovely in his pot, and we let him go. He went staggering off, it not having been too hard of a tolchock really, and we had a snigger at him and then riffled through his pockets, Dim dancing round with his crappy umbrella meanwhile, but there wasn't much in them. There were a few starry letters, some of them dating right back to 1960, with "My dearest dearest" in them and all that chepooka, and a keyring and a starry leaky pen. Old Dim gave up his umbrella dance and of

---

1 **to filly** (N.): (herum)spielen, (herum)albern. | 2 f. **to yank out** (coll.): (mit einem Ruck) herausreißen. | 3 **zooby** (N.): Zahn. | 7 **to chumble:** eigtl.: nagen, knabbern; hier wohl eher lautmalerisch für die Sprechweise eines Zahnlosen (Abwandlung von *to mumble* ›murmeln‹). | **shoom** (N.): Laut, Geräusch. | 8 **goober** (N.): Lippe. | 9 **ringy** (N.): *ringed:* beringt, Ringe tragend. | 12 **platties** (N.): Kleidungsstücke. | 13 **vest:** Unterjacke, -hemd. | 14 **pot** (slang): Kurzform von *pot-belly:* Dick-, Spitzbauch. | 16 **tolchock** (N.): Hieb, Schlag. | **snigger:** Kichern. | 17 **to riffle through s.th.:** etwas durcheinanderbringen, durchwühlen. | 21 **chepooka** (N.): Unsinn. | 22 **leaky:** leck, undicht.

course had to start reading one of the letters out loud, like to show the empty street he could read. "My darling one," he recited, in this very high type goloss, "I shall be thinking of you while you are away and hope you will remember to wrap up warm when you go out at night." Then he let out a very shoomny smeck – "Ho ho ho" – pretending to start wiping his yahma with it. "All right," I said. "Let it go, O my brothers." In the trousers of this starry veck there was only a malenky bit of cutter (money, that is) – not more than three gollies – so we gave all his messy little coin the scatter treatment, it being hen-korm to the amount of pretty polly we had on us already. Then we smashed the umbrella and razrezzed his platties and gave them to the blowing winds, my brothers, and then we'd finished with the starry teacher type veck. We hadn't done much, I know, but that was only like the start of the evening and I make no appy polly loggies to thee or thine for that. The knives in the milk-plus were stabbing away nice and horrorshow now.

The next thing was to do the sammy act, which was one way to unload some of our cutter so we'd have more of an incentive like for some shop-crasting, as well as it being a

3 **to recite:** rezitieren, vortragen. | 6 **shoomny** (N.): laut. | **smeck** (N.): Lachen, Gelächter. | 7 **yahma** (N.): Loch. | 9 **cutter** (N.): Geld. | 10 **golly** (N.): Münzeinheit. | **messy:** unordentlich, schmutzig. | 11 **hen-korm** (N.): Kleingeld. | 12 **to smash:** zerschmettern, zerbrechen. | 16 f. **I make no appy polly loggies to thee or thine:** Ich entschuldige mich weder bei dir, euch noch den deinen, euren (*appy polly loggy* [N.]: *apology; thee* [arch.]: *you; thine* [arch.]: *your, yours*). | 18 **to stab:** stechen. | 20 **to do the sammy act** (slang, obs.): einen ausgeben. | 22 **incentive:** Ansporn, Anreiz. | **shop-crasting** (N.): Ladendiebstahl, -einbruch.

way of buying an alibi in advance, so we went into the Duke
of New York on Amis Avenue and sure enough in the snug
there were three or four old baboochkas peeting their black
and suds on SA (State Aid). Now we were the very good
malchicks, smiling good evening to one and all, though
these wrinkled old lighters started to get all shook, their
veiny old rookers trembling round their glasses and making
the suds spill on the table. "Leave us be, lads," said one of
them, her face all mappy with being a thousand years old,
"we're only poor old women." But we just made with the
zoobies, flash flash flash, sat down, rang the bell, and waited for the boy to come. When he came, all nervous and
rubbing his rookers on his grazzy apron, we ordered us four
veterans – a veteran being rum and cherry brandy mixed,
which was popular just then, some liking a dash of lime
in it, that being the Canadian variation. Then I said to the
boy:

"Give these poor old baboochkas over there a nourishing
something. Large Scotchmen all round and something to
take away." And I poured my pocket of deng all over the
table, and the other three did likewise, O my brothers. So

2 **Amis Avenue:** Anspielung auf den englischen Autor Kingsley A.
(1922–1995). | **snug** (slang): (gemütliche) Sitzecke (in einer Bar o. ä.). |
3 **baboochka** (N.): alte Frau. | 3 f. **black and suds:** Gemeint ist vermutl.
Guinness (*suds* [pl.]: **1.** Seifenlauge; **2.** [AE, slang] Bier). | 6 **wrinkled:**
runzlig. | **lighter** (N.): Trinkende(r). | **to get all shook:** *to get all shaken:*
zittern, beben. | 7 **veiny:** geädert. | 8 **to spill:** (ver)schütten. | 9 **mappy** (N.):
gezeichnet, runzlig (von *map*). | 10 f. **to make with the zoobies**
(slang): etwa: die Zähne blitzen lassen, d. h. lächeln (*to make with s.th.:*
etwas zum Einsatz bringen, einsetzen). | 13 **grazzy** (N.): schmutzig,
schmierig. | 15 **dash:** ,Schuss'. | **lime:** Limone(nsaft). | 18 **nourishing:**
nahrhaft. | 19 **Scotchman** (slang): Whisky.

double firegolds were brought in for the scared starry lighters, and they knew not what to do or say. One of them got out "Thanks, lads," but you could see they thought there was something dirty like coming. Anyway, they were each given a bottle of Yank General, cognac that is, to take away, and I gave money for them to be delivered each a dozen of black and suds that following morning, they to leave their stinking old cheenas' addresses at the counter. Then with the cutter that was left over we did purchase, my brothers, all the meat pies, pretzels, cheese-snacks, crisps and chocbars in that mesto, and those too were for the old sharps. Then we said, "Back in a minoota," and the old ptitsas were still saying, "Thanks, lads," and "God bless you, boys," and we were going out without one cent of cutter in our carmans.

"Makes you feel real dooby, that does," said Pete. You could viddy that poor old Dim the dim didn't quite pony all that, but he said nothing for fear of being called gloopy and a domeless wonderboy. Well, we went off now round the corner to Attlee Avenue, and there was this sweets and cancers shop still open. We'd left them alone near three months now and the whole district had been very quiet on

---

1 **firegold** (N.): Whisky. | 5 **Yank General:** fiktiver Markenname (*Yank*: Amerikaner). | 8 **cheena** (N.): Frau. | 10 **meat pie:** Fleischpastete. | **pretzel:** Brezel. | **crisps:** (Kartoffel-)Chips. | 10 f. **chocbar:** Kurzform von *chocolate bar*: Schokoriegel. | 14 f. **carman** (N.): (Hosen-)Tasche. | 17 **to pony** (N.): verstehen. | 18 **gloopy** (N.): blöd. | 19 **domeless wonderboy** (N.): Schimpfwort für jdn., der keine Ahnung hat. | 20 **Attlee:** Clement A. (1883–1967), englischer Premierminister 1945–1951. In seine Amtszeit fallen die Begründung des Wohlfahrtsstaats und die Unabhängigkeit Indiens. | 21 **cancer** (N.): Zigarette (von *cancer* ›Krebs‹).

the whole, so the armed millicents or rozz patrols weren't round there much, being more north of the river these days. We put our maskies on – new jobs these were, real horrorshow, wonderfully done, really; they were like faces of historical personalities (they have you the name when you bought) and I had Disraeli, Pete had Elvis Presley, Georgie had Henry VIII and poor old Dim had a poet called Peebee Shelley; they were a real like disguise, hair and all, and they were some very special plastic veshch so you could roll up when you'd done with it and hide it in your boot – then the three of us went in, Pete keeping chasso without, not that there was anything to worry about out there. As soon as we launched on the shop we went for Slouse who ran it, a big portwine jelly of a veck who viddied at once what was coming and made straight for the inside where the telephone was and perhaps his well-oiled pooshka, complete with six dirty rounds. Dim was round that counter skorry as a bird, sending packets of snoutie flying and cracking over a big cut-out showing a sharp with all

---

1 **millicent** (N.): Polizist. | **rozz** (N.): Polizist (von [slang] *rozzer*). | **patrol:** Patrouille, Streife. | 3 **maskie:** Diminutiv zu *mask*. | **job:** hier: (Stück) Arbeit. | 6 **Disraeli:** Benjamin D. (1804–1881), englischer Premierminister 1868 und 1874–1880. | 7 **Henry VIII:** Heinrich VIII. (1491–1547), König von England 1509–1547. | 8 **Shelley:** Percy Bysshe S. (1792–1822), englischer romantischer Dichter. | 10 **to have done with s.th.** (auch: *to be done with*) (coll.): mit etwas fertig sein, etwas aufhören. | 11 **chasso** (N.): Wache. | 12 **without** (adv.): draußen, außerhalb. | 13 **to launch on s.th.:** mit etwas beginnen. | **to go for s.o.** (slang): jdn. angreifen. | 14 **portwine jelly:** Portweingelee, -sülze. | 17 **pooshka** (N.): Pistole, Revolver, ‚Kanone'. | **round:** hier: Schuss (Patronen). | 18 **snoutie:** Diminutiv zu (slang) *snout* ›Tabak‹. | 19 **cut-out:** Druck, Abbildung.

her zoobies going flash at the customers and her groodies
near hanging out to advertise some new brand of cancers.
What you could viddy then was a sort of a big ball rolling
into the inside of the shop behind the curtain, this being
old Dim and Slouse sort of locked in a death struggle. Then
you could slooshy panting and snorting and kicking behind
the curtain and veshches falling over and swearing and
then glass going smash smash smash. Mother Slouse, the
wife, was sort of froze behind the counter. We could tell
she would creech murder given one chance, so I was round
that counter very skorry and had a hold of her, and a horrorshow big lump she was too, all nuking of scent and with
flipflop big bobbing groodies on her. I'd got my rooker
round her rot to stop her belting out death and destruction
to the four winds of heaven, but this lady doggie gave me a
large foul big bite on it and it was me that did the creeching,
and then she opened up beautiful with a flip yell for the
millicents. Well, then she had to be tolchocked proper with
one of the weights for the scales, and then a fair tap with a
crowbar they had for opening cases, and that brought the
red out like an old friend. So we had her down on the floor
and a rip of her platties for fun and a gentle bit of boot to
stop her moaning. And, viddying her lying there with her

1 **to go flash at s.o.** (N.): jdn. anfunkeln. | 2 **brand:** Marke, Sorte. | 5 **to
lock:** hier: umschließen, umfassen, ineinanderschlingen. | 6 **to slooshy**
(N.): hören. | **to pant:** keuchen. | **to snore:** schnarchen. | 9 **froze:** *frozen.* |
10 **to creech murder** (coll.): Abwandlung von *to cry blue murder* ›Zeter
und Mordio schreien‹. | 12 **to nuke** (N.): riechen. | 13 **flipflop** (coll.):
sich hin und her, auf und ab bewegend. | **to bob:** baumeln, sich hin und
ab bewegen. | 14 **to belt out** (slang): schmettern, brüllen. | 17 **flip:**
schnell, flink. | 20 **crowbar:** Stemmeisen. | 21 **red** (N.): Blut. | 22 **rip:**
Riss, Reißen.

groodies on show, I wondered should I or not, but that was for later on in the evening. Then we cleaned the till, and there was flip horrorshow takings that nochy, and we had a few packs of the very best top cancers apiece, then off we went, my brothers.

"A real big heavy great bastard he was," Dim kept saying. I didn't like the look of Dim; he looked dirty and untidy, like a veck who'd been in a fight, which he had been, of course, but you should never *look* as though you have been. His cravat was like someone had trampled on it, his maskie had been pulled off and he had floor-dirt on his litso, so we got him in an alleyway and tidied him up a malenky bit, soaking our tashtooks in spit to cheest the dirt off. The things we did for old Dim. We were back in the Duke of New York very skorry, and I reckoned by my watch we hadn't been more than ten minutes away. The starry old baboochkas were still there on the black and suds and Scotchmen we'd bought them, and we said, "Hallo, there, girlies, what's it going to be?" They started on the old "Very kind, lads, God bless you, boys," and so we rang the collocoll and brought a different waiter in this time and we ordered beers with rum in, being sore athirst, my brothers, and whatever the old ptitsas wanted. Then I said to the old baboochkas: "We haven't been out of here, have we? Been here all the time, haven't we?" They all caught on real skorry and said:

"That's right, lads. Not been out of our sight, you haven't. God bless you boys," drinking.

---

4 **apiece:** je, für jeden. | 10 **to trample on s.th.:** auf etwas (herum)trampeln. | 12 **alleyway:** Gässchen, Seitengasse. | 13 **tashtook** (N.): Taschentuch. | **to cheest** (N.): waschen. | 20 **collocoll** (N.): Glocke. | 22 **athirst:** durstig.

Not that it mattered much, really. About half an hour went by before there was any sign of life among the millicents, and then it was only two very young rozzes that came in, very pink under their big copper's shlemmies. One said:

"You lot know anything about the happenings at Slouse's shop this night?"

"Us?" I said, innocent. "Why, what happened?"

"Stealing and roughing. Two hospitalisations. Where've you lot been this evening?"

"I don't go for that nasty tone," I said. "I don't care much for these nasty insinuations. A very suspicious nature all this betokeneth, my little brothers."

"They've been in here all night, lads," the old sharps started to creech out. "God bless them, there's no better lot of boys living for kindness and generosity. Been here all the time they have. Not seen them move we haven't."

"We're only asking," said the other young millicent. "We've got our job to do like anyone else." But they gave us the nasty warning look before they went out. As they were going out we handed them a bit of lip-music: brrrrzzzzrrrr. But, myself, I couldn't help a bit of disappointment at things as they were those days. Nothing to fight against really. Everything as easy as kiss-my-sharries. Still, the night was still very young.

4 **copper** (slang): ‚Bulle‘. | **shlemmy** (auch: *shlem*; N.): Helm. | 6 **happenings**: Ereignisse. | 9 **roughing**: Rauferei. | **hospitalisation**: Krankenhauseinlieferung. | 11 **to go for s.th.** (AE, coll.): etwas mögen. | 12 **nasty**: schmutzig, garstig, unflätig, ekelhaft. | **insinuation**: Einflüsterung, Wink, Andeutung. | 13 **betokeneth** (arch.): *betokens* (*to betoken*: an-, bedeuten). | 24 **kiss-my-sharries** (N.): leck mich am Arsch.

Two

When we got outside of the Duke of New York we viddied, by the main bar's long lighted window, a burbling old
pyahnitsa or drunkie, howling away at the filthy songs of
his fathers and going blerp blerp in between as it might be
a filthy old orchestra in his stinking rotten guts. One veshch
I could never stand was that. I could never stand to see a
moodge all filthy and rolling and burping and drunk, whatever his age might be, but more especially when he was
real starry like this one was. He was sort of flattened to
the wall and his platties were a disgrace, all creased and untidy and covered in cal and mud and filth and stuff. So we
got hold of him and cracked him with a few good horrorshow tolchocks, but he still went on singing. The song
went:

And I will go back to my darling, my darling,
When you, my darling are gone.

But when Dim fisted him a few times on his filthy drunk-
ard's rot he shut up singing and started to creech: "Go on,
do me in, you bastard cowards, I don't want to live anyway,
not in a stinking world like this one." I told Dim to lay off a
bit then, because it used to interest me sometimes to

---

4 **pyahnitsa** (N.): Trinker, Trunkenbold. | **drunkie:** Trunkenbold,
Trinker. | 8 **moodge:** *mooch* (slang): Faulpelz, Bettler, Landstreicher. | **to
burp:** rülpsen, aufstoßen. | 11 **creased:** zerknittert. | 12 **cal** (N.): Dreck,
Kacke, Mist. | 18 **fo fist:** mit der Faust schlagen. | 18 f. **drunkard:** Säufer,
Trunkenbold. | 20 **to do s.o. in** (slang): jdn. ‚um die Ecke bringen', um-
bringen. | 21 **to lay off** (coll.): aufhören.

slooshy what some of these starry decreps had to say about
life and the world. I said:

"Oh. And what's stinking about it?" He cried out:

"It's a stinking world because it lets the young get on to
the old like you done, and there's no law nor order no
more." He was creeching out loud and waving his rookers
and making real horrorshow with the slovos, only the odd
blurp blurp coming from his keeshkas, like something was
orbiting within, or like some very rude interrupting sort of
a moodge making a shoom, so that this old veck kept sort of
threatening it with his fists, shouting: "It's no world for an
old man any longer, and that means that I'm not one bit
scared of you, my boyos, because I'm too drunk to feel the
pain if you hit me, and if you kill me I'll be glad to be dead."
We smecked and then grinned but said nothing, and then
he said: "What sort of a world is it at all? Men on the moon
and men spinning round the earth like it might be midges
round a lamp, and there's not no attention paid to earthly
law nor order no more. So your worst you may do, you
filthy cowardly hooligans." Then he gave us some lip-music – "Prrrrzzzzrrrr" – like we'd done to those young millicents, and then he started singing again:

> O dear dear land, I fought for thee
> And brought thee peace and victory –

---

1 **decreps** (N.): Altersschwäche (vermutl. abgeleitet von *decrepitude*
›Altersschwäche‹, ›Hinfälligkeit‹). | 8 **keeshkas** (N.): Eingeweide. |
9 **to orbit:** (um)kreisen. | 13 **boyo** (slang): Junge, Mann, Freund (meist
als Anrede gebraucht). | 17 **to spin:** sich drehen. | **midge:** kleine Mücke. |
20 **hooligan:** Rowdy, Schläger.

So we cracked into him lovely, grinning all over our litsos, but he still went on singing. Then we tripped him so he laid down flat and heavy and a bucketload of beer-vomit came whooshing out. That was disgusting so we have him the boot, one go each, and then it was blood, not song nor vomit, that came out of his filthy old rot. Then we went on our way.

It was round by the Municipal Power Plant that we came across Billyboy and his five droogs. Now in those days, my brothers, the teaming up was mostly by fours or fives, these being like auto-teams, four being a comfy number for an auto, and six being the outside limit for gang-size. Sometimes gangs would gang up so as to make like malenky armies for big night-war, but mostly it was best to roam in these like small numbers. Billyboy was something that made me want to sick just to viddy his fat grinning litso, and he always had this von of very stale oil that's been used for frying over and over, even when he was dressed in his best platties, like now. They viddied us just as we viddied them, and there was like a very quiet kind of watching each other now. This would be real, this would be proper, this would be the nozh, the oozy, the britva, not just fisties and boots. Billyboy and his droogs stopped what they were do-

---

2 **to trip s.o.:** jdn. zu Fall bringen, jdm. ein Bein stellen. | 3 **beer-vomit:** Bier-Erbrochenes. | 4 **to whoosh** (coll.): (hervor)zischen. | 5 **go:** Versuch. | 10 **teaming up:** Zusammentun. | 11 **comfy:** behaglich, bequem. | 13 **to gang up:** sich zusammenrotten. | 14 **to roam:** umherziehen. | 16 **to sick** (auch: *to sick up*): sich erbrechen, kotzen (eigtl. nicht als Verb gebräuchlich). | 17 **von** (N.): Geruch, Gestank. | **stale:** schal, abgestanden. | 22 **nozh** (N.): Messer. | **oozy** (N.): Kette. | **britva** (N.): Rasiermesser. | **fistie:** Diminutiv zu *fist*.

ing, which was just getting ready to perform something on a weepy young devotchka they had there, not more than ten, she creeching away but with her platties still on, Billy-boy holding her by one rooker and his number-one, Leo, holding the other. They'd probably just been doing the dirty slovo part of the act before getting down to a malenky bit of ultra-violence. When they viddied us a-coming they let go of this boo-hooing little ptitsa, there being plenty more where she came from, and she ran with her thin white legs flashing through the dark, still going "Oh oh oh." I said, smiling very wide and droogie, "Well, if it isn't fat stinking billygoat Billyboy in poison. How art thou, thou globby bottle of cheap stinking chip-oil? Come and get one in the yarbles, if you have any yarbles, you eunuch jelly, thou." And then we started.

There were four of us to six of them, like I have already indicated, but poor old Dim, for all his dimness, was worth three of the others in sheer madness and dirty fighting. Dim had a real horrorshow length of oozy or chain round his waist, twice wound round, and he unwound this and began to swing it beautiful in the eyes or glazzies. Pete and Georgie had good sharp nozhes, but I for my own part had a fine starry horrorshow cut-throat britva which, at that time, I could flash and shine artistic. So there we were

2 **weepy** (coll.): weinerlich. | 7 **ultra-violence** (N.): Vergewaltigung. | 8 **to boo-hoo:** laut weinen, flennen. | 11 **droogie** (N.): nett, freundlich. | 12 **billygoat:** Ziegenbock. | **in poison:** Wortspiel mit *in person.* | **art thou** (arch.): *are you.* | 13 **globby** (N.): vermutl. etwa: kugelförmig, rund (abgeleitet von *globe* bzw. *globular*). | **chip-oil:** Fritierfett. | 14 **yarbles** (N.): Hoden, ,Eier'. | **eunuch:** Eunuch, Kastrat. | 23 **cut-throat:** etwa: mörderisch.

dratsing away in the dark, the old Luna with men on it just coming up, the stars stabbing away as it might be knives anxious to join in the dratsing. With my britva I managed to slit right down the front of one of Billyboy's droog's platties, very neat and not even touching the plott under the cloth. Then in the dratsing this droog of Billyboy's suddenly found himself all opened up like a peapod, with his belly bare and his poor old yarbles showing, and then he got very very razdraz, waving and screaming and losing his guard and letting in old Dim with his chain snaking whisssssshhhhhhhhh, so that old Dim chained him right in the glazzies, and this droog of Billyboy's went tottering off and howling his heart out. We were doing very horrorshow, and soon we had Billyboy's number-one down underfoot, blinded with old Dim's chain and crawling about like an animal, but with one fair boot on the gulliver he was out and out and out.

Of the four of us Dim, as usual, came out the worst in point of looks, that is to say his litso was all bloodied and his platties a dirty mess, but the others of us were still cool and whole. It was stinking fatty Billyboy I wanted now, and there I was dancing about with my britva like I might be a barber on board a ship on a very rough sea, trying to get in at him with a few fair slashes on his unclean oily litso. Billy-

---

1 **to drats** (N.): kämpfen. | **Luna:** Mond. | 4 **to slit:** (auf)schlitzen. | 5 **plott** (N.): Körper. | 7 **peapod:** Erbsenschote. | 9 **razdraz** (N.): wütend, zornig. | 10 **to snake:** sich schlängeln; hier auch: zischen, züngeln. | 11 **to whish:** zischen. | **to chain:** hier: mit der Kette schlagen. | 12 **to totter:** torkeln, wanken. | 14 f. **underfoot:** am Boden. | 20 **mess:** Durcheinander, Unordnung, Schmutz. | 24 **slash:** Hieb, Schmarre, Schlitz.

boy had a nozh, a long flick-type, but he was a malenky bit too slow and heavy in his movements to vred anyone really bad. And, my brothers, it was real satisfaction to me to waltz – left two three, right two three – and carve left cheeky and right cheeky, so that like two curtains of blood seemed to pour out at the same time, one on either side of his fat filthy oily snout in the winter starlight. Down this blood poured like red curtains, but you could viddy Billyboy felt not a thing, and he went lumbering on like a filthy fatty bear, poking at me with his nozh.

Then we slooshied the sirens and knew the millicents were coming with pooshkas pushing out of the police-auto-windows at the ready. That little weepy devotchka had told them, no doubt, there being a box for calling the rozzes not too far behind the Muni Power Plant. "Get you soon, fear not," I called, "stinking billygoat. I'll have your yarbles off lovely." Then off they ran, slow and panting, ex-cept for Number One Leo out snoring on the ground, away north towards the river, and we went the other way. Just around the next turning was an alley, dark and empty and open at both ends, and we rested there, panting fast then slower, then breathing like normal. It was like resting be-tween the feet of two terrific and very enormous moun-tains, these being the flatblocks, and in the windows of all of the flats you could viddy like blue dancing light. This

---

1 **flick-type:** Gemeint ist *flick-knife* (BE): Springmesser (*to flick:* schnel-len). | 2 **to vred** (N.): verletzen. | 3 **bad:** *badly:* sehr, heftig, schlimm. | 4 **to waltz:** walzen, Walzer tanzen. | 5 **cheeky:** Diminutiv zu *cheek.* | 7 **snout:** Schnauze. | 9 **to lumber:** sich schleppen, schwerfällig gehen. | 10 **to poke:** stoßen, stochern. | 23 **terrific:** fürchterlich, großartig. | 24 **flatblock:** Etagenhaus, Wohnblock.

would be the telly. Tonight was what they called a world-cast, meaning that the same programme was being viddied by everybody in the world that wanted to, that being mostly the middle-aged middle-class lewdies. There would be some big famous stupid comic chelloveck or black singer, and it was all being bounced off the special telly satellites in outer space, my brothers. We waited panting, and we could slooshy the sirening millicents going east, so we knew we were all right now. But poor Dim kept looking up at the stars and planets and the Luna with his rot wide open like a kid who'd never viddied any such thing before, and he said:

"What's on them, I wonder. What would be up there on things like that?"

I nudged him hard, saying: "Come, gloopy bastard as thou art. Think thou not on them. There'll be life like down here most likely, with some getting knifed and others doing the knifing. And now, with the nochy still molodoy, let us be on our way, O my brothers." The others smecked at this, but poor old Dim looked at me serious, then up again at the stars and the Luna. So we went on our way down the alley, with the worldcast blueing on on either side. What we needed now was an auto, so we turned left coming out of the alley, knowing right away we were in Priestley Place as soon as we viddied the big bronze statue of some starry

1 **telly** (coll.): Kurzform von *television*. | 1f. **worldcast** (N.): weltweite Fernsehübertragung. | 6 **to bounce off**: abprallen lassen, abstrahlen, senden. | 7 **outer space**: Weltraum. | 15 **to nudge**: anstoßen, -stupsen. | 17 **to knife**: erstechen, erdolchen. | 18 **molodoy** (N.): jung. | 22 **to blue** (N.): blau strahlen. | 24 **Priestley**: John Boynton P. (1894–1984), von Burgess geschätzter englischer Schriftsteller.

poet with an apey upper lip and a pipe stuck in a droopy old rot. Going north we came to the filthy old Filmdrome, peeling and dropping to bits through nobody going there much except malchicks like me and my droogs, and then only for a yell or a razrez or a bit of in-out-in-out in the dark. We could viddy from the poster on the Filmdrome's face, a couple of fly-dirted spots trained on it, that there was the usual cowboy riot, with the archangels on the side of the US marshal six-shooting at the rustlers out of hell's fighting legions, the kind of hound-and-horny veshch put out by Statefilm in those days. The autos parked by the sinny weren't all that horrorshow, crappy starry veshches most of them, but there was a newish Durango 95 that I thought might do. Georgie had one of these ployclefs, as they called them, on his keyring, so we were soon aboard – Dim and Pete at the back, puffing away lordly at their cancers – and I turned on the ignition and started her up and she grumbled away real horrorshow, a nice warm vibraty

1 **apey:** affig, affenartig (von *ape* ›Affe‹). | **droopy:** (herab)hängend, traurig. | 3 **to peel:** abblättern. | 5 **yell:** hier: Spaß, Vergnügen (*yell-play* [coll.]: von ständigem Lachen begleitete Farce). | **razrez** (N.): Wut, Zorn. | **in-out** (AE, slang): Geschlechtsverkehr. | 6 **poster:** Plakat, Anschlag. | 7 **fly-dirted:** voller Fliegendreck. | **spot:** Kurzform von *spotlight*: Scheinwerfer. | **(to be) trained on s.th.:** auf etwas gerichtet sein. | 8 **riot:** Aufstand, Krawall. | **archangel:** Erzengel. | 9 **US marshal:** amerikanischer (Bundes-)Vollzugsbeamter. | **six-shooting:** mit dem Revolver schießend (*six-shooter* [AE, slang]: Revolver). | **rustler:** Viehdieb. | 10 **legion:** Legion, Heerschar. | 10 f. **to put out:** hier: veröffentlichen. | 11 f. **sinny** (N.): Kino (von *cinema*). | 13 **newish** (AE, slang): ziemlich neu. | 14 **to do:** genügen, ausreichen. | **polyclef** (N.): Nachschlüssel, Dietrich. | 17 **ignition:** Zündung. | 18 **vibraty** (N.): *vibratory*: vibrierend, schwingend, pulsierend.

feeling grumbling all through your guttiwuts. Then I made with the noga, and we backed out lovely, and nobody viddied us take off.

We fillied round what was called the backtown for a bit, scaring old vecks and cheenas that were crossing the roads and zigzagging after cats and that. Then we took the road west. There wasn't much traffic about, so I kept pushing the old noga through the floorboards near, and the Durango 95 ate up the road like spaghetti. Soon it was winter trees and dark, my brothers, with a country dark, and at one place I ran over something big with a snarling toothy rot in the headlamps, then it screamed and squelched under and old Dim at the back near laughed his gulliver off – "Ho ho ho" – at that. Then we saw one young malchick with his sharp, lubbilubbing under a tree, so we stopped and cheered at them, then we bashed into them both with a couple of half-hearted tolchocks, making them cry, then on we went. What we were after now was the old surprise visit. That was a real kick and good for smecks and lashings of the ultra-violent. We came at last to a sort of village, and just outside this village was a small sort of a cottage on its own with a bit of a garden. The Luna was well up now, and we could viddy this cottage fine and clear as I eased up and put the brake on, the other three giggling like bezoomny, and we

---

1 **guttiwuts** (N.): Eingeweide (von *guts*). | 2 **noga** (N.): Fuß, Bein. | 6 **to zigzag**: im Zickzack fahren. | 11 **to snarl**: knurren. | 11 f. **headlamp**: Vorderscheinwerfer. | 12 **to squelch**: p(l)atschen, quatschen, glucksen. | 15 **to lubbilub** (N.): küssen. | 16 **to bash**: heftig schlagen. | 19 **kick**: Nervenkitzel. | **lashing**: Peitschenhieb (*to lash*: schlagen, peitschen). | 23 **to ease up**: verlangsamen, langsamer fahren. | 24 **to giggle**: kichern. | **bezoomny** (N.): verrückt.

could viddy the name on the gate of this cottage veshch was HOME, a gloopy sort of a name. I got out of the auto, ordering my droogs to shush their giggles and act like serious, and I opened this malenky gate and walked up to the front
5 door. I knocked nice and gentle and nobody came, so I knocked a bit more and this time I could slooshy somebody coming, then a bolt drawn, then the door inched open an inch or so, then I could viddy this one glaz looking out at me and the door was on a chain. "Yes? Who is it?" It was s
10 sharp's goloss, a youngish devotchka by her sound, so I said in a very refined manner of speech, a real gentleman's goloss:

"Pardon, madam, most sorry to disturb you, but my friend and me were out for a walk, and my friend has taken
15 bad all of a sudden with a very troublesome turn, and he is out there on the road dead out and groaning. Would you have the goodness to let me use your telephone to telephone for an ambulance?"

"We haven't a telephone," said this devotchka. "I'm sor-
20 ry, but we haven't. You'll have to go somewhere else." From inside this malenky cottage I could slooshy the clack clack clacky clack clack clackity clackclack of some veck typing away, and then the typing stopped and there was this chelloveck's goloss calling: "What is it, dear?"

25 "Well," I said, "could you of your goodness please let

---

3 **to shush s.th.:** etwas zum Schweigen bringen, unterdrücken. | **giggle:** Kichern. | 7 **to inch open:** (sich) langsam öffnen. | 11 **refined:** kultiviert. | 14 f. **my friend has taken bad** (coll.): meinem Freund ist übel geworden. | 15 **a troublesome turn:** eine Wendung zum Schlechteren. | 18 **ambulance:** Krankenwagen. | 21 **clack:** Klappern.

him have a cup of water? It's like a faint, you see. It seems as though he's passed out in a sort of a fainting fit."

The devotchka sort of hesitated and then said: "Wait." Then she went off, and my three droogs got out of the auto quiet and crept up horrorshow stealthy, putting their maskies on now, then I put mine on, then it was only a matter of me putting the old rooker and undoing the chain, me having softened up this devotchka with my gent's goloss, so that she hadn't shut the door like she should have done, us being strangers of the night. The four of us then went roaring in, old Dim playing the shoot as usual with his jumping up and down and singing out dirty slovos, and it was a nice malenky cottage, I'll say that. We all went smecking into the room with a light on, and there was this devotchka sort of cowering, a young pretty bit of sharp with real horrorshow groodies on her, and with her was this chelloveck who was her moodge, youngish too with horn-rimmed otchkies on him, and on a table was a typewriter and all papers scattered everywhere, but there was one little pile of paper that must have been what he'd already typed, so here was another intelligent type bookman type like that we'd fillied with some hours back, but this one was a writer not a reader. Anyway he said:

"What is this? Who are you? How dare you enter my house without permission." And all the time his goloss was trembling and his rookers too. So I said:

2 to pass out: ohnmächtig werden. | fit: Anfall. | 5 stealthy: verstohlen, heimlich. | 8 gent: Kurzform von *gentleman.* | 11 shoot (N.): Narr. | 15 to cower: sich hinkauern. | 17 youngish: ziemlich jung. | 18 horn-rimmed: mit Hornrand (*rim:* Rand, Einfassung). | otchkies (N., pl.): Brille.

"Never fear. If fear thou hast in thy heart, O brother, pray banish it forthwith." Then Georgie and Pete went out to find the kitchen, while old Dim waited for orders, standing next to me with his rot wide open. "What is this, then?" I said, picking up the pile like of typing from off of the table, and the horn-rimmed moodge said, dithering:

"That's just what I want to know. What *is* this? What do you want? Get out at once before I throw you out." So poor old Dim, masked like Peebee Shelley, had a good loud smeck at that, roaring like some animal.

"It's a book," I said. "It's a book what you are writing." I made the old goloss very coarse. "I have always had the strongest admiration for them as can write books." Then I looked at its top sheet, and there was the name – A CLOCK-WORK ORANGE – and I said, "That's a fair gloopy title. Who ever heard of a clockwork orange?" Then I read a malenky bit out loud in a sort of very high type preaching goloss: "– The attempt to impose upon man, a creature of growth and capable of sweetness, to ooze juicily at the last round the bearded lips of God, to attempt to impose, I say, laws and conditions appropriate to a mechanical creation, against this I raise my swordpen –" Dim made the old lip-music at that and I had to smeck myself. Then I started to tear up the sheets and scatter the bits over the floor, and this writer moodge went sort of bezoomny and made for me with his zoobies clenched and showing yellow and his nails ready for me like claws. So that was old Dim's cue and

1 **thy** (arch.): *your.* | 2 **to banish**: vertreiben. | **forthwith**: sofort, so-gleich. | 6 **to dither**: bibbern, zittern. | 13 **them as can write books**: *those who can write books.* | 19 **to ooze**: sickern, (langsam) ausströmen. | **juicily**: saftig. | 26 **to clench**: zusammenbeißen. | 27 **cue**: Stichwort.

he went grinning and going er er and a a a for this veck's dithering rot, crack crack, first left fistie then right, so that our dear old droog the red – red vino on tap and the same in all places, like it's put out by the same big firm – started to pour and spot the nice clean carpet and the bits of his book that I was still ripping away at, razrez razrez. All this time this devotchka, his loving and faithful wife, just stood like froze by the fireplace, and then she started letting out malenky little creeches, like in time to the music of old Dim's fisty work. Then Georgie and Pete came in from the kitchen, both munching away, though with their maskies on, you could do that with them on and no trouble, Georgie with like a cold leg of something in one rooker and half a loaf of kleb with a big dollop of maslo on it in the other, and Pete with a bottle of beer frothing its gulliver off and a hor- rorshow rookerful of like plum cake. They went haw haw haw, viddying old Dim dancing round and fisting the writ- er veck so that the writer veck started to platch like his life's work was ruined, going boo hoo hoo with a very square bloody rot, but it was haw haw haw in a muffled eater's way and you could see bits of what they were eating. I didn't like that, it being dirty and slobbery, so I said:

"Drop that mounch. I gave no permission. Grab hold of this veck here so he can viddy all and not get away." So they put down their fatty pishcha on the table among all the fly-

---

3 **vino** (slang): Wein. | 11 **to munch:** mit vollen Backen, geräuschvoll kauen. | 14 **kleb** (N.): Brot. | **maslo** (N.): Butter. | 15 **to froth:** schäumen. | 18 **to platch** (N.): jammern. | 20 **muffled:** gedämpft (Geräusch). | 22 **slobbery:** sabberig. | 23 **mounch** (N.): Essen, Speise (viell. abgeleitet von *to munch*). | **to grab hold of s.o.:** jdn. packen, greifen, festhalten. | 25 **pishcha** (N.): Essen, Nahrung.

ing paper and they clopped over to the writer veck whose horn-rimmed otchkies were cracked but still hanging on, with old Dim still dancing round and making ornaments shake on the mantelpiece (I swept them all off then and they couldn't shake no more, little brothers) while he fillied with the author of *A Clockwork Orange*, making his litso all purple and dripping away like some very special sort of a juicy fruit. "All right, Dim," I said. "Now for the other veshch, Bog help us all." So he did the strong-man on the devotchka, who was still creech creech creeching away in very horrorshow four-in-a-bar, locking her rookers from the back, while I ripped away at this and that and the other, the others going haw haw haw still, and real good horror-show groodies they were that then exhibited their pink glazzies, O my brothers, while I untrussed and got ready for the plunge. Plunging, I could slooshy cries of agony and this writer bleeding veck that Georgie and Pete held on to nearly got loose howling bezoomny with the filthiest of slovos that I already knew and others he was making up. Then after me it was right old Dim should have his turn, which he did in a beasty snorty howly sort of a way with his Peebee Shelley maskie taking no notice, while I held on to her. Then there was a changeover, Dim and me grabbing the slobbering writer veck who was past struggling really,

1 **to clop:** hoppeln. | 4 **mantelpiece:** Kaminsims. | 11 **four-in-a-bar** (N.): Viervierteltakt (*bar:* Takt). | 15 **to untruss:** aufschnüren, ausziehen. | 16 **plunge:** Sturz, Sprung. | 17 **bleeding** (slang): verflucht. | 19 **to make up:** ersinnen, erfinden. | 21 **beasty** (N.): *beastly:* tierisch, viehisch, ekelhaft. | **snorty:** gereizt, naserümpfend; hier wohl eher: schnaubend (von *to snort* ›schnauben‹). | **howly** (N.): *howling.* | 24 **to slobber:** geifern, sabbern.

only just coming out with slack sort of slovos like he was in the land in a milk-plus bar, and Pete and Georgie had theirs. Then there was like quiet and we were full of like hate, so smashed what was left to be smashed – typewriter, lamp, chairs – and Dim, it was typical of old Dim, watered the fire out and was going to dung on the carpet, there being plenty of paper, but I said no. "Out out out out," I howled. The writer veck and his zheena were not really there, bloody and torn and making noises. But they'd live.

So we got into the waiting auto and I left it to Georgie to take the wheel, me feeling that malenky bit shagged, and we went back to town, running over odd squealing things on the way.

---

1 **slack**: nachlässig. | 5 **to water out**: hier: (mit Urin) auslöschen; Anspielung auf eine Episode in J. Swifts *Gullivers Travels, Part I: A Voyage to Lilliput.* | 6 **to dung**: düngen; hier: scheißen. | 8 **zheena** (N.): Ehefrau. | 11 **wheel**: *steering-wheel*. | **shagged** (slang): erschöpft. | 12 **to run over** (auch: *to run down*): überfahren. | **to squeal**: grell schreien, winseln, quieken.

Three

We yeckated back townwards, my brothers, but just outside, not far from what they called the Industrial Canal, we viddied the fuel needle had like collapsed, like our own ha ha ha needles had, and the auto was coughing kashl kashl kashl. Not to worry overmuch, though, because a rail station kept flashing blue – on off on off – just near. The point was whether to leave the auto to be sobiratted by the rozzes or, us feeling like in a hate and murder mood, to give it a fair tolchock into the starry waters for a nice heavy loud plesk before the death of the evening. This latter we decided on, so we got out and, the brakes off, all four tolchocked it to the edge of the filthy water that was like treacle mixed with human hole products, then one good horrorshow tolchock and in she went. We had to dash back for fear of the filth splashing out platties, but splussshhh and glolp she went, down and lovely. "Farewell, old droog," called Georgie, and Dim obliged with a clowny great guff – "Huh huh huh huh." Then we made for the station to ride the one stop to Center, as the middle of town was called. We paid our fares nice and polite and waited gentlemanly and quiet on the platform, old Dim fillying with the slot machines, his carmans being full of small malenky coin, and ready if need be to distribute chocbars to the poor and starving, though there was none such about, and then the

2 **to yeckat** (N.): fahren. | 4 **to collapse:** zusammenbrechen, schlappmachen. | 8 **to sobirat** (N.): aufnehmen, auflesen. | 11 **plesk** (N.): Platsch. | 13 **treacle:** Sirup. | 18 **to oblige with s.th.** (coll.): etwas zum besten geben. | **guff:** Kurzform von *guffaw:* schallendes Gelächter. | 22 f. **slot machine:** Spielautomat.

old espresso rapido came lumbering in and we climbed aboard, the train looking to be near empty. To pass the three-minute ride we fillied about with what they called the upholstery, doing some nice horrorshow tearing-out of the seats' guts and old Dim chaining the okno till the glass cracked and sparkled in the winter air, but we were all feeling that bit shagged and fagged and fashed, it having been an evening of some energy expenditure, my brothers, only Dim, like the clowny animal he was, full of the joys-of but looking all dirtied over and too much von of sweat on him, which was one thing I had against old Dim.

We got out at Center and walked slow back to the Korova Milkbar, all going yawwwww a malenky bit and exhibiting to moon and star and lamplight our back fillings, because we were still only growing malchicks and had school in the daytime, and when we got into the Korova we found it fuller than when we'd left earlier on. But the chelloveck that had been burbling away, in the land, on white and synthemesc or whatever, was still on at it, going: "Urchins and deadcast in the way-ho-hay glill platonic tide weatherborn." It was probable that this was his third or fourth lot that evening, for he had that pale inhuman look, like he'd become a *thing*, and like his litso was really a piece of chalk carved. Really, if he wanted to spend so long in the land, he

1 **espresso rapido** (N.): Expresszug. | 4 **upholstery**: Bezüge, Polsterung. | 5 **okno** (N.): Fenster, Scheibe. | 7 **fagged / fashed**: ermüdet, erschöpft; verärgert, geplagt; Anspielung auf das Gedicht »The Leaden Echo and the Golden Echo« von Gerard Manley Hopkins (1844–1889). | 8 **expenditure**: Aufwand, Verbrauch. | 14 **fillings**: (Zahn-)Füllungen, Plomben. | 19 **urchin**: Bengel, Balg. | 20 **deadcast**: Nonsens-Wort. | **way-hohay**: *way*. | **glill**: Nonsens-Wort. | **platonic**: platonisch. | **tide**: Flut. | 22 **inhuman**: unmenschlich.

should have gone into one of the private cubies at the back
and not stayed in the big mesto, because here some of the
malchickies would filly about with him a malenky bit,
though not too much because there were powerful bruise-
5 boys hidden away in the old Korova who could stop any riot. Anyway, Dim squeezed in next to this veck and, with
his big clown's yawp that showed his hanging grape, he
stabbed this veck's foot with his own large filthy sabog. But
the veck, my brothers, heard nought, being now all above
10 the body.

It was nadsats mostly milking and coking and fillying
around (nadsats were what we used to call the teens), but
there were a few of the more starry ones, vecks and cheenas
alike (but not of the boorjoyce, never them) laughing and
15 govoreeting at the bar. You could tell from their barberings
and loose platties (big string sweaters mostly) that they'd
been on rehearsal at the TV studios round the corner. The
devotchkas among them had these very lively litsos and
wide big rots, very red, showing a lot of teeth, and smeck-
20 ing away and not caring about the wicked world one whit.
And then the disc on the stereo twanged off and out (it was

1 **cuby**: Nische, Kabine (Wortspiel mit *cubicle* ›Zelle‹, ›Nische‹, ›Kabine‹
und *cubbyhole* ›gemütliches Plätzchen‹, ›Kämmerchen‹, ›Kabuff‹). |
4f. **bruiseboy**: Schläger, Rauswerfer (von *bruiser* ›Schläger‹). | 7 **yawp**
(coll.): Schrei, heiserer oder harter Laut. | **hanging grape** (N.): Zäpfchen
im weichen Gaumen. | 8 **sabog** (N.): Schuh. | 9 **nought**: nichts. | 11 **nad-
sat** (N.): Teenager (von russ. *-nadcat* ›-zehn‹). | **milking and coking** (N.):
Milch und Cola trinkend. | 12 **teen**: *teenager*. | 15 **to govoreet** (N.): reden,
sprechen. | **barbering** (N.): Haarschnitt. | 16 **string sweater**: grob-
gestrickter Pullover. | 17 **rehearsal**: (Theater-, Film-)Probe. | 20 **not
one whit**: kein Jota, kein bisschen. | 21 **to twang**: schwirren, (scharf)
klingen.

Johnny Zhivago, a Russky koshka, singing "Only Every Other Day"), and in the like interval, the short silence before the next one came on, one of these devotchkas – very fair and with a big smiling red rot and in her late thirties I'd say – suddenly came with a burst of singing, only a bar and a half and as though she was like giving an example of something they'd all been govoreeting about, and it was like for a moment, O my brothers, some great bird had flown into the milkbar, and I felt all the malenky hairs on my plott standing endwise and the shivers crawling up like slow malenky lizards and then down again. Because I knew what she sang. It was from an opera by Friedrich Gitterfenster called *Das Bettzeug*, and it was the bit where she's snuffing it with her throat cut, and the slovos are "Better like this maybe". Anyway, I shivered.

But old Dim, as soon as he'd slooshied this dollop of song like a lomtick of red hot meat plonked on your plate, let off one of his vulgarities, which in this case was a lip-trump followed by a dog-howl followed by two fingers pronging twice at the air followed by a clowny guffaw. I felt myself all of a fever and like drowning in redhot blood, slooshying and viddying Dim's vulgarity, and I said: "Bas-

---

1 **Zhivago:** Anklang an den Roman *Doktor Schiwago* (1957) des russischen Schriftstellers Boris Pasternak (1890–1960). | **Russky** (N.): russisch. | **koshka** (N.): Katze; hier (fig.): analoge Wortbildung zu (AE, slang) *cat* ›Jazzmusiker‹. | 10 **endwise** (N.): aufrecht. | **shiver:** Schauer, Erschauern. | 11 **lizard:** Eidechse. | 12 f. **Gitterfenster / "Das Bettzeug":** Komponist und Oper fiktiv. | 13 f. **to snuff it** (slang): sterben. | 17 **lomtick** (N.): Stück. | **to plonk:** knallen, hinpacken, heftig setzen, stellen, legen. | 18 **vulgarity:** Ungezogenheit, Pöbelhaftigkeit. | 18 f. **lip-trump** (N.): Trompetenstoß mit den Lippen. | 20 **to prong:** stechen.

tard. Filthy drooling mannerless bastard." Then I leaned across Georgie, who was between me and horrible Dim, and fisted Dim skorry on the rot. Dim looked very surprised, his rot open, wiping the krovvy off of his goober with his rook and in turn looking surprised at the red flowing krovvy and at me. "What for did you do that for?" he said in his ignorant way. Not many viddied what I'd done, and those that viddied cared not. The stereo was on again and was playing a very sick electronic guitar veshch. I said:

"For being a bastard with no manners and not the dook of an idea how to comport yourself publicwise, O my brother."

Dim put on a hound-and-horny look of evil, saying, "I don't like you should do what you done then. And I'm not your brother no more and wouldn't want to be." He'd taken a big snotty tashtook from his pocket and was mopping the red flow puzzled, keeping on looking at it frowning as if he thought that blood was for other vecks and not for him. It was like he was singing blood to make up for his vulgarity when that devotchka was singing music. But that devotchka was smecking away ha ha ha now with her droogs at the bar, her red rot working and her zoobies ashine, not having noticed Dim's filthy vulgarity. It was me really Dim had done wrong to. I said:

"If you don't like this and you wouldn't want that, then

1 **to drool:** sabbern. | **mannerless:** ohne Benehmen, ohne Manieren. | 4 **krovvy** (N.): Blut. | 11 f. **not the dook of an idea** (N.): keinen blassen Schimmer. | 12 **to comport o.s.:** sich betragen. | 17 **snotty** (coll.): rotzig. | **to mop:** auf-, abwischen. | 20 **to make up for s.th.:** etwas wiedergutmachen, wettmachen. | 23 **ashine:** leuchtend, glänzend.

you know what to do, little brother." Georgie said, in a sharp way that made me look:

"All right. Let's not be starting."

"That's clean up to Dim," I said. "Dim can't go on all his jeezny being as a little child." And I looked sharp at Georgie. Dim said, and the red krovvy was easing its flow now:

"What natural right does he have to think he can give the orders and tolchock me whenever he likes? Yarbles is what I say to him, and I'd chain his glazzies out soon as look."

"Watch that," I said, as quiet as I could with the stereo bouncing all over the walls and ceiling and the in-the-land veck beyond Dim getting loud now with his "Spark nearer, ultoptimate." I said, "Do watch that, O Dim, if continue to be on live thou dost wish."

"Yarbles," said Dim, sneering, "great bolshy yarblockos to you. What you done then you had no right. I'll meet you with chain or nozh or britva any time, not having you aiming tolchocks at me reasonless, it stands to reason I won't have it."

"A nozh scrap any time you say," I snarled back. Pete said:

"Oh now, don't, both of you malchicks. Droogs, aren't we? It isn't right droogs should behave thiswise. See, there are some loose-lipped malchicks over there smecking at us, leering like. We mustn't let ourselves down."

---

5 **jeezny** (N.): Leben, Dasein. | 12 **to bounce**: springen, hüpfen; aufprallen, heftig schlagen. | 14 **ultoptimate**: Nonsens-Wort. | 15 **thou dost** (arch.): *you do.* | 16 **sneering**: höhnisch, spöttisch. | **bolshy** (N.): groß. | 21 **scrap**: Streit, Auseinandersetzung. | 24 **loose-lipped**: mit lockerer Zunge, frech. | 25 **to leer**: (lüstern) schielen, boshaft herüberschauen. | **to let o.s. down**: sich unter sein Niveau begeben.

"Dim, I said, "has got to learn his place. Right?"

"Wait," said Georgie. "What's all this about place? This is the first I ever hear about lewdies learning their place." Pete said:

"If the truth is known, Alex, you shouldn't have given old Dim that uncalled-for tolchock. I'll say it once and no more. I say it with all respect, but if it had been me you'd given it to you'd have to answer. I say no more." And he drowned his litso in his milk-glass.

I could feel myself getting all razdraz inside, but I tried to cover it, saying calm: "There has to be a leader. Discipline there has to be. Right?" None of them skazatted a word or nodded even. I got more razdraz inside, calmer out. "I," I said, "have been in charge long now. We are all droogs, but somebody has to be in charge. Right? Right?" They all like nodded, wary like. Dim was osooshing the last of the krovvy off. It was Dim who said now:

"Right, right. Doobidoob. A bit tired, maybe, everybody is. Best not to say more." I was surprised and just that malenky bit poogly to sloosh Dim govoreeting that wise. Dim said: "Bedways is rightways now, so best we go homeways. Right?" I was very surprised. The other two nodded, going right right right. I said:

"You understand about the tolchock on the rot, Dim. It was the music, see. I get all bezoomny when any veck interferes with a ptitsa singing, as it might be. Like that then."

6 **uncalled-for:** unverlangt. | 12 **to skazat** (N.): sagen, sprechen. | 15 **to be in charge:** leiten, die Führung haben. | 16 **wary:** vorsichtig, bedachtsam. | **to osoosh** (N.): wischen. | 18 **doobidoob:** Dubidu. | 21f. **homeways** (N.): *homewards:* heimwärts.

"Best we go off homeways and get a bit of spatchka," said Dim. "A long night for growing malchicks. Right?" Right right nodded the other two. I said:

"I think it's best we go home now. Dim has made a real horrorshow suggestion. If we don't meet daywise, O my brothers, well then – same time same place tomorrow?"

"Oh yes," said Georgie. "I think that can be arranged."

"I might," said Dim, "be just that malenky bit late. But same place and near same time tomorrow surely." He was still wiping away at his goober, though no krovvy flowed any longer now. "And," he said, "it's to be hoped that there won't be no more of them singing ptitsas in here." Then he gave his old Dim guff, a clowny big hohohohoho. It seemed like he was too dim to take much offence.

So off we went our several ways, me belching arrrrgh on the cold coke I'd peeted. I had my cut-throat britva handy in case any of Billyboy's droogs should be around near the flat-block waiting, or for that matter any of the other bandas or gruppas or shaikas that from time to time were at war with one. Where I lived was with my dadda and mum in the flats of Municipal Flatblock 18A, between Kingsley Avenue and Wilsonsway. I got to the big main door with no trouble, though I did pass one young malchick sprawling and creech-

---

1 **spatchka** (N.): Schlaf, Ruhe, Nickerchen. | 15 **to belch**: aufstoßen, rülpsen. | 16 **handy**: zur Hand, griffbereit. | 19 **shaika** (N.): Bande, Horde. | 20 **dadda** (coll.): Vater. | **mum** (coll.): Mutter. | 21 **Kingsley**: Charles K. (1819–1875), anglikanischer Geistlicher und Autor mehrerer sozial engagierter Romane. | 22 **Wilsonsway**: Anspielung auf John Burgess Wilson, den Taufnamen von Anthony Burgess, oder den englischen Schriftsteller Angus Wilson (1913–1991). | 23 **to sprawl**: ausgestreckt daliegen.

ing and moaning in the gutter, all cut about lovely, and saw in the lamplight also streaks of blood here and there like signatures, my brothers, of the night's fillying. And too I saw just by 18A a pair of devotchka's neezhnies doubtless rudely wrenched off in the heat of the moment, O my brothers. And so in. In the hallway was the good old municipal painting on the walls – vecks and ptitsas very well-developed, stern in the dignity of labour, at workbench and machine with not one stitch of platties on their well-developed plotts. But of course some of the malchicks living in 18A had, as was to be expected, embellished and decorated the said big painting with handy pencil and ballpoint, adding hair and stiff rods and dirty ballooning slovos out of the dignified rots of these nagoy (bare, that is) cheenas and vecks. I went to the lift, but there was no need to press the electric knopka to see if it was working or not, because it had been tolchocked real horrorshow this night, the metal doors all buckled, some feat of rare strength indeed, so I had to walk the ten floors up. I cursed and panted climbing, being tired in plott if not so much in brain. I wanted music very bad this evening, that singing devotchka in the Korova having perhaps started me off. I wanted a big feast of it before getting my passport stamped, my brothers, at sleep's frontier and the stripy shest lifted to let me through.

1 **gutter**: Rinnstein, Gosse. | 4 **neezhnies** (N., pl.): Unterhose. | 5 **to wrench off**: entwinden. | 6 **hallway**: Flur. | 8 **workbench**: Werkbank. | 9 f. **with not one stitch … plotts**: splitterfasernackt (*stitch*: Faden). | 11 **to embellish**: verschönern. | 12 **said**: besagt. | **ballpoint**: *ballpoint pen*: Kugelschreiber. | 13 **ballooning slovos**: Wörter in Sprechblasen. | 14 **nagoy** (N.): nackt. | 18 **buckled**: verbogen. | 24 **stripy**: streifig, gestreift. | **shest** (N.): Schranke.

I opened the door of 10-8 with my own little klootch, and inside our malenky quarters all was quiet, the pee and em both being in sleepland, and mum had laid out on the table my malenky bit of supper – a couple of lomticks and tinned spongemeat with a shive or so of kleb and butter, a glass of the old cold moloko. Hohoho, the old cold moloko, with no knives or synthemesc or drencrom in it. How wicked, my brothers, innocent milk must always seem to me now. Still, I drank and ate growling, being more hungry than I thought at first, and I got a fruitpie from the larder and tore chunks off it to stuff into my greedy rot. Then I tooth-cleaned and clicked, cleaning out the old rot with my yahzick or tongue, then I went into my own little room or den, easing off my platties as I did so. Here was my bed and my stereo, pride of my jeezny, and my discs in their cupboard, and banners and flags on the wall, these being like remembrances of my corrective school life since I was eleven, O my brothers, each one shining and blazoned with name or number: SOUTH 4; METRO CORSKOL BLUE DIVISION; THE BOYS OF ALPHA.

The little speakers of my stereo were all arranged round the room, on ceiling, walls, floor, so, lying on my bed slooshying the music, I was like netted and meshed in the

---

1 **klootch** (N.): Schlüssel. | 2 f. **pee and em:** P und M, Vater und Mutter. | 5 **tinned spongemeat:** Büchsenfleisch. | **shive** (N.): Scheibe, Stück (vgl. [Romani] *chiv* ›Klinge‹). | 10 **fruitpie:** Obstkuchen. | **larder:** Speisekammer. | 11 **chunk:** Klumpen, dickes Stück. | 12 **to click:** schnalzen. | 13 **yahzick** (N.): Zunge. | 14 **den:** Höhle. | **to ease off:** hier: abstreifen. | 17 **corrective school:** Besserungsanstalt. | 18 **to blazon:** schmücken, zieren. | 21 **speaker:** Lautsprecher. | 23 **to net:** einfangen, mit einem Netz umgeben. | **to mesh:** in einem Netz fangen, verwickeln.

orchestra. Now what I fancied first tonight was this new violin concerto by the American Geoffrey Plautus, played by Odysseus Choerilos with the Macon (Georgia) Philharmonic, so I slid it from where it was neatly filed and switched on and waited.

Then, brothers, it came. Oh, bliss, bliss and heaven. I lay all nagoy to the ceiling, my gulliver on my rookers on the pillow, rot open in bliss, slooshying the sluice of lovely sounds. Oh, it was gorgeousness and gorgeosity made flesh. The trombones crunched redgold under my bed, and behind my gulliver the trumpets threewise silverflamed, and there by the door the timps rolling through my guts and out again crunched like candy thunder. Oh, it was wonder of wonders. And then, a bird of like rarest heavenmetal, or like silvery wine flowing into a spaceship, gravity all nonsense now, came the violin solo above all the other strings, and those strings were like a cage of silk around my bed. Then flute and oboe bored, like worms of like platinum, into the thick thick toffee gold and silver. I was in such bliss, my brothers. Pee and em in their bedroom next door had learnt now not to knock on the wall with complaints of what they called noise. I had taught them. Now

2 f. **Plautus / Choerilos:** fiktive Namen. | 6 **bliss:** Seligkeit, Wonne. | 8 **sluice:** eigtl.: Schleuse; hier: Strom. | 9 **gorgeousness:** Pracht, Glanz. | **gorgeosity** (N.): *gorgeousness*. | 9 f. **made flesh:** fleischgeworden, leibhaftig. | 10 **trombone:** Posaune. | **to crunch:** knirschen. | 11 **to silverflame:** silbern flammen, lodern, leuchten. | 12 **timps:** Kurzform von *timpani* (pl.): Kessel-, Orchesterpauke. | 13 **candy:** Kandis. | 15 **spaceship:** Raumschiff. | **gravity:** Schwerkraft. | 17 **strings:** Streichinstrumente, Streicher. | 18 **flute:** Flöte. | 18 f. **platinum:** Platin. | 19 **toffee:** Sahnebonbon.

they would take sleep-pills. Perhaps, knowing the joy I had in my night music, they had already taken them. As I slooshied, my glazzies tight shut to shut in the bliss that was better than any synthemesc Bog or God, I knew such lovely pictures. There were vecks and ptitsas, both young and starry, lying on the ground screaming for mercy, and I was smecking all over my rot and grinding my boot in their litsos. And there were devotchkas ripped and creeching against the walls and I plunging like a shlaga into them, and indeed when the music, which was one movement only, rose to the top of its big highest tower, then, lying there on my bed with glazzies tight shut and rookers behind my gulliver, I broke and spattered and cried aaaaaaah with the bliss of it. And so the lovely music glided to its glowing close.

After that I had lovely Mozart, the Jupiter, and there were new pictures of different litsos to be ground and splashed, and it was after this that I thought I would have just one last disc only before crossing the border, and I wanted something starry and strong and very firm, so it was J. S. Bach I had, the Brandenburg Concerto just for middle and lower strings. And, slooshying with different bliss than before, I viddied again this name on the paper I'd razrezzed that night, a long time ago it seemed, in that cottage called HOME. The name was about a clockwork orange. Lis-

7 **to grind:** hier: hineindrehen. | 9 **shlaga** (N.): Keule, Knüppel. | 10 **movement:** Satz (Musik). | 13 **to spatter:** spritzen. | 16 **Jupiter:** »Jupitersinfonie«, Sinfonie C-Dur mit großer Fuge im Schlusssatz von W. A. Mozart (KV 551). | 21 **Brandenburg Concerto:** Gemeint ist hier das letzte der sechs dem Markgrafen Christian Ludwig von Brandenburg gewidmeten Konzerte von J. S. Bach.

tening to the J.S. Bach, I began to pony better what that meant now, and I thought, slooshying away to the brown gorgeousness of the starry German master, that I would like to have tolchocked them both harder and ripped them to ribbons on their own floor.

Four

The next morning I woke up at oh eight oh oh hours, my brothers, and as I still felt shagged and fagged and fashed and bashed and my glazzies were stuck together real horrorshow with sleepglue, I thought I would not go to school. I thought how I would have a malenky bit longer in the bed, an hour or two say, and then get dressed nice and easy, perhaps even having a splosh about in the bath, and then brew a pot of real strong horrorshow chai and make toast for myself and slooshy the radio or read the gazetta, all on my oddy knocky. And then in the afterlunch I might perhaps, if I still felt like it, itty off to the old skolliwoll and see what was vareeting in that great seat of gloopy useless learning, O my brothers. I heard my papapa grumbling and trampling and then ittying off to the dyeworks where he rabbited, and then my mum called in in a very respectful goloss as she did now I was growing up big and strong:

"It's gone eight, son. You don't want to be late again." So I called back:

"A bit of a pain in the gulliver. Leave us be and I'll try to sleep it off and then I'll be right as dodgers for this after." I slooshied her give a sort of a sigh and she said:

"I'll put your breakfast in the oven then, son. I've got to

8 **splosh** (coll.): Platsch. | 9 **chai:** Chai (Gewürztee). | 10 **gazetta** (N.): Zeitung. | 10 f. **on one's oddy knocky** (N.): allein. | 11 **afterlunch** (N.): Nachmittag. | 12 **to itty** (N.): gehen. | 12 **skolliwoll** (N.): Schule. | 13 **to vareet** (N.): ,emporkochen', sich zusammenbrauen. | 15 **dyeworks** (pl.): Färberei. | 15 f. **to rabbit** (N.): arbeiten. | 21 **to sleep s.th. off:** etwas (z. B. einen Rausch) ausschlafen. | **right as dodgers** (N.): völlig in Ordnung.

be off myself." Which was true, there being this law for everybody not a child nor with child nor ill to go out rabbiting. My mum worked at one of the Statemarts, as they called them, filling up the shelves with tinned soup and beans and all that cal. So I slooshied her clank a plate in the gas-oven like and then she was putting her shoes on and then getting her coat from behind the door and then sighing again, then she said: "I'm off now, son." But I let on to be back in sleepland and then I did doze off real horrorshow, and I had a queer and very real like sneety, dreaming for some reason of my droog Georgie. In this sneety he'd got like very much older and very sharp and hard and was govoreeting about discipline and obedience and how all the malchicks under his control had to jump hard at it and throw up the old salute like being in the army, and there was me in line like the rest saying yes sir and no sir, and then I viddied clear that Georgie had these stars on his pletchoes and he was like a general. And then he brought in old Dim with a whip, and Dim was a lot more starry and grey and had a few zoobies missing as you could see when he let out a smeck, viddying me, and then my droog Georgie said, pointing like at me, "That man has filth and cal all over his platties," and it was true. Then I creeched, "Don't hit, please don't, brothers," and started to run. And I was running in like circles and Dim after me, smecking his gulliver off, cracking with the old whip, and each time I got a real horrorshow tolchock with this whip there was like a

2 **with child:** schwanger. | 3 **Statemart:** staatlicher Supermarkt. |
5 **to clank:** rasseln, klirren. | 9 **to doze off:** einschlummern. | 10 **sneety**
(N.): Traum. | 14 **to jump hard at it** (coll.): fest mitanpacken.

very loud electric bell ringringringing, and this bell was like a sort of a pain, too.

Then I woke up real skorry, my heart going bap bap bap, and of course there was really a bell going brrrrr, and it was our front-door bell. I let on that nobody was at home, but this brrrrr still ittied on, and then I heard a goloss shouting through the door, "Come on then, get out of it, I know you're in bed." I recognised the goloss right away. It was the goloss of P. R. Deltoid (a real gloopy nazz, that one), what they called my Post-Corrective Adviser, an over-worked veck with hundreds on his books. I shouted right right right, in a goloss of like pain, and I got out of bed and attired myself, O my brothers, in a very lovely over-gown of like silk, with designs of like great cities all over this over-gown. Then I put my nogas into very comfy woolly toofles, combed my luscious glory, and was ready for P. R. Deltoid. When I opened up he came shambling in looking shagged, a battered old shlapa on his gulliver, his raincoat filthy. "Ah, Alex boy," he said to me. "I met your mother, yes. She said something about a pain somewhere. Hence not at school, yes."

"A rather intolerable pain in the head, brother, sir," I said in my gentleman's goloss. "I think it should clear by this afternoon."

---

5 **to let on:** vorgeben, so tun als ob. | 9 **nazz:** Kurzform von *nazzard* (obs.): (körperlich oder geistig) schwache, unbedeutende Person. | 10 **post-corrective adviser:** etwa: Bewährungshelfer. | 12 **to attire o.s.:** sich ankleiden, anziehen. | 15 **toofles** (N.): Pantoffeln, Hausschuhe. | 16 **luscious:** köstlich, prachtvoll. | 17 **to shamble:** watscheln. | 18 **battered:** schäbig, mitgenommen. | **shlapa** (N.): Hut. | 22 **intolerable:** unerträglich.

"Or certainly by this evening, yes," said P.R. Deltoid. "The evening is the great time, isn't it, Alex boy? Sit," he said, "sit, sit," as though this was his domy and me his guest. And he sat in this starry rocking-chair of my dad's and began rocking, as if that was all he'd come for. I said:

"A cup of the old chai, sir? Tea, I mean."

"No time," he said. And he rocked, giving me the old glint under frowning brows, as if with all the time in the world. "No time, yes," he said, gloopy. So I put the kettle on. Then I said:

"To what do I owe the extreme pleasure? Is anything wrong, sir?"

"Wrong?" he said, very skorry and sly, sort of hunched looking at me but still rocking away. Then he caught sight of an advert in the gazetta, which was on the table – a lovely smecking young ptitsa with her groodies hanging out to advertise, my brothers, the Glories of the Jugoslav Beaches. Then, after sort of eating her up in two swallows, he said, "Why should you think in terms of there being anything wrong? Have you been doing something you shouldn't, yes?"

"Just a manner of speech," I said, "sir."

"Well," said P.R. Deltoid, "it's just a manner of speech from me to you that you watch out, little Alex, because next time, as you very well know, it's not going to be the corrective school any more. Next time it's going to be the barry

---

3 **domy** (N.): Haus. | 4 **rocking-chair**: Schaukelstuhl. | 8 **glint**: Schimmern, Schein, Glitzern. | 13 **to hunch**: (sich) krümmen, einen Buckel machen. | 15 **advert** (coll.): Kurzform von *advertisement*: Anzeige. | 19 **in terms of** (pl.): im Sinne von. | 26 f. **barry place** (N.): Gefängnis (von *bars* [pl.] ›Gitter‹).

place and all my work ruined. If you have no consideration for your horrible self you might at least have some for me, who have sweated over you. A big black mark, I tell you in confidence, for every one we don't reclaim, a confession of failure for every one of you that ends up in the stripy hole."

"I've been doing nothing I shouldn't, sir," I said. "The millicents have nothing on me, brother, sir I mean."

"Cut out this clever talk about millicents," said P. R. Deltoid very weary, but still rocking. "Just because the police have not picked you up lately doesn't, as you very well know, mean you've not been up to some nastiness. There was a bit of a fight last night, wasn't there? There was a bit of shuffling with nozhes and bike-chains and the like. One of a certain fat boy's friends was ambulanced off late from near the Power Plant and hospitalised, cut about very unpleasantly, yes. Your name was mentioned. The word has got through to me by the usual channels. Certain friends of yours were named also. There seems to have been a fair amount of assorted nastiness last night. Oh, nobody can prove anything about anybody, as usual. But I'm warning you, little Alex, being a good friend to you as always, the one man in this sore and sick community who wants to save you from yourself."

"I appreciate all that, sir," I said, "very sincerely."

"Yes, you do, don't you?" he sort of sneered. "Just watch

---

4 **to reclaim:** bessern, (wieder) in die Gesellschaft integrieren. | 8 **to cut out s.th.** (coll.): mit etwas aufhören. | 10 **to pick s.o. up:** jdn. erwischen. | 11 **to be up to s.th.:** etwas im Schilde führen. | 12 f. **bit of shuffling:** kleines Gerangel. | 13 **bike-chain:** Fahrradkette. | 14 **to ambulance off:** mit dem Krankenwagen wegbringen. | 15 **to hospitalise:** ins Krankenhaus einliefern. | 19 **assorted:** verschiedenartig.

it, that's all, yes. We know more than you think, little Alex." Then he said, in a goloss of great suffering, but still rocking away, "What gets into you all? We study the problem and we've been studying it for damn well near a century, yes, but we get no further with our studies. You've got a good home here, good loving parents, you've got not too bad of a brain. Is some devil that crawls inside you?"

"Nobody's got anything on me, sir," I said. "I've been out of the rookers of the millicents for a long time now."

"That's just what worries me," sighed P.R. Deltoid. "A bit too long of a time to be healthy. You're about due now by my reckoning. That's why I'm warning you, little Alex, to keep your handsome young proboscis out of the dirt, yes. Do I make myself clear?"

"As an unmuddied lake, sir," I said. "Clear as an azure sky of deepest summer. You can rely on me, sir." And I gave him a nice zooby smile.

But when he'd ookadeeted and I was making this very strong pot of chai, I grinned to myself over this thing that P.R. Deltoid and his droogs worried about. All right, I do bad, what with crasting and tolchocks and carves with the britva and the old in-out-in-out, and if I get loveted, well, too bad for me, O my little brothers, and you can't run a country with every chelloveck comporting himself in my manner of the night. So if I get loveted and it's three months in this mesto and another six in that, and then, as P.R. Deltoid so kindly warns, next time, in spite of the

---

12 **reckoning**: Berechnung. | 13 **proboscis**: Rüssel. | 15 **unmuddied**: unverschmutzt. | **azure**: azurblau, himmelblau. | 18 **to ookadeet** (N.): weggehen. | 21 **carve**: Schnitt (von *to carve*). | 22 **to lovet** (N.): erwischen.

great tenderness of my summers, brothers, it's the great unearthly zoo itself, well, I say, "Fair, but a pity, my lords, because I just cannot bear to be shut in. My endeavour shall be, in such future as stretches out its snowy and lilywhite arms to me before the nozh overtakes or the blood spatters its final chorus in twisted metal and smashed glass on the highroad, to not get loveted again." Which is fair speeching. But, brothers, this biting of their toenails over what is the *cause* of badness is what turns me into a fine laughing malchick. They don't go into what is the cause of *goodness*, so why of the other shop? If lewdies are good that's because they like it, and I wouldn't ever interfere with their pleasures, and so of the other shop. And I was patronising the other shop. More, badness is of the self, the one, the you or me on our oddy knockies, and that self is made by old Bog or God and is his great pride and radosty. But the not-self cannot have the bad, meaning they of the government and the judges and the schools cannot allow the bad because they cannot allow the self. And is not our modern history, my brothers, the story of brave malenky selves fighting these big machines? I am serious with you, brothers, over this. But what I do I do because I like to do.

So now, this smiling winter morning. I drank this very strong chai with moloko and spoon after spoon of sugar, me having a sladky tooth, and I dragged out of the oven the

---

2 **unearthly:** überirdisch, übernatürlich, unheimlich. | **zoo** (slang): etwa: Tollhaus; gemeint ist die Haftanstalt (vgl. S. 102, Z. 7). | 4 **lilywhite:** lilienweiß. | 5 **to overtake:** *to take over.* | 7 f. **speeching** (N.): Sprache, Rede (von *speech*). | 11 **the other shop** (slang): etwa: das rivalisierende Etablissement. | 13 **to patronise:** fördern, bevorzugen. | 16 **radosty** (N.): Freude. | 25 **sladky** (N.): süß. | **tooth:** Vorliebe.

breakfast my poor old mum had cooked for me. It was an egg fried, that and no more, but I made toast and ate egg and toast and jam, smacking away at it while I read the gazetta. The gazetta was the usual about ultra-violence and bank robberies and strikes and footballers making everybody paralytic with fright by threatening not to play next Saturday if they did not get higher wages, naughty malchickiwicks as they were. Also there were more space-trips and bigger stereo TV screens and offers of free packets of soapflakes in exchange for the labels on soup-tins, amazing offer for one week only, which made me smeck. And there wa a bolshy big article on Modern Youth (meaning me, so I gave the old bow, grinning like bezoomny) by some very clever bald chelloveck. I read this with care, my brothers, slurping away at the old chai, cup after tass after chasha, crunching my lomticks of black toast dipped in jammiwam and eggiweg. This learned veck said the usual veshches, about no parental discipline, as he called it, and the shortage of real horrorshow teachers who would lambast bloody beggary out of their innocent poops and make them go boohoohoo for mercy. All this was gloopy and made me smeck, but it was like nice to go on knowing that one was making the news all the time, O my brothers. Every day there was something about Modern Youth, but the best

---

3 **to smack:** schmatzen. | 6 **paralytic:** paralytisch, gelähmt. | 8 **space-trip:** Raumfahrt. | 9 **TV screen:** Fernsehbildschirm. | 10 **soapflakes:** Seifenflocken. | 14 **bald:** kahl, glatzköpfig. | 15 **to slurp** (slang): schmatzen, schlürfen. | **chasha** (N.): Tasse. | 16 **to crunch:** (geräuschvoll) knabbern. | **jammiwam** (N.): *jam.* | 17 **eggiweg** (N.): *egg.* | 18 **parental:** elterlich. | 19 **to lambast:** vermöbeln, herunterputzen. | 20 **beggary:** Bettelarmut. | **poop:** Kurzform von *nincompoop:* Einfaltspinsel, Dummkopf.

veshch they ever had in the old gazetta was by some starry pop in a doggy collar who said that in his considered opinion and he was govoreeting as a man of Bog IT WAS THE DEVIL THAT WAS ABROAD and was like ferreting his way into like young innocent flesh, and it was the adult world that could take the responsibility for this with their wars and bombs and nonsense. So that was all right. So he knew what he talked of, being a Godman. So we young innocent malchicks could take no blame. Right right right.

When I'd gone erk erk a couple of razzes on my full innocent stomach, I started to get out the day platties from my wardrobe, turning the radio on. There was music playing, a very nice malenky string quartet, my brothers, by Claudius Birdman, one that I knew well. I had to have a smeck, though, thinking of what I'd viddied once in one of these like articles on Modern Youth, about how Modern Youth would be better off if A Lively Appreciation Of the Arts could be like encouraged. Great Music, it said, and Great Poetry would like quieten Modern Youth down and make Modern Youth more Civilised. Civilised my syphilised yarbles. Music always sort of sharpened me up, O my brothers, and made me feel like old Bog himself, ready to make with the old donner and blitzen and have vecks and ptitsas creeching away in my ha ha power. And when I'd cheested up my litso and rookers a bit and done dressing (my day platties were like student-wear: the old blue

---

2 **pop** (coll.): Papa, Paps. | **doggy collar** (slang): runder Stehkragen (wie bei Geistlichen). | 4 **to ferret one's way:** sich (hinein)schleichen. | 10 **raz** (N.): Mal. | 13 **string quartet:** Streichquartett. | 14 **Birdman:** fiktiver Komponist. | 19 **to quieten down:** beruhigen. | 20 f. **syphilised:** *syphilitic:* syphilisiert (Anklang an *civilised*).

pantalonies with sweater with A for Alex) I thought here at least was time to itty off to the disc-bootick (and cutter too, my pockets being full of pretty polly) to see about this long-promised and long-ordered stereo Beethoven Number Nine (the Choral Symphony, that is), recorded on Masterstroke by the Esh Sham Sinfonia under L. Muhaiwir. So I went out, brothers.

The day was very different from the night. The night belonged to me and my droogs and all the rest of the nadsats, and the starry boorjoyce lurked indoors drinking in the gloopy worldcasts, but the day was for the starry ones, and there always seemed to be more rozzes or millicents about during the day, too. I got the autobus from the corner and rode to Center, and then I walked back to Taylor Place, and there was the disc-bootick I favoured with my inestimable custom, O my brothers. It had the gloopy name of MELODIA, but it was a real horrorshow mesto and skorry, most times, at getting the new recordings. I walked in and the only other customers were two young ptitsas sucking away at ice-sticks (and this, mark, was dead cold winter) and sort of shuffling through the new popdiscs – Johnny Burnaway,

1 **pantalonies** (N., pl.): Hose. | 2 **disc-bootick** (N.): Schallplattenladen. | 5 **Choral Symphony:** Beethovens Sinfonie d-Moll, op. 125, die im Chorsatz, der Vertonung von Schillers Ode »An die Freude«, kulminiert. | 5f. **Masterstroke:** sprechender Name der Schallplattenfirma (wörtl.: Meisterstück). | 6 **Esh Sham Sinfonia / Muhaiwir:** fiktive Eigennamen. | 10 **to lurk:** sich versteckt halten. | 14 **Taylor Place:** vermutl. Anspielung auf den Historiker A. J. P. Taylor (1906–1990), der zu den Universitätslehrern von Burgess gehörte, oder auf die von Burgess geschätzte englische Romanautorin Elizabeth Taylor (1912–1975). | 15 **inestimable:** unschätzbar. | 18 **recording:** (Schallplatten-)Aufnahme. | 21 **to shuffle through s.th.:** etwas flüchtig erledigen; etwas durcheinanderbringen.

Stash Kroh, The Mixers, Lie Quiet Awhile With Ed and Id Molotov, and all the rest of that cal. These two ptitsas couldn't have been more than ten, and they too, like me, it seemed, evidently, had decided to take a morning off from the old skolliwoll. They saw themselves, you could see, as real grown-up devotchkas already, what with the old hipswing when they saw your Faithful Narrator, brothers, and padded groodies and red all ploshed on their goobers. I went up to the counter, making with the polite zooby smile at old Andy behind it (always polite himself, always helpful, a real horrorshow type of a veck, though bald and very very thin). He said:

"Aha, I know what thou wantest, I thinkest. Good news, good news. It have arrived." And with like big conductor's rookers beating time he went to get it. The two young ptitsas started giggling, as they will at that age, and I gave them a like cold glazzy. Andy was back real skorry, waving the great shiny white sleeve of the Ninth, which had on it, brothers, the frowning like thunderbottled litso of Ludwig van himself. "Here," said Andy. "Shall we give it the trial spin?" But I wanted it back home on my stereo to slooshy on my oddy knocky, greedy as hell. I fumbled out the deng to pay and one of the little ptitsas said:

"Who you getten, bratty? What biggy, what only?"

---

7 **hipswing:** Hüftschwung. | **narrator:** Erzähler. | 8 **padded:** gepolstert. | **to plosh:** spritzen, klatschen. | 14 **conductor:** Dirigent. | 15 **to beat time:** den Rhythmus schlagen. | 18 **sleeve:** hier: Schallplattenhülle. | 19 **thunderbottled:** vermutl. Wortspiel mit *thunderbolted*: Adjektivbildung zu *thunderbolt* ›Blitz und Donnerschlag‹. | 20 f. **to give s.th. a spin** (slang): etwas (Schallplatte) abspielen. | 22 **to fumble out:** hervorkramen. | 24 **getten:** *getting*. | **bratty** (auch: *brat*; N.): Bruder (Wortspiel mit *brat* ›Balg‹, Gör‹). | **biggy** (N.): vermutl.: Star.

These young devotchkas had their own way of like govo-reeting. "The Heaven Seventeen? Luke Sterne? Goggly Gogol?" And both giggles, rocking and hippy. Then an idea hit me and made me near fall over with the anguish and ec-stasy of it, O my brothers, so I could not breathe for near ten seconds. I recovered and made with my new-clean zoo-bies and said:

"What you got back home, little sisters, to play your fuzzy warbles on?" Because I could viddy the discs they were buying were with teeny pop veshches. "I bet you got little save tiny portable like picnic spinners." And they sort of pushed their lower lips out at that. "Come with uncle," I said, "and hear all proper. Hear angel trumpets and devil trombones. You are invited." And I like bowed. They gig-gled again and one said:

"Oh, but we're so hungry. Oh, but we could so eat." The other said, "Yah, she can say that, can't she just." So I said:

"Eat with uncle. Name your place."

Then they viddied themselves as real sophistoes, which was like pathetic, and started talking in big-lady golosses about the Ritz and the Bristol and Il Restorante Granturco. But I stopped that with "Follow uncle," and I led them to the Pasta Parlour just round the corner and let them fill their innocent young litsos on spaghetti and cream-puffs

3 **rocking and hippy** (N.): die Hüften wiegend. | 6 **new-clean** (N.): frisch geputzt. | 9 **fuzzy**: undeutlich (Geräusch). | **warble**: Trillern, Ge-sang. | 10 **teeny pop**: Pop-Musik für Teenager. | 11 **save**: hier wohl: er-spart, billig. | **portable picnic spinner** (N.): tragbarer Plattenspieler. | 19 **sophisto** (N.): erfahrene, kultivierte Person (von *sophisticated* ›erfah-ren‹, ›weltoffen‹, ›kultiviert‹). | 21 **restorante**: *ristorante*. | 23 **pasta par-lour**: etwa: Pasta-Salon, Nudelrestaurant. | 24 **cream-puff**: Windbeutel.

and banana-splits and hot choc-sauce, till I near sicked with the sight of it, I, brothers, lunching but frugally off a cold ham-slice and a growling dollop of chilli. These two young ptitsas were much alike, though not sisters. They had the same ideas or lack of, and the same colour hair – a like dyed strawy. Well, they would grow up real today. Today I would make a day of it. No school this afterlunch, but education certainly, Alex as teacher. Their names, they said, were Marty and Sonietta, bezoomny enough and in the heighth of their childish fashion, so I said: 10

"Righty right, Marty and Sonietta. Time for the big spin. Come." When we were outside on the cold street they thought they would not go by autobus, oh no, but by taxi, so I have them the humour, though with a real horror-show in-grin, and I called a taxi from the rank near Center. 15 The driver, a starry whiskery veck in very stained platties, said:

"No tearing up, now. No nonsense with them seats. Just re-upholstered they are." I quieted his gloopy fears and off we spun to Municipal Flatblock 18A, these two bold little 20 ptitsas giggling and whispering. So, to cut all short, we arrived, O my brothers, and I led the way up to 10-8, and they panted and smecked away the way up, and then they were thirsty, they said, so I unlocked the treasure-chest in my room and gave these ten-year-young devotchkas a real hor- 25

2 **to lunch:** eine Zwischenmahlzeit einnehmen. | **frugally:** genügsam, einfach, sparsam. | 7 **to make a day of it** (coll.): sich einen schönen Tag machen. | 14 **humour:** Laune, Willen. | 15 **in-grin** (N.): inwendiges Lächeln. | 16 **whiskery** (slang): einen Backenbart tragend (*whiskers* [pl.]: Backenbart). | 19 **re-upholstered:** frisch gepolstert. | 20 **to spin off:** lossausen. | 21 **to cut short:** abkürzen.

rorshow Scotchman apiece, though well filled with sneezy pins-and-needles soda. They sat on my bed (yet unmade) and leg-swung, smecking and peeting their highballs, while I spun their like pathetic malenky discs through my stereo. Like peeting some sweet scented kid's drink, that was, in like very beautiful and lovely and costly gold goblets. But they went oh oh oh and said, "Swoony" and "Hilly" and other weird slovos that were the heighth of fashion in that youth-group. While I spun this cal for them I encouraged them to drink up and have another, and they were nothing loath, O my brothers. So by the time their pathetic pop-discs had been twice spun each (there were two: "Honey Nose", sung by Ike Yard, and "Night After Day After Night", moaned by two horrible yarbleless like eunuchs whose names I forget) they were getting near the pitch of like young ptitsa's hysterics, what with jumping all over my bed and me in the room with them.

What was actually done that afternoon there is no need to describe, brothers, as you may easily guess all. Those two were unplatted and smecking fit to crack in no time at all, and they thought it the bolshiest fun to viddy old Uncle Alex standing there all nagoy and pan-handled, squirting

---

1f. **sneezy pins-and-needles soda** (N.): die Nase reizendes, kribbelndes Sodawasser. | 3 **highball:** Whisky mit Soda. | 5 **scented:** duftend. | 6 **costly:** kostbar; kostspielig. | **goblet:** Glas mit Fuß, Becher. | 7 **swoony** (AE, slang): ,stark', toll (*to swoon:* ohnmächtig werden). | **hilly** (slang, obs.): schwierig; hier: Bedeutung unklar. | 8 **weird:** unheimlich, sonderbar. | 11 **loath:** abgeneigt. | 15 **pitch:** (fig.) Tonhöhe; Gipfel, Höhepunkt. | 16 **hysterics** (pl.): hysterischer Anfall, Hysterie. | 20 **unplatted** (N.): ausgezogen, nackt. | 22 **pan-handled:** Adjektiv zu *panhandle* ›Pfannenstiel‹; gemeint ist hier eine Erektion. | **to squirt:** spritzen.

the hypodermic like some bare doctor, then giving myself the old jab of growling jungle-cat secretion in the rooker. Then I pulled the lovely Ninth out of its sleeve, so that Ludwig van was now nagoy too, and I set the needle hissing on to the last movement, which was all bliss. There it was then, the bass strings like govoreeting away from under my bed at the rest of the orchestra, and then the male human goloss coming in and telling them all to be joyful, and then the lovely blissful tune all about Joy being a glorious spark like of heaven, and then I felt the old tigers leap in me and then I leapt on these two young ptitsas. This time they thought nothing fun and stopped creeching with high mirth, and had to submit to the strange and weird desires of Alexander the Large which, what with the Ninth and the hypo jab, were choodessny and zammechat and very demanding, O my brothers. But they were both very very drunken and could hardly feel very much.

When the last movement had gone round for the second time with all the banging and creeching about Joy Joy Joy Joy, then these two young ptitsas were not acting the big lady sophisto no more. They were like waking up to what

---

1 **hypodermic:** Kurzform von *hypodermic syringe* oder *hypodermic needle:* Spritze bzw. Injektionsnadel. | 2 **jab** (coll.): Stich, Stoß. | **jungle-cat:** Rohrkatze, Sumpfluchs (in Asien beheimatet). | **secretion:** Sekretion, Absonderung; gemeint ist hier offenkundig die von Alex injizierte Droge. | 6 **bass:** Bass. | 9 **blissful:** (glück)selig, wonnig. | 9 f. **Joy being a glorious spark like of heaven:** Schiller, »An die Freude«, Z. 1: »Freude, schöner Götterfunken«. | 14 **Alexander the Large:** Wortspiel mit *Alexander the Great*; gemeint ist der erigierte Penis. | 15 **choodessny** (N.): wunderbar. | **zammechat** (N.): bemerkenswert. | 19 **to bang:** (zu)schlagen, knallen; hier wohl: dröhnen. | 21 **to wake up to s.th.:** sich einer Sache bewusst werden.

was being done to their malenky persons and saying that they wanted to go home and like I was a wild beast. They looked like they had been in some big bitva, as indeed they had, and were all bruised and pouty. Well, if they would not go to school they must still have their education. And education they had had. They were creeching and going ow ow ow as they put their platties on, and they were like punchipunching me with their teeny fists as I lay there dirty and nagoy and fair shagged and fagged on the bed. This young Sonietta was creeching: "Beast and hateful animal. Filthy horror." So I let them get their things together and get out, which they did, talking about how the rozzes should be got on to me and all that cal. Then they were going down the stairs and I dropped off to sleep, still with the old Joy Joy Joy Joy crashing and howling away.

---

3 **bitva** (N.): Schlacht. | 4 **bruised:** mit blauen Flecken übersät. | **pouty:** schmollend. | 7 f. **punchipunching:** von to punch ›stoßen, puffen‹.

Five

What happened, though, was that I woke up late (near seven-thirty by my watch) and, as it turned out, that was not so clever. You can viddy that everything in this wicked world counts. You can pony that one thing always leads to another. Right right right. My stereo was no longer on about Joy and I Embrace Ye O Ye Millions, so some veck had dealt it the off, and that would be either pee or em, both of them now being quite clear to the slooshying in the living-room and, from the clink clink of plates and slurp slurp of peeting tea from cups, at their tired meal after the day's rabbiting in the factory the one, the store the other. The poor old. The pitiable starry. I put on my over-gown and looked out, in guise of loving only son, to say:

"Hi hi hi, there. A lot better after the day's rest. Ready now for evening work to earn that little bit." For that's what they said they believed I did these days. "Yum yum, mum. Any of that for me?" It was like some frozen pie that she'd unfroze and then warmed up and it looked not so very appetitish, but I had to say what I said. Dad looked at me with a not-so-pleased suspicious like look but said nothing, knowing he dared not, and mum gave me a tired like little smeck, to thee fruit of my womb, my only son sort of. I

7 I Embrace Ye O Ye Millions: Schiller, »An die Freude«, Z. 9: »Seid umschlungen, Millionen!« | 8 to deal s.th. the off (N.): etwas abstellen, ausmachen. | 10 to clink: klingen, klimpern, klirren. | 13 pitiable: erbärmlich, kläglich, bemitleidenswert. | 14 guise: Erscheinung; Gestalt, Maske. | 17 yum yum (coll.): mmh!, prima!, lecker! | 19 to unfreeze: auftauen. | 19 f. appetitish (N.): *appetizing:* appetitlich. | 23 womb: Mutterleib, Schoß.

danced to the bathroom and had a real horrorshow cheest all over, feeling dirty and gluey, then back to my den for the evening's platties. Then, shining, combed, brushed and gorgeous, I sat to my lomtick of pie. Papapa said:

"Not that I want to pry, son, but where exactly is it you go to work of evenings?"

"Oh," I chewed, "it's mostly odd things, helping like. Here and there, as it might be." I gave him a straight dirty glazzy, as to say to mind his own and I'd mind mine. "I never ask for money, do I? Not money for clothes or for pleasures? All right, then, why ask?"

My dad was like humble mumble chumble. "Sorry, son," he said. "But I get worried sometimes. Sometimes I have dreams. You can laugh if you like, but there's a lot in dreams. Last night I had this dream with you in it and I didn't like it one bit."

"Oh?" He had gotten me interessovatted now, dreaming of me like that. I had like a feeling I had had a dream, too, but I could not remember proper what. "Yes?" I said, stopping chewing my gluey pie.

"It was vivid," said my dad. "I saw you lying on the street and you had been beaten by other boys. These boys were like the boys you used to go around with before you were sent to that last Corrective School."

"Oh?" I had an in-grin at that, papapa believing I had real reformed or believing he believed. And then I remembered my own dream, which was a dream of that morning, of

---

1 **cheest** (N.): Waschen, Wäsche. | 2 **gluey**: klebrig. | 5 **to pry**: spähen, neugierig sein, schnüffeln. | 9 **to mind one's own (business)**: sich um seine eigenen Angelegenheiten kümmern. | 17 **to interessovat** (N.): interessieren.

Georgie giving his general's orders and old Dim smecking around toothless as he wielded the whip. But dreams go by opposites I was once told. "Never worry about thine only son and heir, O my father," I said. "Fear not. He canst take care of himself, verily."

"And," said my dad, "you were like helpless in your blood and you couldn't fight back." That was real opposites, so I had another quiet malenky grin within and then I took all the deng out of my carmans and tinkled it on the saucy tablecloth. I said:

"Here, dad, it's not much. It's what I earned last night. But perhaps for the odd peet of Scotchman in the snug somewhere for you and mum."

"Thanks, son," he said. "But we don't go out much now. We daren't go out much, the streets being what they are. Young hooligans and so on. Still, thanks. I'll bring her home a bottle of something tomorrow." And he scooped this ill-gotten pretty into his trouser carmans, mum being at the cheesting and the dishes in the kitchen. And I went out with loving smiles all round.

When I got to the bottom of the stairs of the flatblock I was somewhat surprised. I was more than that. I opened my rot like wide in the old stony gapes. They had come to meet me. They were waiting by the all scrawled over municipal wall painting of the nagoy dignity of labour, bare vecks and cheenas stern at the wheels of industry, like I

---

2 **to wield:** schwingen. | 4 **canst:** *can.* | 5 **verily:** wahrlich, fürwahr. | 9 **to tinkle:** klingeln. | 11 **saucy:** hier: mit Sauce bekleckert. | 12 **peet** (N.): Getränk, Trunk. | 17 **to scoop:** schaufeln. | 18 **ill-gotten:** unrechtmäßig erworben. | 23 **stony gapes:** etwa: steinerne Figuren mit aufgerissenem Mund (*gape:* Gaffen, Glotzen). | 24 **scrawled over:** bekritzelt.

said, with all this dirt pencilled from their rots by naughty
malchicks. Dim had a big thick like stick of black grease-
paint and was tracing filthy slovos real big over our municipal painting and doing the old Dim guff – with whu huh
huh – while he did it. But he turned round when Georgie
and Pete gave me the well hello, showing off their shining droogy zoobies, and he horned out, "He are here, he
have arrived, hooray," and did a clumsy turnitoe bit of
dancing.

"We got worried," said Georgie. "There we were,
a-waiting and peeting away at the old knify moloko, and
you had not turned up. So then Pete here thought how you
might have been like offended by some veshch or other, so
round we come to your abode. That's right, Pete, right?"

"Oh, yes, right," said Pete.

"Appy polly loggies," I said, careful. "I had something of
pain in the gulliver so had to sleep. I was not wakened
when I gave orders for wakening. Still, here we all are, ready
for what the old nochy offers, yes?" I seemed to have picked
up that yes? from P. R. Deltoid, my Post-Corrective Adviser. Very strange.

"Sorry about the pain," said Georgie, like very concerned. "Using the gulliver too much like, maybe. Giving
orders and discipline and such, perhaps. Sure the pain is
gone? Sure you'll not be happier going back to the bed?"
And they all had a bit of a malenky grin.

2 f. **greasepaint:** Schminke. | 3 **to trace:** zeichnen, malen. | 6 **to give s.o.
the well hello** (N.): jdn. begrüßen. | 7 **to horn out** (N.): trompeten,
röhren. | 8 **hooray:** hurra! | **clumsy:** unbeholfen, plump. | 8 f. **turnitoe
bit of dancing** (N.): Tanz auf den Zehenspitzen, Ballett. | 11 **knify** (N.):
gespickt. | 14 **abode:** Wohnung. | 18 **wakening:** Wecken.

"Wait," I said. "Let's get things nice and sparkling clear. This sarcasm, if I may call it such, does not become you, O my little friends. Perhaps you have been having a bit of a quiet govoreet behind my back, making your own little jokes and such-like. As I am your droog and leader, surely I am entitled to know what goes on, eh? Now then, Dim, what does that great big horsy gape of a grin portend?" For Dim had his rot open in a sort of bezoomny soundless smeck. Georgie got in very skorry with:

"All right, no more picking on Dim, brother. That's part of the new way."

"New way?" I said. "What's this about a new way? There's been some very large talk behind my sleeping back and no error. Let me slooshy more." And I sort of folded my rookers and leaned comfortable to listen against the broken banister-rail, me being still higher than them, droogs as they called themselves, on the third stair.

"No offence, Alex," said Pete, "but we wanted to have things more democratic like. Not like you saying what to do and what not all the time. But no offence." Georgie said:

"Offence is neither here nor elsewhere. It's a matter of who has ideas. What ideas has he had?" And he kept his very bold glazzies turned full on me. "It's all the small stuff, malenky veshches like last night. We're growing up, brothers."

2 **sarcasm:** Sarkasmus, beißender Spott. | **to become s.o.:** jdm. (an)stehen. | 4 **govoreet** (N.): Gespräch. | 7 **horsy:** pferdeartig. | **to portend:** anzeigen, bedeuten. | 10 **to pick on s.o.:** an jdm. herummäkeln, -nörgeln. | 16 **banister-rail:** Geländer(stange). | 20 **no offence:** nichts für ungut. | 21 **is neither here nor elsewhere:** *is neither here nor there:* gehört nicht zur Sache, besagt nichts.

"More," I said, not moving. "Let me slooshy more."

"Well," said Georgie, "if you must have it, have it then. We itty round, shop-crasting and the like, coming out with a pitiful rookerful of cutter each. And there's Will the Eng-
5 lish in the Muscleman coffee mesto saying he can fence anything that any malchick cares to try to crast. The shiny stuff, the ice," he said, still with these like cold glazzies on me. "The big big big money is available is what Will the Eng-lish says."

> "So," I said, very comfortable out but real razdraz with-in. "Since when have you been consorting and comporting with Will the English?"

"Now and again," said Georgie, "I get around all on my oddy knocky. Like last Sabbath for instance. I can live my
5 own jeezny, droogie, right?"

I didn't really care for any of this, my brothers. "And what will you do," I said, "with the big big big deng or mon-ey as you so highfaluting call it? Have you not every veshch you need? If you need an auto you pluck it from the trees. If
> you need pretty polly you take it. Yes? Why this sudden shilarny for being the big bloated capitalist?"

"Ah," said Georgie, "you think and govoreet sometimes like a little child." Dim went huh huh huh at that. "To-night," said Georgie, "we pull a mansize crast."
5 So my dream had told the truth, then. Georgie the gen-

---

5 **to fence** (slang): Hehlerei treiben. | 11 **to consort with s.o.:** mit jdm. verkehren. | 11 f. **to comport with s.o.:** zu jdm. passen. | 18 **highfaluting:** hochtrabend, hochgestochen. | 21 **shilarny** (N.): Interesse, Sorge. | **bloated:** (fig.) aufgeblasen. | 24 **to pull** (slang): (Ding) drehen. | **mansize:** männlich, für Männer. | **crast** (N.): Einbruch, Diebstahl.

eral saying what we should do and what not do, Dim with the whip as mindless grinning bulldog. But I played with great care, the greatest, saying, smiling: "Good. Real horrorshow. Initiative comes to them as wait. I have taught you much, little droogie. Now tell me what you have in mind, Georgieboy."

"Oh," said Georgie, cunning and crafty in his grin, "the old moloko-plus first, would you not say? Something to sharpen us up, boy, but you especially, we having the start of you."

"You have govoreeted my thoughts for me," I smiled away. "I was about to suggest the dear old Korova. Good good good. Lead, little Georgie." And I made like a deep bow, smiling like bezoomny but thinking all the time. But when we got into the street I viddied that thinking is for the gloopy ones and that the oomny ones use like inspiration and what Bog sends. For now it was lovely music that came to my aid. There was an auto ittying by and it had its radio on, and I could just slooshy a bar or so of Ludwig van (it was the Violin Concerto, last movement), and I viddied right at once what to do. I said, in like a thick deep goloss, "Right, Georgie, now," and I whished out my cut-throat britva. Georgie said, "Uh?" but he was skorry enough with his nozh, the blade coming sleesh out of the handle, and we were on to each other. Old Dim said, "Oh, no, not right that isn't," and made to uncoil the chain around his tally, but

---

2 **mindless:** unbekümmert, geistlos. | 4 **initiative:** Unternehmungsgeist. | 7 **crafty:** geschickt, listig. | 16 **oomny** (N.): geistreich, gescheit, clever. | 22 **to whish out:** hervorzischen lassen, zücken. | 24 **sleesh** (N.): etwa: husch! | 26 **to uncoil:** abwickeln, abspulen. | **tally** (N.): Taille.

Pete said, putting his rooker firm on old Dim, "Leave them. It's right like that." So then Georgie and Your Humble did the old quiet cat-stalk, looking for openings, knowing each other's style a bit too horrorshow really, Georgie now and then going lurch lurch lurch with his shining nozh but not no wise connecting. And all the time lewdies passed by and viddied all this but minded their own, it being perhaps a common street-sight. But then I counted odin dva tree and went ak ak ak with the britva, though not at litso or glazzies but at Georgie's nozh-holding rooker and, my little brothers, he dropped. He did. He dropped his nozh with a tinkle tankle on the hard winter sidewalk. I had just ticklewickled his fingers with my britva, and there he was looking at the malenky dribble of krovvy that was redding out in the lamplight. "Now," I said, and it was me that was starting, because Pete had given old Dim the soviet not to uncoil the oozy from round his tally and Dim had taken it, "NOW, Dim, let's thou and me have all this now, shall us?" Dim went, "Aaaaaaarhg," like some bolshy bezoomny animal, and snaked out the chain from his waist real horrorshow and skorry, so you had to admire. Now the right style for me here was to keep low like in frog-dancing to protect litso and glazzies, and this I did, brothers, so that poor old Dim was a malenky bit surprised, him being accustomed to

3 **cat-stalk:** katzenartiger Gang. | **opening:** Bresche, Spalt, Blöße. | 5 **to lurch:** schlingern, taumeln, torkeln. | 8 **odin dva tree** (N.): eins, zwei, drei. | 9 **ak** (N.): zack! | 11f. **tinkle tankle** (N.): Geklingel. | 12 **side-walk:** Gehweg, Bürgersteig (AE). | 14 **to ticklewickle** (N.): leicht berühren, kitzeln (von *to tickle* ›kitzeln‹). | 14 **dribble:** Tröpfeln. | **to red out** (N.): rot ausströmen. | 16 **soviet** (N.): Rat. | 20 **to snake s.th. out:** etwas hervorschlängeln lassen.

the straight face-on lash lash lash. Now I will say that he whished me horrorshow on the back so that it stung like bezoomny, but that pain told me to dig in skorry once and for all and be done with old Dim. So I swished with the britva at his left noga in its very tight tight and I slashed two inches of cloth and drew a malenky drop of krovvy to make Dim real bezoomny. Then while he went hauwwww hauwww hauwww like a doggie I tried the same style as for Georgie, banking all on one move – up, cross, cut – and I felt the britva go just deep enough in the meat of old Dim's wrist and he dropped his snaking oozy yelping like a little child. Then he tried to drink in all the blood from his wrist and howl at the same time, and there was too much krovvy to drink and he went bubble bubble bubble, the red like fountaining out lovely, but not for very long. I said:

"Right, my droogies, now we should know. Yes, Pete?"

"I never said anything," said Pete. "I never govoreeted one slovo. Look, old Dim's bleeding to death."

"Never," I said. "One can die but once. Dim died before he was born. That red red krovvy will soon stop." Because I had not cut into the like main cables. And I myself took a clean tashtook from my carman to wrap around poor old dying Dim's rooker, howling and moaning as he was, and the krovvy stopped like I said it would, O my brothers. So they knew now who was master and leader, sheep, thought I.

---

1 **face-on:** direkt, geradeheraus. | **lash:** Hieb. | 3 **to dig in:** sich verschanzen. | 4 **to swish:** schwirren, zischen, sausen. | 5 **to slash:** aufschlitzen. | 9 **to bank on s.th.:** auf etwas setzen. | 14 **to bubble:** blubbern. | 15 **to fountain out:** hervorsprudeln (von *fountain*). | 19 **One can die but once:** Anspielung auf Shakespeare, *Julius Caesar* II,2,32 f.

It did not take long to quieten these two wounded soldiers down in the snug of the Duke of New York, what with large brandies (bought with their own cutter, me having given all to my dad) and a wipe with tashtooks dipped in the water-jug. The old ptitsas we'd bee so horrorshow to last night were there again, going, "Thanks, lads" and "God bless you, boys" like they couldn't stop, though we had not repeated the old sammy act with them. But Pete said, "What's it to be, girls?" and bought black and suds for them, him seeming to have a fair amount of pretty polly in his carmans, so they were on louder than ever with their "God bless and keep you all, lads" and "We'd never split on you, boys" and "The best lads breathing, that's what you are." At last I said to Georgie:

"Now we're back to where we were, yes? Just like before and all forgotten, right?"

"Right right right," said Georgie. But old Dim still looked a bit dazed and he even said, "I could have got that big bastard, see, with my oozy, only some veck got in the way," as though he'd been dratsing not with me but with some other malchick. I said:

"Well, Georgieboy, what did you have in mind?"

"Oh," said Georgie, "not tonight. Not this nochy, please."

"You're a big strong chelloveck," I said, "like us all. We're not little children, are we, Georgieboy? What, then, didst thou in thy mind have?"

"I could have chained his glazzies real horrorshow," said

4 **wipe:** Wischen. | 12 f. **to split on s.o.** (slang): jdn. verraten. | 18 **dazed:** betäubt, benommen.

Dim, and the old baboochkas were still on with their "Thanks, lads."

"It was this house, see," said Georgie. "The one with the two lamps outside. The one with the gloopy name, like."

"What gloopy name?"

"The Mansion or the Manse or some such piece of gloop. Where this very starry ptitsa lives with her cats and all these very starry valuable veshches."

"Such as?"

"Gold and silver and like jewels. It was Will the English who like said."

"I viddy," I said. "I viddy horrorshow." I knew where he meant – Oldtown, just beyond Victoria Flatblock. Well, the real horrorshow leader knows always when like to give and show generous to his like unders. "Very good, Georgie," I said. "A good thought, and one to be followed. Let us at once itty." And as we were going out the old baboochkas said, "We'll say nothing, lads. Been here all the time you have, boys." So I said, "Good old girls. Back to buy more in ten minutes." And so I led my three droogs out to my doom.

---

4 **gloop** (N.): Blödsinn, Unsinn. | 13 **Victoria:** (1819–1901), Königin von England 1837–1901. | 15 **under** (N.): Untergebener. | 21 **doom:** (böses) Geschick, Verhängnis, Verderben.

Six

Just past the Duke of New York going east was offices and then there was the starry beat-up biblio and then was the bolshy flatblock called Victoria Flatblock after some victory or other, and then you came to the like starry type houses of the town in what was called Oldtown. You got some of the real horrorshow ancient domies here, my brothers, with starry lewdies living in them, thin old barking like colonels with sticks and old ptitsas who were widows and deaf starry damas with cats who, my brothers, had felt not the touch of any chelloveck in the whole of their pure like jeeznies. And here, true, there were starry veshches that would fetch their share of cutter on the tourist market – like pictures and jewels and other starry pre-plastic cal of that type. So we came nice and quiet to this domy called the Manse, and there were globe lights outside on iron stalks, like guarding the front door on each side, and there was a light like dim on in one of the rooms on the ground level, and we went to a nice patch of street dark to watch through the window what was ittying on. This window had iron bars in front of it, like the house was a prison, but we could viddy nice and clear what was ittying on.

What was ittying on was that this starry ptitsa, very grey in the voloss and with a very liny like litso, was pouring the old moloko from a milk-bottle into saucers and then setting these saucers down on the floor, so you could tell there

---

3 **beat-up** (slang): heruntergekommen. | 10 **dama** (N.): Dame. | 13 **to fetch**: hier: einbringen. | 14 **pre-plastic**: aus der Vorplastikzeit. | 24 **voloss** (N.): Haar(e). | **liny**: faltig, runzlig. | 25 **saucer**: Untertasse.

were plenty of mewing kots and koshkas writhing about down there. And we could viddy one or two, great fat scoteenas, jumping up on to the table with their rots open going mare mare mare. And you could viddy this old baboochka talking back to them, govoreeting in like scoldy language to her pussies. In the room you could viddy a lot of old pictures on the walls and starry very elaborate clocks, also some like vases and ornaments that looked starry and dorogoy. Georgie whispered, "Real horrorshow deng to be gotten for them, brothers. Will the English is real anxious." Pete said, "How in?" Now it was up to me, and skorry, before Georgie started telling us how. "First veshch," I whispered, "is to try the regular way, the front. I will go very polite and say that one of my droogs has had a like funny fainting turn on the street. Georgie can be ready to show, when she opens, thatwise. Then to ask for water or to phone the doc. Then in easy." Georgie said:

"She may not open." I said:

"We'll try it, yes?" And he sort of shrugged his pletchoes, making with a frog's rot. So I said to Pete and old Dim, "You two droogies get either side of the door. Right?" They nodded in the dark right right right. "So," I said to Georgie, and I made bold straight for the front door. There was a bellpush and I pushed, and brrrrrr brrrrrr sounded down the hall inside. A like sense of slooshying followed, as though the ptitsa and her koshkas all had their ears back

1 **to mew:** miauen. | **kot** (N.): Kater. | **to writhe:** sich krümmen, winden. | 2 f. **scoteena** (N.): ‚Kuh‘. | 5 **scoldy** (N.): scheltend (von *to scold*). | 6 **pussy** (coll.): Kurzform von *pussycat:* Mieze. | 9 **dorogoy** (N.): teuer, wertvoll. | 17 **doc:** Kurzform von *doctor:* Arzt. | 24 **bellpush:** Klingelknopf.

at the brrrrrr brrrrrr, wondering. So I pushed the old zvo-
nock a malenky bit more urgent. I then bent down to the
letter-slit and called through in a refined like goloss, "Help,
madam, please. My friend has just had a funny turn on the
street. Let me phone a doctor, please." Then I could viddy a
light being put on in the hall, and then I could hear the old
baboochka's nogas going flip flap in flipflap slippers to
nearer the front door, and I got the idea, I don't know why,
that she had a big fat pussycat under each arm. Then she
called out in a very surprising deep like goloss:

"Go away. Go away or I shoot." Georgie heard that and
wanted to giggle. I said, with like suffering and urgency in
my gentleman's goloss:

"Oh, please help, madam. My friend's very ill."

"Go away," she called. "I know your dirty tricks, making me open the door and then buy things I don't want.
Go away, I tell you." That was real lovely innocence, that
was. "Go away," she said again, "or I'll set my cats on
to you." A malenky bit bezoomny she was, you could tell
that, through spending her jeezny all on her oddy knocky.
Then I looked up and I viddied that there was a sash-
window above the front door and that it would be a lot
more skorry to just do the old pletcho climb and get in that
way. Else there'd be this argument all the long nochy. So I
said:

"Very well, madam. If you won't help I must take my
suffering friend elsewhere." And I winked my droogies all
away quiet, only me crying out, "All right, old friend, you

1f. **zvonock** (N.): Klingelknopf. | 3 **letter-slit:** Briefschlitz. | 7 **flip flap:**
lautmalerisch für das Geräusch der Schritte (*to flip:* klapsen; *to flap:*
schlagen, klapsen). | 21f. **sash-window:** Schiebefenster.

will surely meet some good samaritan some place other. This old lady perhaps cannot be blamed for being suspicious with so many scoundrels and rogues of the night about. No, indeed not." Then we waited again in the dark and I whispered, "Right. Return to the door. Me stand on Dim's pletchoes. Open that window and me enter, droogies. Then to shut up that old ptitsa and open up for all. No trouble." For I was like showing who was leader and the chelloveck with the ideas. "See," I said. "Real horrorshow bit of stonework over that door, a nice hold for my nogas." They viddied all that, admiring perhaps I thought, and said and nodded Right right right in the dark.

So back tiptoe to the door. Dim was our heavy strong malchick and Pete and Georgie like heaved me up on to Dim's bolshy manly pletchoes. All this time, O thanks to worldcasts on the gloopy TV and, more, lewdies' nightfear through lack of night-police, dead lay the street. Up there on Dim's pletchoes I viddied that this stonework above the door would take my boots lovely. I kneed up, brothers, and there I was. The window, as I had expected, was closed, but I outed with my britva and cracked the glass of the window smart with the bony handle thereof. All the time below my droogies were hard breathing. So I put in my rooker through the crack and made the lower half of the window sail up open silver-smooth and lovely. And I was, like getting into the bath, in. And there were my

1 **good samaritan:** barmherziger Samariter (vgl. Lukas 10,30–37). | 3 **scoundrel:** Schurke. | **rogue:** Schurke, Schelm. | 10 **stonework:** Steinmetzarbeit. | 13 **tiptoe:** auf Zehenspitzen. | 19 **to knee up** (N.): mit den Knien hochdrücken. | 21 **to out with s.th.:** etwa: etwas hervorholen, zücken.

sheep down below, their rots open as they looked up, O brothers.

I was in bumpy darkness, with beds and cupbaords and bolshy heavy stoolies and piles of boxes and books about. But I strode manful towards the door of the room I was in, seeing a like crack of light under it. The door went squeeeeeeeeeeak and then I was on a dusty corridor with other doors. All this waste, brothers, meaning all these rooms and but one starry sharp and her pussies, but perhaps the kots and koshkas had like separate bedrooms, living on cream and fish-heads like royal queens and princes. I could hear the like muffled goloss of this old ptitsa down below saying, "Yes yes yes, that's it," but she would be govoreeting to these mewing sidlers going maaaaaaah for more moloko. Then I saw the stairs going down to the hall and I thought to myself that I would show these fickle and worthless droogs of mine that I was worth the whole three of them and more. I would do all on my oddy knocky. I would perform the old ultra-violence on the starry ptitsa and on her pusspots if need be, then I would take fair rookerfuls of what looked like real polenzy stuff and go waltzing to the front door and open up showering gold and silver on my waiting droogs. They must learn all about leadership.

So down I ittied, slow and gentle, admiring in the stair-

---

3 **bumpy:** holperig, uneben; hier etwa: mit lauter Ecken und Kanten. | 4 **stooly:** Schemel (von *stool*). | 6 f. **to squeak:** quietschen. | 8 **waste:** Verschwendung, Abfall. | 14 **sidler** (N.): Katze (von *to sidle* ›schleichen‹). | 16 **fickle:** wankelmütig, unbeständig. | 21 **polenzy** (N.): nützlich, wertvoll. | 22 **to shower s.th. on s.o.:** jdn. mit etwas übergießen, überschütten. | 25 f. **stair-well:** Treppenhaus.

well grahzny pictures of old time – devotchkas with long hair and high collars, and the country with trees and horses, the holy bearded veck all nagoy hanging on a cross. There was a real musty von of pussies and pussyfish and starry dust in this domy, different from the flatblocks. And then I was downstairs and I could viddy the light in this front room where she had been doling moloko to the kots and koshkas. More, I could viddy these great over-stuffed scoteenas going in and out with their tails waving and like rubbing themselves on the door-bottom. On a like big wooden chest in the dark hall I could viddy a nice malenky statue that shone in the light of the room, so I crasted this for my own self, it being like of a young thin devotchka standing on one noga with her rookers out, and I could see this was made of silver. So I had this when I ittied into the lit-up room, saying, "Hi hi hi. At last we meet. Our brief govoreet through the letter-hole was not, shall we say, satisfactory, yes? Let us admit not, oh verily not, you stinking starry old sharp." And I like blinked in the light at this room and the old ptitsa in it. It was full of kots and koshkas all crawling to and fro over the carpet, with bits of fur floating in the lower air, and these fat scoteenas were all different shapes and colours, black, white, tabby, ginger, tortoise-shell, and of all ages, too, so that there were kittens fillying about with each other and there were pussies full-grown and there were real dribbling starry ones very bad-tempered. Their mistress, this old ptitsa, looked at me fierce like a man and said:

1 **grahzny** (N.): schmutzig. | 4 **musty**: modrig, verstaubt. | 7 **to dole**: aus-, verteilen. | 8 **over-stuffed**: überfüttert. | 19 **to blink**: blinzeln. | 23 **tabby**: getigert (Katze). | **ginger**: rötlich(gelb), ingwerfarben. | **tortoise-shell**: Schildpatt. | 26 **to dribble**: sabbern, geifern.

"How did you get in? Keep your distance, you villainous young toad, or I shall be forced to strike you."

I had a real horrorshow smeck at that, viddying that she had in her veiny rooker a crappy wood walking-stick which she raised at me threatening. So, making with my shiny zoobies, I ittied a bit nearer to her, taking my time, and on the way I saw on a like sideboard a lovely little veshch, the loveliest malenky veshch any malchick fond of music like myself could ever hope to viddy with his own two glazzies, for it was like the gulliver and pletchoes of Ludwig van himself, what they call a bust, a like stone veshch with long hair and blind glazzies and the big flowy cravat. I was off for that right away, saying, "Well, how lovely and all for me." But ittying towards it with my glazzies like full on it and my greedy rooker held out, I did not see the milk saucers on the floor and into one I went and sort of lost balance. "Whoops," I said, trying to steady, but this old ptitsa had come up behind me very sly and with great skorriness for her age and then she went crack crack on my gulliver with her bit of a stick. So I found myself on my rookers and knees trying to get up and saying, "Naughty naughty naughty." And then she was going crack crack again, saying, "Wretched little slummy bed-bug, breaking into *real* people's houses." I didn't like this crack crack eegra, so I grasped hold of one end of her stick as it came down again and then she lost her balance and was trying to steady herself against a table, but then the table-cloth came off with a milk-jug and a

---

1 villainous: schändlich, schurkisch. | 2 toad: Kröte. | 7 sideboard: Büfett, Anrichtetisch. | 11 bust: Büste. | 17 whoops: hoppla! | 18 skorriness (N.): Schnelligkeit. | 23 slummy: elend, dreckig, schmutzig (von *slum* ›Elendsviertel‹). | bed-bug: Wanze. | 24 eegra (N.): Spiel.

milk-bottle going all drunk then scattering white splosh in all directions, then she was down on the floor grunting, going, "Blast you, boy, you shall suffer." Now all the cats were getting spoogy and running and jumping in a like cat-panic, and some were blaming each other, hitting out cat-tolchocks with the old naga and ptaaaaa and grrrrr and kraaaaark. I got up on to my nogas, and there was this nasty vindictive starry forella with her wattles ashake and grunting as she like tried to lever herself up from the floor, so I gave her a malenky fair kick in the litso, and she didn't like that, crying, "Waaaaah," and you could viddy her veiny mottled litso going purplewurple where I'd landed the old noga.

As I stepped back from the kick I must have like trod on the tail of one of these dratsing creeching pusspots, because I shooshied and gromky yauuuuuuuuw and found that like fur and teeth and claws had like fastened themselves round my leg, and there I was cursing away and trying to shake it off holding this silver malenky statue in one rooker and trying to climb over this old ptitsa on the floor to reach lovely Ludwig van in frowning like stone. And then I was into another saucer brimful of creamy moloko and near went flying again, the whole veshch really a very humorous one if you could imagine it sloochatting to some other veck

---

2 **to grunt:** grunzen. | 3 **blast you:** zum Teufel mit dir! (*to blast:* sprengen, vernichten). | 4 **spoogy** (N.): erschreckt, verängstigt. | 6 **naga** (N.): Pfote. | 8 **vindictive:** rachsüchtig. | **forella** (N.): ‚Forelle'. | **wattles** (pl.): Bart, Kehllappen. | **ashake:** zitternd, bebend. | 9 **to lever o.s. up:** sich hochdrücken. | 12 **mottled:** gesprenkelt, gefleckt, bunt. | **purplewurple:** *purple.* | 16 **gromky** (N.): laut. | 22 **brimful:** randvoll, übervoll. | 24 **to sloochat** (N.): sich ereignen, geschehen.

and not to Your Humble Narrator. And then the starry ptitsa on the floor reached over all the dratsing yowling pusscats and grabbed at my noga, still going "Waaaaah" at me,
and, my balance being a bit gone, I went really crash this
time, on to sploshing moloko and skriking koshkas, and the
old forella started to fist me on the litso, both of us being
on the floor, creeching, "Thrash him, beat him, pull out his
finger-nails, the poisonous young beetle," addressing her
pusscats only, and then, as if like obeying the starry old
ptitsa, a couple of koshkas got on to me and started scratch-
ing like bezoomny. So then I got real bezoomny myself,
brothers, and hit out at them, but this baboochka said,
"Toad, don't touch my kitties," and like scratched my litso.
So then I creeched: "You filthy old soomka," and upped
with the little malenky like silver statue and cracked her a
fine fair tolchock on the gulliver and that shut her up real
horrorshow and lovely.

Now as I got up from the floor among all the crarking
kots and koshkas what should I slooshy but the shoom of
the old police-auto siren in the distance, and it dawned on
me skorry that the old forella of the pusscats had been on
the phone to the millicents when I thought she'd been govoreeting to the mewlers and mowlers, her having got her
suspicions skorry on the boil when I'd rung the old zvo-

2 **to yowl:** jaulen, heulen. | 5 **to splosh:** platschen, (ver)spritzen. |
to skrike (N.): kratzen. | 7 **to thrash:** (ver)dreschen, (ver)prügeln. |
13 **kitty:** Kätzchen. | 14 **soomka** (N.): Schlampe. | 14 f. **to up with s.th.:**
etwas hochheben. | 18 **to crark** (N.): jaulen, heulen. | 20 **to dawn on
s.o.:** jdm. ,dämmern', klarwerden. | 23 **mewler** (N.): Maunzer, Miauen
(von *to mew*). | **mowler** (N.): *mewler.* | 24 **boil:** *boiling-point:* (fig.)
Siedepunkt.

nock pretending for help. So now, slooshying this fearsome shoom of the rozz-van, I belted for the front door and had a rabbiting time undoing all the locks and chains and bolts and other protective veshches. Then I got it open, and who should be on the doorstep but old Dim, me just being able to viddy the other two of my so-called droogs belting off. "Away," I creeched to Dim. "The rozzes are coming." Dim said, "You stay to meet them huh huh huh," and then I viddied that he had his oozy out, and then he upped with it and it snaked whishhhhh and he chained me gentle and artistic like on the glazzies, me just closing them up in time. Then I was howling around trying to viddy with this howling great pain, and Dim said, "I don't like you should do what you done, old droogy. Not right it wasn't to get on to me like the way you done, brat." And then I could slooshy his bolshy lumpy boots beating off, him going huh huh huh into the darkmans, and it was only about seven seconds after that I slooshied the millicent-van draw up with a filthy great dropping siren-howl, like some bezoomny animal snuffing it. I was howling too and like yawing about and I banged my gulliver smack on the hall-wall, my glazzies being tight shut and the juice astream from them, very agonising. So there I was like groping in the hallway as the millicents arrived. I couldn't viddy them, of course, but I could slooshy and damn near smell the von of the bastards, and

---

1 **fearsome**: fürchterlich, grässlich. | 2 **to belt** (slang): eilen, rasen. | 16 **lumpy**: klumpig, klobig. | **to beat off** (slang): abhauen, sich entfernen. | 17 **darkmans** (slang, pl.): Nacht. | 20 **to yaw**: schwanken. | 21 **smack**: 1. klatsch!, platsch!; 2. (adv.) gerade, direkt. | 22 **astream**: strömend, fließend. | 22 f. **agonising**: quälend, herzzerreißend. | 23 **to grope**: tasten, tappen.

soon I could feel the bastards as they got rough and did the old twist-arm act, carrying me out. I could also slooshy one millicent goloss saying from like the room I'd come out of with all the kots and koshkas in it, "She's been nastily knocked about but she's breathing," and there was loud mewing all the time.

"A real pleasure this is," I heard another millicent goloss say as I was tolchocked very rough and skorry into the auto. "Little Alex all to our own selves." I creeched out:

"I'm blind, Bog bust and bleed you, you grahzny bastards."

"Language, language," like smecked a goloss, and then I got a like backhand tolchock with some ringy rooker or other full on the rot. I said:

"Bog murder you, you vonny stinking bratchnies. Where are the others? Where are my stinking traitorous droogs? One of my cursed grahzny bratties chained me on the glazzies. Get them before they get away. It was all their idea, brothers. They like forced me to do it. I'm innocent, Bog butcher you." By this time they were all having a good smeck at me with the heighth of like callousness, and they'd tolchocked me into the back of the auto, but I still kept on about these so-called droogs of mine and then I viddied it would be no good, because they'd all be back now in the snug of the Duke of New York forcing black and suds and double Scotchmen down the unprotesting

10 **to bust:** ruinieren. | **to bleed s.o.:** jdn. zur Ader lassen, bluten lassen, schröpfen. | 13 **backhand:** mit dem Handrücken. | 15 **vonny** (N.): stinkig. | **bratchny** (N.): Bastard. | 16 **traitorous:** verräterisch. | 20 **to butcher:** schlachten, morden. | 21 **callousness:** Gleichgültigkeit, Gefühllosigkeit. | 26 **unprotesting:** nicht widersprechend, nicht widerstrebend.

gorloes of those stinking starry ptitsas and they saying, "Thanks, lads. God bless you, boys. Been here all the time you have, lads. Not been out of our sight you haven't."

All the time we were sirening off to the rozz-shop, me being wedged between two millicents and being given the odd thump and malenky tolchock by these smecking bullies. Then I found I could open up my glaz-lids a malenky bit and viddy like through all tears a kind of streamy city going by, all the lights like having run into one another. I could viddy now through smarting glazzies these two smecking millicents at the back with me and the thin-necked driver and the fat-necked bastard next to him, this one having a sarky like govoreet at me, saying, "Well, Alex boy, we all look forward to a pleasant evening together, don't we not?" I said:

"How do you know my name, you stinking vonny bully? May Bog blast you all to hell, grahzny bratchny as you are, you sod." So they all had a smeck at that and I had my ooko like twisted by one of these stinking millicents at the back with me. The fat-necked not-driver said:

"Everybody knows little Alex and his droogs. Quite a famous young boy our Alex has become."

"It's those others," I creeched. "Georgie and Dim and Pete. No droogs of mine, the bastards."

"Well," said the fat-neck, "you've got the evening in

---

1 **gorlo** (N.): Kehle. | 4 **to siren** (N.): mit Sirengeheul fahren. | **rozz-shop** (N.): Polizeistation. | 5 **to wedge**: einzwängen. | 6 **thump**: (heftiger) Schlag. | 6 f. **bully**: brutaler Kerl, Maulheld, Tyrann. | 8 **streamy**: etwa: verschwommen. | 10 **to smart**: schmerzen, leiden. | 13 **sarky** (N.): *sarcastic*: sarkastisch. | 18 **sod** (taboo slang): Sodomit, Saukerl, Schweinehund.

front of you to tell the whole story of the daring exploits of those young gentlemen and how they led poor little innocent Alex astray." Then there was the shoom of another like police siren passing this auto but going the other way.

"Is that for those bastards?" I said. "Are they being picked up by you bastards?"

"That," said fat-neck, "is an ambulance. Doubtless for your old lady victim, you ghastly wretched scoundrel."

"It was all their fault," I creeched, blinking my smarting glazzies. "The bastards will be peeting away in the Duke of New York. Pick them up, blast you, you vonny sods." And then there was more smecking and another malenky tolchock, O my brothers, on my poor smarting rot. And then we arrived at the stinking rozz-shop and they helped me get out of the auto with kicks and pulls and they tolchocked me up the steps and I knew I was going to get nothing like fair play from these stinking grahzny bratchnies, Bog blast them.

1 **exploit**: Heldentat. | 2 **to lead s.o. astray**: jdn. in die Irre führen. | 8 **ghastly**: grässlich, grausig; geisterhaft.

Seven

They dragged me into this very bright-lit whitewashed cantora, and it had a strong von that was a mixture of like sick and lavatories and beery rots and disinfectant, all coming from the barry places near by. You could hear some of the plennies in their cells cursing and singing and I fancied I could slooshy one belting out:

And I will go back to my darling, my darling,
When you, my darling are gone.

But there were the golosses of millicents telling them to shut it and you could even slooshy the zvook of like somebody being tolchocked real horrorshow and going owwwwwwww, and it was like the goloss of a drunken starry ptitsa, not a man. With me in this cantora were four millicents, all having a good loud peet of chai, a big pot of it being on the table and they sucking and belching away over their dirty bolshy mugs. They didn't offer me any. All that they gave me, my brothers, was a crappy starry mirror to look into, and indeed I was not your handsome young Narrator any longer but a real strack of a sight, my rot swollen and my glazzies all red and my nose bumped a bit also. They all had a real horrorshow smeck when they viddied

2 to whitewash: tünchen. | 3 cantora (N.): Büro. | 4 sick: Erbrochenes. | lavatory: Waschraum, Toilette. | beery: hier: nach Bier riechend. | disinfectant: Desinfektionsmittel. | 6 plenny (N.): Gefangener, Gefängnisinsasse. | 11 zvook (N.): Klang, Geräusch. | 17 mug: Krug, Becher. | 20 strack (N.): Schrecken, Horror. | 21 bumped: zerstoßen.

my like dismay, and one of them said, "Love's young nightmare, like." And then a top millicent came in with like stars on his pletchoes to show me he was high high high, and he viddied me and said, "Hm." So then they started. I said:

"I won't say one single solitary slovo unless I have my lawyer here. I know the law, you bratchnies." Of course they all had a good gromky smeck at that and the stellar top millicent said:

"Righty right, boys, we'll start off by showing him that we know the law, too, but that knowing the law's not everything." He had a like gentleman's goloss and spoke in a very weary sort of a way, and he nodded with a like droogy smile at one very big fat bastard. This big fat bastard took off his tunic and you could viddy he had a real big starry pot on him, then he came up to me not too skorry and I could get the von of the milky chai he'd been peeting when he opened his rot in a like very tired leery grin at me. He was not too well shaved for a rozz and you could viddy like patches of dried sweat on his short under the arms, and you could get this von of like earwax from him as he came close. Then he clenched his stinking red rooker and let me have it right in the belly, which was unfair, and all the other millicents smecked their gullivers off at that, except the top one and he kept on with this weary like bored grin. I had to lean against the whitewashed wall so that all the white got on to my platties, trying to drag the old breath back and in great agony, and then I wanted to sick up the gluey pie I'd had be-

1f. **nightmare:** Alptraum. | 5 **solitary:** einzig, einzeln. | 7 **stellar: 1.** mit den Sternen, Stern(en)…; **2.** (fig.) führend, herausragend. | 14 **tunic:** Tunika, Waffenrock. | 17 **leery:** schlau, gerissen; argwöhnisch. | 20 **earwax:** Ohrenschmalz. | 21 **to clench:** fest zusammenpressen, ballen.

fore the start of the evening. But I couldn't stand that sort of veshch, sicking all over the floor, so I held it back. Then I saw that this fatty bruiseboy was turning to his millicent droogs to have a real horrorshow smeck at what he'd done, so I raised my right noga and before they could creech at him to watch out I'd kicked him smart and lovely on the shin. And he creeched murder, hopping around.

But after that they all had a turn, bouncing me from one to the other like some very weary bloody ball, O my brothers, and fisting me in the yarbles and the rot and the belly and dealing out kicks, and then at last I had to sick up on the floor and, like some real bezoomny veck, I even said, "Sorry, brothers, that was not the right thing at all. Sorry sorry sorry." But they handed me starry bits of gazetta and made me wipe it, then they made me make with the sawdust. And then they said, almost like dear old droogs, that I was to sit down and we'd all have a quiet like govoreet. And then P. R. Deltoid came in to have a viddy, his office being in the same building, looking very tired and grahzny, to say, "So it's happened, Alex boy, yes?" Then he turned to the millicents to say, "Evening, inspector. Evening, sergeant. Evening, evening all. Well, this is the end of the line for me, yes. Dear dear, this boy does look messy, doesn't he? Just look at the state of him."

"Violence makes violence," said the top millicent in a very holy type goloss. "He resisted his lawful arresters."

"End of the line, yes," said P. R. Deltoid again. He looked at me with very cold glazzies like I had become like a thing

---

7 **shin:** Schienbein. | 15 **sawdust:** Sägemehl. | 18 **viddy** (N.): Blick. | 26 **arrester:** jd., der verhaftet.

and was no more a bleeding very tired battered chelloveck. "I suppose I'll have to be in court tomorrow."

"It wasn't me, brother, sir," I said, a malenky bit weepy. "Speak up for me, sir, for I'm not so bad. I was led on by the treachery of others, sir."

"Sings like a linnet," said the top rozz, sneery. "Sings the roof off lovely, he does that."

"I'll speak," said cold P. R. Deltoid. "I'll be there tomorrow, don't worry."

"If you'd like to give him a bash in the chops, sir," said the top millicent, "don't mind us. We'll hold him down. He must be another great disappointment to you."

P. R. Deltoid then did something I never thought any man like him who was supposed to turn us baddiwads into real horrorshow malchicks would do, especially with all those rozzes around. He came a bit nearer and he spat. He spat. He spat full in my litso and then wiped his wet spitty rot with the back of his rooker. And I wiped and wiped and wiped my spat-on litso with my bloody tashtook, saying, "Thank you, sir, thank you." And then P. R. Deltoid walked out without another slovo.

The millicents now got down to making this long statement for me to sign, and I thought to myself, Hell and blast you all, if all you bastards are on the side of the Good then I'm glad I belong to the other shop. "All right," I said to them, "you grahzny bratchnies as you are, you vonny sods,

---

4 **to speak up for s.o.:** sich für jdn. einsetzen. | 6 **linnet:** Hänfling. | **sneery** (N.): *sneering.* | 10 **bash:** heftiger Schlag. | **chops** (pl.): Kiefer; Maul, Rachen. | 14 **baddiwads** (N.): schlechte Kerle, Übeltäter. | 17 **spitty** (N.): mit Spucke benetzt (von *to spit*).

Take it, take the lot. I'm not going to crawl around on my brooko any more, you merzky gets. Where do you want it taken from, you cally vonning animals? From my last corrective? Horrorshow, horrorshow, here it is, then." So I gave it to them, and I had this shorthand millicent, a very quiet and scared type chelloveck, no real rozz at all, covering page after page after page after. I gave them the ultraviolence, the crasting, the dratsing, the old in-out in-out, the lot, right up to this night's veshch with the bugatty starry ptitsa with the mewing kots and koshkas. And I made sure my so-called droogs were in it, right up to the shiyah. When I'd got through the lot the shorthand millicent looked a bit faint, poor old veck. The top rozz said to him, in a kind type goloss:

"Right, son, you go off and get a nice cup of chai for yourself and then type all that filth and rottenness out with a clothes-peg on your nose, three copies. Then they can be brought to our handsome young friend here, for signature. And you," he said to me, "can now be shown to your bridal suite with running water and all conveniences. All right," in this weary goloss to two of the real tough rozzes, "take him away."

So I was kicked and punched and bullied off to the cells and put in with about ten or twelve other plennies, a lot of them drunk. There were real oozhassny animal type vecks

---

2 **brooko** (N.): Bauch. | **merzky** (N.): Drecks…, dreckig. | **get** (slang): Kerl. | 3 **cally** (N.): dreckig, beschissen. | 5 **shorthand**: Kurzschrift. | 9 **bugatty** (N.): reich. | 12 **shiyah** (N.): Hals. | 16 **rottenness**: Verkommenheit, Verderbtheit. | 17 **clothes-peg**: Wäscheklammer. | 19 f. **bridal suite**: Hochzeitssuite. | 23 **to bully**: einschüchtern, tyrannisieren, schikanieren. | 25 **oozhassny** (N.): schrecklich.

among them, one with his nose all ate away and his rot open like a big black hole, one that was lying on the floor snoring away and all like slime dribbling all the time out of his rot, and one that had like done all cal on his pantalonies.
Then there were two like queer ones who both took a fancy to me, and one of them made a jump on to my back, and I had a real nasty bit of dratsing with him and the von on him, like of meth and cheap scent, made me want to sick again, only my belly was empty now, O my brothers. Then the other queer one started putting his rookers on to me, and then there was a snarling bit of dratsing between these two, both of them wanting to get at my plott. The shoom became very loud, so that a couple of millicents came along and cracked into these two with like truncheons, so that both sat quiet then, looking into space, and there was the old krovvy going drip drip drip down the litso of one of them. There were bunks in this cell, but all filled. I climbed up to the top of one tier of bunks, there being four in a tier, and there was a starry drunken veck snoring away, most probably heaved up there to the top by the millicents. Anyway, I heaved him down again, him not being all that heavy, and he collapsed on top of a fat drunk chelloveck on the floor, and both woke and started creeching and punching pathetic at each other. So I lay down on this vonny bed, my brothers, and went to very tired and exhausted and hurt sleep. But it was not really like sleep, it was like passing out to another better world. And in this

1 ate away: *eaten away*: zerfressen. | 3 slime: Schleim, Schlamm. | 5 queer (slang): schwul. | 8 meth (slang): Methylalkohol. | 14 truncheon: Gummiknüppel. | 17 bunk: Schlafbank, -stelle, -koje. | 18 tier: Reihe, Lage.

other better world, O my brothers, I was in like a big field with all flowers and trees, and there was a like goat with a man's litso playing away on a like flute. And then there rose like the sun Ludwig van himself with thundery litso and cravat and wild windy voloss, and then I heard the Ninth, last movement, with the slovos all a bit mixed-up, like they knew themselves they had to be mixed-up, this being a dream:

> Boy, thou uproarious shark of heaven,
>   Slaughter of Elysium,
> Hearts on fire, aroused, enraptured,
>   We will tolchock you on the rot and kick
>   your grahzny vonny bum.

But the tune was right, as I knew when I was being woke up two or ten minutes or twenty hours or days or years later, my watch having been taken away. There was a millicent like miles and miles down below and he was prodding at me with a long stick with a spike on the end, saying:

"Wake up, son. Wake up, my beauty. Wake to real trouble." I said:

"Why? Who? Where? What is it?" And the tune of the

---

4 **thundery:** donnernd, donnergleich. | 9 f. **uproarious shark of heaven, / Slaughter of Elysium:** Verballhornung der Anfangszeilen von Schillers »Ode an die Freude« (*uproarious:* lärmend, laut, stürmisch; tosend; tobend; *shark:* Hai; *slaughter:* Gemetzel; *Elysium:* Elysium [in der griechischen Sage das Land der Seligen in der Unterwelt]). | 11 **to arouse:** (fig.) wecken. | **to enrapture:** entzücken, hinreißen. | 13 **bum** (coll.): Hintern. | 17 **to prod:** stechen, stoßen; antreiben, anspornen. | 18 **spike:** Stift, Dorn, Stachel.

Joy ode in the Ninth was singing away real lovely and horrorshow within. The millicent said:

"Come down and find out. There's some real lovely news for you, my son." So I scrambled down, very stiff and sore and not like real awake, and this rozz, who had a strong von of cheese and onions on him, pushed me out of the filthy snoring cell, and then along corridors, and all the time the old tune Joy Thou Glorious Spark of Heaven was sparking away within. Then we came to a very neat like cantora with typewriters and flowers on the desks, and at the like chief desk the top millicent was sitting, looking very serious and fixing a like very cold glazzy on my sleepy litso. I said:

"Well well well. What makes, bratty? What gives, this fine bright middle of the nochy?" He said:

"I'll give you just ten seconds to wipe that stupid grin off of your face. Then I want you to listen."

"Well, what?" I said, smecking. "Are you not satisfied with beating me near to death and having me spat upon and making me confess to crimes for hours on end and then shoving me among bezoomnies and vonny perverts in that grahzny cell? Have you some new torture for me, you bratchny?"

"It'll be your own torture," he said, serious. "I hope to God it'll torture you to madness."

And then, before he told me, I knew what it was. The old ptitsa who had all the kots and koshkas had passed on to a

9 **to spark:** funkeln. | 14 **what gives:** was gibt's?, was ist los? | 20 **on end:** ununterbrochen. | 21 **bezoomny** (N.): Verrückter. | **pervert:** Perverser.

better world in one of the city hospitals. I'd cracked her a bit too hard, like. Well, well, that was everything. I thought of all those kots and koshkas mewing for moloko and getting none, not any more from their starry forella of a mistress. That was everything. I'd done the lot, now. And me still only fifteen.

Part Two

One

"What's it going to be then, eh?"

I take it up now, and this is the real weepy and like tragic part of the story beginning, my brothers and only friends, in Staja (State Jail, that is) Number 84F. You will have little desire to slooshy all the cally and horrible raskazz of the shock that sent my dad beating his bruised and krovvy rookers against unfair like Bog in His Heaven, and my mum squaring her rot for owwwww owwwww owwwww in her mother's grief at her only child and son of her bosom like letting everybody down real horrorshow. Then there was the starry very grim magistrate in the lower court govoreeting some very hard slovos against your Friend and Humble Narrator, after all the cally and grahzny slander spat forth by P. R. Deltoid and the rozzes, Bog blast them. Then there was being remanded in filthy custody among vonny perverts and prestoopnicks. Then there was the trial in the higher court with judges and a jury, and some very very nasty slovos indeed govoreeted in a very like solemn way, and then Guilty and my mum boohoohooing when they said Fourteen Years, O my brothers. So here I was now, two years just to the day of being kicked and clanged into Staja 84F, dressed in the heighth of prison fashion, which was a one-

7 **raskazz** (N.): Geschichte. | 12 **to let s.o. down:** jdn. im Stich lassen, enttäuschen. | 15 **slander:** Verleumdung. | 17 **to remand:** zurückschicken. | **custody:** Gewahrsam, Haft. | 18 **prestoopnick** (N.): Verbrecher, Krimineller. | 23 **to clang:** hier: schmettern, werfen. | 24 f. **one-piece:** einteilig.

piece suit of a very filthy like cal colour, and the number sewn on the groody part just above the old tick-tocker and on the back as well, so that going and coming I was 6655321 and not your little droog Alex not no longer.

"What's it going to be then, eh?"

It had not been like edifying, indeed it had not, being in this grahzny hellhole and like human zoo for two years, being kicked and tolchocked by brutal bully warders and meeting vonny leering like criminals, some of them real perverts and ready to dribble all over a luscious young malchick like your story-teller. And there was having to rabbit in the workshop at making matchboxes and itty round and round and round the yard for like exercise, and in the evenings sometimes some starry prof type veck would give a talk on beetles or the Milky Way or the Glorious Wonders of the Snowflake, and I had a good smeck at this last one, because it reminded me of that time of the tolchocking and Sheer Vandalism with that ded coming from the public biblio on a winter's night when my droogs were still not traitors and I was like happy and free. Of those droogs I had slooshied but one thing, and that was one day when my pee and em came to visit and I was told that Georgie was dead. Yes, dead, my brothers. Dead as a bit of dog-cal on the road. Georgie had led the other two into a like very bugatty chelloveck's house, and there they had kicked and tolchocked the owner on the floor, and then Georgie had started to razrez the cushions and curtains, and then old Dim had

2 **tick-tocker** (N.): Herz, ‚Ticker'. | 6 **edifying**: erbaulich, belehrend. | 8 **warder**: Wächter. | 12 **matchbox**: Streichholzschachtel. | 15 **Milky Way**: Milchstraße. | 18 **vandalism**: Vandalismus, Zerstörungswut. | **ded** (N.): alter Mann.

cracked at some very precious ornaments, like statues and so on, and this rich beat-up chelloveck had raged like real bezoomny and gone for them all with a very heavy iron bar. His being all razdraz had given him like gigantic strength, and Dim and Pete had got out through the window but Georgie had tripped on the carpet and then bought this terrific swinging iron bar crack and splooge on the gulliver, and that was the end of traitorous Georgie. The starry murderer had got off with Self Defence, as was really right and proper. Georgie being killed, though it was more than one year after me being caught by the millicents, it all seemed right and proper and like Fate.

"What's it going to be then, eh?"

I was in the Wing Chapel, it being Sunday morning, and the prison charlie was govoreeting the Word of the Lord. It was my rabbit to play the starry stereo, putting on solemn music before and after and in the middle too when hymns were sung. I was at the back of the Wing Chapel (there were four altogether in Staja 84F) near where the warders or chassos were standing with their rifles and their dirty bolshy blue brutal jowls, and I could viddy all the plennies sitting down slooshying the Slovo of the Lord in their horrible cal-coloured prison platties, and a sort of filthy von rose from them, not like real unwashed, not grazzy, but like a special real stinking von which you only got with the criminal types, my brothers, a like dusty, greasy, hopeless sort of

7 **splooge** (N.): Krach, Knall. | 15 **charlie** (auch: *charles*; N.): Kaplan, Geistlicher; Wortspiel mit (slang) *charlie* ›Nachtwächter‹ und ›Narr‹, ›Dummkopf‹; viell. auch Anklang an *charlatan* ›Scharlatan‹. | 16 **rabbit** (N.): Arbeit. | 21 **jowl**: (Unter-)Kiefer; Wange, Backe. | 26 **greasy**: fettig, schmierig.

a von. And I was thinking that perhaps I had this von too, having become a real plenny myself, though still very young. So it was very important to me, O my brothers, to get out of this stinking grahzny zoo as soon as I could. And, as you will viddy if you keep reading on, it was not long before I did.

"What's it going to be then, eh?" said the prison charlie for the third raz. "Is it going to be in and out and in and out of institutions like this, though more in than out for most of you, or are you going to attend to the Divine Word and 10 realise the punishments that await the unrepentant sinner in the next world, as well as in this? A lot of blasted idiots you are, most of you, selling your birthright for a saucer of cold porridge. The thrill of theft, of violence, the urge to live easy – is it worth it when we have undeniable proof, yes 15 yes, incontrovertible evidence that hell exists? I know, I know, my friends, I have been informed in visions that there is a place, darker than any prison, hotter than any flame of human fire, where souls of unrepentant criminal sinners like yourselves – and don't leer at me, damn you, 20 don't laugh – like yourselves, I say, scream in endless and intolerable agony, their noses choked with the smell of filth, their mouths crammed with burning ordure, their skin peeling and rotting, a fireball spinning in their screaming guts. Yes, yes, yes, I know." 25

At this point, brothers, a plenny somewhere or other

11 **unrepentant**: reuelos, unbußfertig. | 12 **blasted** (slang): verflucht. | 13 **birthright**: (Erst-)Geburtsrecht. | 14 **thrill**: Nervenkitzel. | **theft**: Diebstahl. | **urge**: Drang, Trieb. | 16 **incontrovertible**: unbestreitbar. | 23 **crammed**: vollgestopft. | **ordure**: Schmutz, Unflat. | 24 **to peel**: (sich) (ab)schälen.

near the back row let out a shoom of lip-music – "Prrrrrp" –
and then the brutal chassos were on the job right away,
rushing real skorry to what they thought was the scene of
the shoom, then hitting out nasty and delivering tolchocks
left and right. Then they picked out one poor trembling
plenny, very thin and malenky and starry too, and dragged
him off, but all the time he kept creeching, "It wasn't me,
it was him, see," but that made no difference. He was tolchocked real nasty and then dragged out of the Wing Chapel creeching his gulliver off.

"Now," said the prison charlie, "listen to the Word of the
Lord." Then he picked up the big book and flipped over the
pages, keeping on wetting his fingers to do this by licking
them splurge splurge. He was a bolshy great burly bastard
with a very red litso, but he was very fond of myself, me
being young and also now very interested in the big book.
It had been arranged as part of my like further education to
read in the book and even have music on the chapel stereo
while I was reading, O my brothers. And that was real horrorshow. They would like lock me in and let me slooshy holy music by J. S. Bach and G. F. Handel, and I would read of
these starry yahoodies tolchocking each other and then
peeting their Hebrew vino and getting on to the bed with
their wives' like handmaidens, real horrorshow. That kept

2 **on the job:** in Aktion. | 12 **to flip over:** umdrehen, umblättern. |
14 **splurge:** hier: lautmalerisch für den Vorgang des Fingerbenetzens. |
burly: stämmig, kräftig. | 21 **Handel:** englische Schreibweise des Namens
Händel; der Komponist Georg Friedrich H. (1685–1759) war die größere
Zeit seines Lebens in London tätig und ist dort begraben. | 22 **yahoodies**
(N.): Juden; Anspielung auf *yahoos*, menschenähnliche Wesen im Land
der weisen Pferde in Swifts *Gulliver's Travels*. | 24 **handmaiden:** Diene-
rin, Magd.

me going, brothers. I didn't so much kopat the later part of
the book, which is more like all preachy govoreeting than
fighting and the old in-out. But one day the charles said to
me, squeezing me like tight with his bolshy beefy rooker,
"Ah 6655321, think on the divine suffering. Meditate on
that, my boy." And all the time he had this rich manny von
of Scotch on him, and then he went off to his little cantora
to peet some more. So I read all about the scourging and the
crowning with thorns and then the cross veshch and all that
cal, and I viddied better that there was something in it. 10
While the stereo played bits of lovely Bach I closed my
glazzies and viddied myself helping out and even taking
charge of the tolchocking and the nailing in, being dressed
in a like toga that was the heighth of Roman fashion. So being in Staja 84F was not all that wasted, and the Governor 15
himself was very pleased to hear that I had taken to like Religion, and that was where I had my hopes.

This Sunday morning the charlie read out from the book
about chellovecks who slooshied the slovo and didn't take a
blind bit being like a domy built on sand, and then the rain 20
came splash and the old boomaboom cracked the sky and
that was the end of that domy. But I thought only a very
dim veck would build his domy upon sand, and a right lot
of real sneering droogs and nasty neighbours a veck like
that would have, them not telling him how dim he was do- 25

---

1 **to kopat** (N.): verstehen. | 2 **preachy:** salbadernd, moralisierend. |
4 **beefy:** fleischig, kräftig, bullig. | 6 **manny** (N.): *manly:* männlich. |
8 **to scourge:** geißeln. | 12 f. **to take charge of s.th.:** die Aufsicht,
Leitung über etwas übernehmen. | 14 **toga:** Toga (im alten Rom von den
vornehmen Bürgern getragenes Obergewand). | 21 **boomaboom** (N.):
Donner (von *boom* ›Dröhnen‹, ›Donner‹).

ing that sort of building. Then the charles creeched, "Right, you lot. We'll end with Hymn Number 435 in the Prisoner's Hymnal." Then there was a crash and plop and a whish whish whish while the plennies picked up and dropped and
5 lickturned the pages of their grazzy malenky hymnbooks, and the bully fierce warders creeched, "Stop talking there, bastards. I'm watching you, 920537." Of course I had the disc ready on the stereo, and then I let the simple music for organ only come belting out with a growwwwowwwwwow-
10 www. Then the plennies started to sing real horrible:

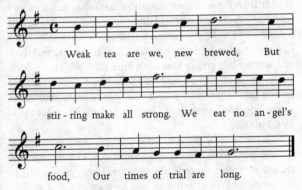

Weak tea are we, new brewed, But stir-ring make all strong. We eat no an-gel's food, Our times of trial are long.

Weak tea are we, new brewed,
15 But stirring make all strong.
We eat no angel's food,
  Our times of trial are long.

---

3 **hymnal**: Gesangbuch. | **plop**: Plumps. | 5 **to lickturn** (N.): mit ange-feuchteten Fingern umblättern. | 11 **to brew**: brauen; sich zusammen-brauen.

They sort of howled and wept these stupid slovos with the charlie like whipping them on with "Louder, damn you, sing up," and the warders creeching, "Just you wait, 7749222" and "One on the turnip coming up for you, filth." Then it was all over and the charlie said, "May the Holy Trinity keep you always and make you good, amen," and the shamble out began to a nice choice bit of Symphony No. 2 by Adrian Schweigselber, chosen by your Humble Narrator, O my brothers. What a lot they were, I thought, as I stood there by the starry chapel stereo, viddying them all shuffle out going marrrrre and baaaaaa like animals and up-your-piping with their grahzny fingers at me, because it looked like I was very special favoured. When the last one had slouched out, his rookers hanging like an ape and then one warder left giving him a fair loud tolchock on the back of the gulliver, and when I had turned off the stereo, the charlie came up to me, puffing away at a cancer, still in his starry bogman's platties, all lacy and white like a devotchka's. He said:

"Thank you as always, little 6655321. And what news have you got for me today?" The idea was, I knew, that this charlie was after becoming a very great holy chelloveck in the world of Prison Religion, and he wanted a real horror-show testimonial from the Governor, so he would go and govoreet quietly to the Governor now and then about what

---

2 **to whip s.o. on:** jdn. antreiben. | 4 **turnip:** Rübe. | 5 f. **Holy Trinity:** Heilige Dreieinigkeit. | 7 **shamble:** Watscheln, Torkeln. | 8 **Schweigselber:** fiktiver Komponist. | 11 **to shuffle:** schlurfen. | 12 **up-your-piping** (N.): Euphemismus für *up your arse:* steck's dir in den Arsch (*piping:* Rohrleitung). | 14 **to slouch:** schlottrig gehen. | 18 **bogman** (N.): Geistlicher. | **lacy:** spitzenbesetzt. | 24 **testimonial:** Zeugnis, Attest.

dark plots were brewing among the plennies, and he would get a lot of this cal from me. A lot of it would be all like made up, but some of it would be true, like for instance the time it had come through to our cell on the waterpipes knock knock knockiknockiknock knockknock that big Harriman was going to break. He was going to tolchock the warder at sloptime and get out in the warder's platties. Then there was going to be a big throwing about of the horrible pishcha we got in the dining-hall, and I knew about that and told. Then the charlie passed it on and was complimented like by the Governor for his Public Spirit and Keen Ear. So this time I said, and this was not true:

"Well, sir, it has come through on the pipes that a consignment of cocaine has arrived by irregular means and that a cell somewhere along Tier 5 is to be the centre of distribution." I made all that up as I went along, like I made up many of these stories, but the prison charlie was very grateful, saying, "Good, good, good. I shall pass that on to Himself," this being what he called the Governor. Then I said:

"Sir, I have done my best, have I not?" I always used my very polite gentleman's goloss govoreeting with those at the top. "I've tried, sir, haven't I?"

"I think," said the charlie, "that on the whole you have, 6655321. You've been very helpful and, I consider, shown a genuine desire to reform. You will, if you continue in this manner, earn your remission with no trouble at all."

"But sir," I said, "how about this new thing they're talking about? How about this new like treatment that gets

---

4 **waterpipe**: Wasserrohr. | 7 **sloptime**: Essenszeit (*slops* [pl.]: Krankenspeise, ‚dünnes Zeug'). | 9 **dining-hall**: Speisesaal. | 13 f. **consignment**: Sendung, Ladung. | 26 **remission**: Straferlass.

you out of prison in no time at all and makes sure that you never get back in again?"

"Oh," he said, very like wary. "Where did you hear this? Who's been telling you these things?"

"These things get around, sir," I said. "Two warders talk, as it might be, and somebody can't help hearing what they say. And then somebody picks up a scrap of newspaper in the workshops and the newspaper says all about it. How about you putting me in for this thing, sir, if I may make so bold as to make the suggestion?"

You could viddy him thinking about that while he puffed away at his cancer, wondering how much to say to me about what he knew about this veshch I mentioned. Then he said, "I take it you're referring to Ludovico's Technique." He was still very wary. "I don't know what it's called, sir," I said. "All I know is that it gets you out quickly and makes sure that you don't get in again."

"That is so," he said, his eyebrows like all beetling while he looked down at me. "That is quite so, 6655321. Of course, it's only in the experimental stage at the moment. It's very simple but very drastic."

"But it's being used here, isn't it, sir?" I said. "Those new like white buildings by the South Wall, sir. We've watched those being built, sir, when we've been doing our exercise."

"It's not been used yet," he said, "not in this prison, 6655321. Himself has grave doubts about it. I must confess I

---

1 **to make sure:** sicherstellen. | 9 f. **to make so bold as to do s.th.:** sich erdreisten, etwas zu tun. | 14 **Ludovico** (Ital.): Ludwig; Anspielung auf den italienischen Bösewicht in John Websters Rachetragödie *The White Devil* (1612) und auf Beethoven. | 21 **drastic:** drastisch, durchgreifend, gründlich.

share those doubts. The question is whether such a technique can really make a man good. Goodness comes from within, 6655321. Goodness is something chosen. When a man cannot choose he ceases to be a man." He would have gone on with a lot more of this cal, but we could slooshy the next lot of plennies marching clank clank down the iron stairs to come for their bit of Religion. He said, "We'll have a little chat about this some other time. Now you'd better start the voluntary." So I went over to the starry stereo and put on J. S. Bach's *Wachet Auf* Choral Prelude and in these grahzny vonny bastard criminals and perverts came shambling like a lot of broke-down apes, the warders or chassos like barking at them and lashing them. And soon the prison charlie was asking them, "What's it going to be then, eh?" And that's where you came in.

We had four of these lomticks of like Prison Religion that morning, but the charles said no more to me about this Ludovico's Technique, whatever it was, O my brothers. When I'd finished my rabbit with the stereo he just govoreeted a few slovos of thanks and then I was privodeeted back to the cell on Tier 6 which was my very vonny and crammed home. The chasso was not really too bad of a veck and he did not tolchock or kick me in when he'd opened up, he just said, "Here we are, sonny, back to the old waterhole." And there I was with my new type droogs, all very criminal but, Bog be praised, not given to perversions of

8 **chat:** Geplauder. | 9 **voluntary:** hier: (improvisiertes) Orgelvor- oder -nachspiel. | 10 **"Wachet Auf" Choral Prelude:** Bachs Kantate Nr. 140 »Wachet auf, ruft uns die Stimme« (1731). | 12 **broke-down:** *broken-down:* ruiniert, erschöpft. | 20 **to privodeet** (N.): führen. | 24 **sonny** (coll.): Söhnchen, Kleiner (Anrede).

the body. There was Zophar on his bunk, a very thin and brown veck who went on and on and on in his like cancery goloss, so that nobody bothered to slooshy. What he was saying now like to nobody was "And at that time you couldn't get hold of a poggy" (whatever that was, brothers) "not if you was to hand over ten million archibalds, so what I do eh, I goes down to Turkey's and says I've got this sproog on that morrow, see, and what can he do?" It was all this very old-time real criminal's slang he spoke. Also there was Wall, who had only one glazzy, and he was tearing bits off his toe-nails in honour of Sunday. Also there was Big Jew, a very fat sweaty veck lying flat on his bunk like dead. In addition there was Jojohn and The Doctor. Jojohn was very mean and keen and wiry and had specialised in like Sexual Assault, and The Doctor had pretended to be able to cure syph and gon and gleet but he had only injected water, also he had killed off two devotchkas instead, like he had promised, of getting rid of their unwanted loads for them. They were a terrible grahzny lot really, and I didn't enjoy being with them, O my brothers, any more than you do now, but it won't be for much longer.

Now what I want you to know is that this cell was intended for only three when it was built, but there were six of us there, all jammed together sweaty and tight. And that

2 **cancery** (N.): rauchig. | 5 **poggy** (slang, obs.): Schnaps. | 6 **to hand over:** aushändigen, übergeben. | **archibald** (slang): hier: vermutl. Bezeichnung für eine Geldeinheit. | 7 **Turkey's:** turkey-merchant (slang): Hehler. | 8 **sproog:** vermutl. etwa ‚Bruch'. | **morrow:** folgender Tag. | 12 **Jew:** Jude. | **sweaty:** schweißig, verschwitzt. | 14 **wiry:** drahtig; zäh, sehnig. | 16 **syph:** Kurzform von syphilis. | **gon:** Kurzform von gonorrhoea: Gonorrhöe, Tripper. | **gleet:** Harnröhrenausfluss.

was the state of all the cells in all the prisons in those days, brothers, and a dirty cally disgrace it was, there not being decent room for a chelloveck to stretch his limbs. And you will hardly believe what I say now, which is that on this Sunday they brosatted in another plenny. Yes, we had our horrible pishcha of dumplings and vonny stew and were smoking a quiet cancer each on our bunks when this veck was thrown into our midst. He was a chinny starry veck and it was him who started creeching complaints before we even had a chance to viddy the position. He tried to like shake the bars, creeching, "I demand my sodding rights, this one's full up, it's a bleeding imposition, that's what it is." But one of the chassos came back to say that he had to make the best of it and share a bunk with whoever would let him, otherwise it would have to be the floor. "And," said the warder, "it's going to get worse, not better. A right dirty criminal world you lot are trying to build."

---

5 **to brosat** (N.): werfen. | 6 **dumpling:** Kloß, Knödel. | **stew:** Schmorgericht, Eintopf. | 8 **chinny** (N.): mit einem ausgeprägten Kinn (von *chin*). | 11 **sodding** (taboo slang): verdammt. | 12 **imposition:** Auf(er)legung, Bürde.

Two

Well, it was the letting-in of this new chelloveck that was
really the start of my getting out of the old Staja, for he was
such a nasty quarrelsome type of plenny, with a very dirty
mind and filthy intentions, that trouble nachinatted that
very same day. He was also very boastful and started to
make with a very sneery litso at us all and a loud and proud
goloss. He made out that he was the only real horrorshow
prestoopnick in the whole zoo, going on that he'd done this
and done the other and killed ten rozzes with one crack of
his rooker and all that cal. But nobody was very impressed,
O my brothers. So then he started on me, me being the
youngest there, trying to say that as the youngest I ought
to be the one to zasnoot on the floor and not him. But all
the others were for me, creeching, "Leave him alone, you
grahzny bratchny," and then he began the old whine about
how nobody loved him. So that same nochy I woke up to
find this horrible plenny actually lying with me on my
bunk, which was on the bottom of the three-tier and also
very narrow, and he was govoreeting dirty like love-slovos
and stroke stroke stroking away. So then I got real bezoomny and lashed out, though I could not viddy all that horrorshow, there being only this malenky little red light outside
on the landing. But I knew it was this one, the vonny bastard, and then when the trouble really got under way and
the lights were turned on I could viddy his horrible litso

4 **quarrelsome:** zänkisch. | 5 **to nachinat** (N.): beginnen. | 6 **boastful:**
prahlerisch. | 8 **to make out:** 1. behaupten; 2. vorgeben. | 14 **to zasnoot**
(N.): schlafen. | 16 **whine:** Gewinsel. | 19 **three-tier:** hier: Dreistockbett. |
24 **landing:** Treppenabsatz.

with all krovvy dripping from his rot where I'd hit out with my clawing rooker.

What sloochatted then, of course, was that my cell-mates woke up and started to join in, tolchocking a bit wild in the near dark, and the shoom seemed to wake up the whole tier, so that you could slooshy a lot of creeching and banging about with tin mugs on the wall, as though all the plennies in all the cells thought a big break was about to commence, O my brothers. So then the lights came on and the chassos came along in their shirts and trousers and caps, waving big sticks. We could viddy each other's flushed lit-sos and the shaking of fisty rookers, and there was a lot of creeching and cursing. Then I put in my complaint and every chasso said it was probably Your Humble Narrator, brothers, that started it all anyway, me having no mark of a scratch on me but this horrible plenny dripping red red krovvy from the rot where I'd got him with my clawing rooker. That made me real bezoomny. I said I would not sleep another nochy in that cell if the Prison Authorities were going to allow horrible vonny stinking perverted prestoopnicks to leap on my plott when I was in no posi-tion to defend myself, being asleep. "Wait till the morn-ing," they said. "Is it a private room with bath and televi-sion that your honour requires? Well, all that will be seen to in the morning. But for the present, little droog, get your bleeding gulliver down on your straw-filled podooshka

---

2 **to claw**: kratzen, reißen, zerren. | 5 **near dark**: Halbdunkel. | 12 **fisty** (N.): (zur Faust) geballt (von *fist*). | 16 **scratch**: Kratzer, Schramme. | 20 **perverted**: pervers, verkehrt, widernatürlich; schlecht, böse. | 24 **your honour**: hier (iron.): Euer Ehren. | 24 f. **to see to s.th.**: für etwas Sorge tragen. | 26 **podooshka** (N.): Kissen.

and let's have no more trouble from anyone. Right right right?" Then off they went with stern warnings for all, then soon after the lights went out, and then I said I would sit up all the rest of the nochy, saying first to this horrible prestoopnick, "Go on, get on my bunk if you wish it. I fancy it no longer. You have made it filthy and cally with your horrible vonny plott lying on it already." But then the others joined in. Big Jew said, still sweating from the bit of a bitva we'd had in the dark:

"Not having that we're not, brotherth. Don't give in to the thquirt." So this new one said:

"Crash your dermott, yid," meaning to shut up, but it was very insulting. So then Big Jew got ready to launch a tolchock. The Doctor said:

"Come on gentlemen, we don't want any trouble, do we?" in his very high-class goloss, but this new prestoopnick was really asking for it. You could viddy that he thought he was a very big bolshy veck and it was beneath his dignity to be sharing a cell with six and having to sleep on the floor till I made this gesture at him. In his sneery way he tried to take off The Doctor, saying:

"Owwww, yew wahnt noo moor trabble, is that it, Archiballs?" So Jojohn, mean and keen and wiry, said:

"If we can't have sleep let's have some education. Our new friend here had better be taught a lesson." Although he like specialised in Sexual Assault he had a nice way of

---

10 **brotherth:** *brothers.* Die Schreibweise kennzeichnet das Lispeln des Sprechers. | 11 **thquirt:** *squirt* (coll.): Wichtigtuer. | 12 **crash your dermott** (N.): halt den Mund. | 13 **yid** (slang): Jude. | 14 **to launch:** vom Stapel lassen, abschießen, schleudern; hier: ,landen'. | 21 **to take s.o. off:** jdn. nachahmen.

govoreeting, quiet and like precise. So the new plenny sneered:

"Kish and kosh and koosh, you little terror." So then it all really started, but in a queer like gentle way, with nobody raising his goloss much. The new plenny creeched a malenky bit at first, but then Wall fisted his rot while Big Jew held him up against the bars so that he could be viddied in the malenky red light from the landing, and he just went oh oh oh. He was not a very strong type of veck, being very feeble in his trying to tolchock back, and I suppose he made up for this by being shoomny in the goloss and very boastful. Anyway, seeing the old krovvy flow red in the red light, I felt the old joy like rising up in my keeshkas and I said:

"Leave him to me, go on, let me have him now, brothers." So Big Jew said:

"Yeth, yeth, boyth, that'th fair. Thlosh him then, Alekth."

So they all stood around while I cracked at this prestoopnick in the near dark. I fisted him all over, dancing about with my boots on though unlaced, and then I tripped him and he went crash crash onto the floor. I gave him one real horrorshow kick on the gulliver and he went ohhhhh, then he sort of snorted off to like sleep, and The Doctor said:

"Very well, I think that will be enough of a lesson," squinting to viddy this downed and beaten-up veck on the floor. "Let him dream perhaps about being a better boy in the future." So we all climbed back into our bunks, being very tired now. What I dreamt of, O my brothers, was of being in some very big orchestra, hundreds and hundreds

---

3 **kish and kosh and koosh:** Bedeutung unklar. | 16 **to thlosh:** *to slosh* (slang): verdreschen. | 19 **to unlace:** aufschnüren. | 24 **to squint:** schielen; blinzeln.

strong, and the conductor was a like mixture of Ludwig van and G. F. Handel, looking very deaf and blind and weary of the world. I was with the wind instruments, but what I was playing was like a white pinky bassoon made of flesh and growing out of my plott, right in the middle of my belly, and when I blew into it I had to smeck ha ha ha very loud because it like tickled, and then Ludwig van G.F. got very razdraz and bezoomny. Then he came right up to my litso and creeched loud in my ooko, and then I woke up like sweating. Of course, what the loud shoom really was was the prison buzzer going brrrrr brrrrr brrrrr. It was winter morning and my glazzies were all cally with sleepglue, and when I opened up they were very sore in the electric light that had been switched on all over the zoo. Then I looked down and viddied this new prestoopnick lying on the floor, very bloody and bruisy and still out out out. Then I remembered about last night and that made me smeck a bit.

But when I got off the bunk and moved him with my bare noga, there was a feel of like stiff coldness, so I went over to The Doctor's bunk and shook him, him always being very slow at waking up in the morning. But he was off his bunk skorry enough this time, and so were the others, except for Wall who slept like dead meat. "Very unfortunate," The Doctor said. "A heart attack, that's what it must have been." Then he said, looking round at us all, "You really shouldn't have gone for him like that. It was most ill-advised really." Jojohn said:

3 **wind instrument:** Blasinstrument. | 4 **pinky:** rötlich, rosa. | **bassoon:** Fagott. | 11 **buzzer:** Summer. | 16 **bruisy** (N.): *bruised.* | 24 **heart attack:** Herzanfall. | 26 f. **ill-advised:** schlecht beraten, unbesonnen, unklug.

"Come come, doc, you weren't all that backward your-self in giving him a sly bit of fist." Then Big Jew turned on me, saying:

"Alexth, you were too impetuouth. That latht kick wath a very very nathty one." I began to get razdraz about this and said:

"Who started it, eh? I only got in at the end, didn't I?" I pointed at Jojohn and said, "It was your idea." Wall snored a bit loud, so I said, "Wake that vonny bratchny up. It was him that kept on at his rot while Big Jew here had him up against the bars." The Doctor said:

"Nobody will deny having a gentle little hit at the man, to teach him a lesson so to speak, but it's apparent that you, my dear boy, with the forcefulness and, shall I say, heedlessness of youth, dealt him the coo de grass. It's a great pity."

"Traitors," I said "Traitors and liars," because I could vid-dy it was all like before, when my so-called droogs had left me to the brutal rookers of the millicents. There was no trust anywhere in the world, O my brothers, the way I could see it. And Jojohn went and woke up Wall, and Wall was only too ready to swear that it was Your Humble Nar-rator that had done the real dirty tolchocking and brutality. When the chassos came along, and then the Chief Chasso, and the Governor himself, all these cell-droogs of mine were very shoommy with tales of what I've done to oobivat this worthless pervert whose krovvy-covered plott lay sacklike on the floor.

4 **impetuouth:** *impetuous:* ungestüm. | 13 **so to speak:** sozusagen. | 14 **forcefulness:** Eindringlichkeit, Ungestüm. | **heedlessness:** Unacht-samkeit. | 15 **coo de gras:** *coup de grâce* (Fr.): Gnadenstoß. | 25 **to oobi-vat** (N.): umbringen, töten.

That was a very queer day, O my brothers. The dead plott was carried off, and then everybody in the whole prison had to stay locked up till further orders, and there was no pishcha given out, not even a mug of hot chai. We all just sat there, and the warders or chassos sort of strode up and down the tier, now and then creeching "Shut it" or "Close that hole" whenever they slooshied even a whisper from any of the cells. Then about eleven o'clock in the morning there was a sort of like stiffening and excitement and like the von of fear spreading from outside the cell, and then we could viddy the Governor and the Chief Chasso and some very bolshy important-looking chellovecks walking by real skorry, govoreeting like bezoomny. They seemed to walk right to the end of the tier, then they could be slooshied walking back again, more slow this time, and you could slooshy the Governor, a very sweaty fatty fair-haired veck, saying slovos like "But, sir –" and "Well, what can be done, sir?" and so on. Then the whole lot stopped at our cell and the Chief Chasso opened up. You could viddy who was the real important veck right away, very tall and with blue glazzies and with real horrorshow platties on him, the most lovely suit, brothers, I had ever viddied, absolutely in the heighth of fashion. He just sort of looked right through us poor plennies, saying, in a very beautiful real educated goloss, "The government cannot be concerned any longer with outmoded penological theories. Cram criminals together and see what happens. You get concentrated criminality, crime in the midst of punishment. Soon we may be

9 **stiffening:** Erstarren. | 26 **outmoded:** unmodern, veraltet, überholt. | **penological:** kriminalkundlich, Strafvollzugs… | 27 f. **criminality:** Kriminalität, Verbrechertum. | 28 **crime in the midst of punishment:** An-

needing all our prison space for political offenders." I didn't pony this at all, brothers, but after all he was not govoreeting to me. Then he said, "Common criminals like this unsavoury crowd – " (that meant me, brothers, as well as the others, who were real prestoopnick and treacherous with it) " – can best be dealt with on a purely curative basis. Kill the criminal reflex, that's all. Full implementation in a year's time. Punishment means nothing to them, you can see that. They enjoy their so-called punishment. They start murdering each other." And he turned his stern blue glazzies on me. So I said, bold:

"With respect, sir, I object very strongly to what you said then. I am not a common criminal, sir, and I am not unsavoury. The others may be unsavoury but I am not." The Chief Chasso went all purple and creeched:

"You shut your bleeding hole, you. Don't you know who this is?"

"All right, all right" said the big veck. Then he turned to the Governor and said, "You can use him as a trail-blazer. He's young, bold, vicious. Brodsky will deal with him tomorrow and you can sit in and watch Brodsky. It works all right, don't worry about that. This vicious young hoodlum will be transformed out of all recognition."

And those hard slovos, brothers, were like the beginning of my freedom.

spielung auf *Crime and Punishment*, den englischen Titel eines 1866 veröffentlichten Romans (dt. *Schuld und Sühne*) des russischen Schriftstellers Fjodor Michailowitsch Dostojewski (1821–1881). | 3 f. **unsavoury:** widerwärtig, widerlich. | 6 **curative:** heilend. | 7 **implementation:** Aus-, Durchführung. | 19 **trail-blazer:** Bahnbrecher, Pionier. | 22 **hoodlum** (slang): Strolch, Rowdy; Ganove, Gangster.

Three

That very same evening I was dragged down nice and gentle by brutal tolchocking chassos to viddy the Governor in his holy of holies holy office. The Governor looked very weary at me and said, "I don't suppose you know who that was this morning, do you, 6655321?" And without waiting for me to say no he said, "That was no less a personage than the Minister of the Interior, the new Minister of the Interior and what they call a very new broom. Well, these new ridiculous ideas have come at last and orders are orders, though I may say to you in confidence that I do not approve. I most emphatically do not approve. An eye for an eye, I say. If someone hits you you hit back, do you not? Why then should not the State, very severely hit by you brutal hooligans, not hit back also? But the new view is to say no. The new view is that we turn the bad into the good. All of which seems to me grossly unjust. Hm?" So I said, trying to be like respectful and accommodating:

"Sir." And then the Chief Chasso, who was standing all red and burly behind the Governor's chair, creeched:

"Shut your filthy hole, you scum."

"All right, all right," said the like tired and fagged-out Governor. "You, 6655321, are to be reformed. Tomorrow you go to this man Brodsky. It is believed that you will be able to leave State Custody in a little over a fortnight. In a

---

4 **holy of holies:** das Allerheiligste. | 7 **personage:** Persönlichkeit. | 12 **emphatically:** nachdrücklich. | 12 f. **an eye for an eye:** Auge um Auge (Anspielung auf 2 Mose 21,24). | 17 **grossly:** sehr, höchst; ungeheuerlich. | 18 **accommodating:** gefällig, entgegenkommend. | 21 **scum:** Abschaum. | 25 **custody:** 1. Gewahrsam, Haft; 2. Obhut.

little over a fortnight you will be out again in the big free world, no longer a number. I suppose," and he snorted a bit here, "that prospect pleases you?" I said nothing so the Chief Chasso creeched:

5 "Answer, you filthy young swine, when the Governor asks you a question." So I said:

"Oh, yes, sir. Thank you very much, sir. I've done my best here, really I have. I'm very grateful to all concerned."

"Don't be," like sighed the Governor. "This is not a re-
10 ward. This is far from being a reward. Now, there is a form here to be signed. It says you are willing to have the residue of your sentence commuted to submission to what is called here, ridiculous expression, Reclamation Treatment. Will you sign?"

15 "Most certainly I will sign," I said, "sir. And very many thanks." So I was given an ink-pencil and I signed my name nice and flowy. The Governor said:

"Right. That's the lot, I think." The Chief Chasso said:

"The Prison Chaplain would like a word with him, sir."
20 So I was marched out and off down the corridor towards the Wing Chapel, tolchocked on the back and the gulliver all the way by one of the chassos, but in a very like yawny and bored manner. And I was marched across the Wing Chapel to the little cantora of the charles and then made to
25 go in. The charles was sitting at his desk, smelling loud and clear of a fine manny von of expensive cancers and Scotch. He said:

11 **residue:** Rest, Rückstand. | 12 **to commute:** ein-, umtauschen, umwandeln. | 13 **reclamation:** Besserung, Heilung. | 17 **flowy** (N.): *flowing:* fließend, flüssig. | 19 **chaplain:** Kaplan. | 22 **yawny** (N.): *yawning:* gähnend.

"Ah, little 6655321, be seated." And to the chassos, "Wait outside, eh?" Which they did. Then he spoke in a very like earnest way to me, saying: "One thing I want you to understand, boy, is that this is nothing to do with me. Were it expedient, I would protest about it, but it is not expedient. There is the question of my own career, there is the question of the weakness of my own voice when set against the shout of certain more powerful elements in the polity. Do I make myself clear?" He didn't, brothers, but I nodded that he did. "Very hard ethical questions are involved," he went on. "You are to be made into a good boy, 6655321. Never again will you have the desire to commit acts of violence or to offend in any way whatsoever against the State's Peace. I hope you take all that in. I hope you are absolutely clear in your mind about that." I said:

"Oh, it will be nice to be good, sir." But I had a real horrorshow smeck at that inside, brothers. He said:

"It may not be nice to be good, little 6655321. It may be horrible to be good. And when I say that to you I realise how self-contradictory that sounds. I know I shall have many sleepless nights about this. What does God want? Does God want goodness or the choice of goodness? Is a man who chooses the bad perhaps in some way better than a man who has the good imposed upon him? Deep and hard questions, little 6655321. But all I want to say to you now is this: if at any time in the future you look back to these times and remember me, the lowest and humblest of

---

4 f. **expedient:** zweckmäßig, ratsam, tunlich. | 7 **to set against:** entgegenstellen. | 8 **polity:** Regierungsform, politische Ordnung; Staats-, Gemeinwesen. | 10 **ethical:** ethisch, moralisch, sittlich. | 14 **to take s. th. in:** etwas begreifen. | 20 **self-contradictory:** widerspruchsvoll.

all God's servitors, do not, I pray, think evil of me in your heart, thinking me in any way involved in what is now about to happen to you. And now, talking of praying, I realise sadly that there will be little point in praying for you. You are passing now to a region where you will be beyond the reach of the power of prayer. A terrible terrible thing to consider. And yet, in a sense, in choosing to be deprived of the ability to make an ethical choice, you have in a sense really chosen the good. So I shall like to think. So, God help us all, 6655321, I shall like to think." And then he began to cry. But I didn't really take much notice of that, brothers, only having a bit of a quiet smeck inside, because you could viddy that he had been peeting away at the old whisky, and now he took a bottle from a cupboard in his desk and started to pour himself a real horrorshow bolshy slog into a very greasy and grahzny glass. He downed it and then said, "All may be well, who knows? God works in a mysterious way." Then the door opened and the chassos came in to tolchock me back to my vonny cell, but the old charles still went on singing this hymn.

Well, the next morning I had to say goodbye to the old Staja, and I felt a malenky bit sad as you always will when you have to leave a place that you've like got used to. But I didn't go very far, O my brothers. I was punched and kicked along to the new white building just beyond the yard where we used to do our bit of exercise. This was a very new building and it had a new cold like sizy smell which gave

---

1 **servitor** (obs.): Diener, Gefolgsmann. | 15 **slog**: wilder, harter Schlag (Cricket); hier: ordentlicher ‚Schuss'. | 16 **to down** (coll.): (Getränk) herunterstürzen, hinter die Binde gießen. | 27 **sizy:** klebrig, leimartig.

you a bit of the shivers. I stood there in the horrible bolshy bare hall and I got new vons, sniffing away there with my like very sensitive morder or sniffer. These were like hospital vons, and the chelloveck the chassos handed me over to had a white coat on, as he might be a hospital man. He signed for me, and one of the brutal chassos who had brought me said, "You will watch this one, sir. A right brutal bastard he has been and will be again, in spite of all his sucking up to the Prison Chaplain and reading the Bible." But this new chelloveck had real horrorshow blue glazzies which like smiled when he govoreeted. He said:

"Oh, we don't anticipate any trouble. We're going to be friends, aren't we?" And he smiled with his glazzies and his fine big rot which was full of shining white zoobies and I sort of took to this veck right away. Anyway, he passed me on to a like lesser veck in a white coat, and this one was very nice too, and I was led off to a very nice white clean bedroom with curtains and a bedside lamp, and just the one bed in it, all for Your Humble Narrator. So I had a real horrorshow inner smeck at that, thinking I was really a very lucky young malchickiwick. I was told to take off my horrible prison platties and I was given a really beautiful set of pyjamas, O my brothers, in plain green, the heighth of bedwear fashion. And I was given a nice warm dressing-gown too and lovely toofles to put my bare nogas in, and I thought, "Well, Alex boy, little 6655321 as was, you have

3 **morder** (N.): Nase. | **sniffer** (N.): Nase (von *to sniff*). | 9 **to suck up to s.o.** (slang): jdm. in den Arsch kriechen. | 12 **to anticipate**: erwarten. | 16 **lesser**: rangniedrige(r, s). | 23 f. **bedwear** (N.): Nachtbekleidung (Analogiebildung zu *footwear* ›Schuhwerk‹). | 24 **dressing-gown**: Morgen-, Schlafrock.

copped it lucky and no mistake. You are really going to enjoy it here."

After I had been given a nice chasha of real horrorshow coffee and some old gazettas and mags to look at while peeting it, this first veck in white came in, the one who had like signed for me, and said: "Aha, there you are," a silly sort of a veshch to say but it didn't sound silly, this veck being so like nice. "My name," he said, "is Dr Branom. I'm Dr Brodsky's assistant. With your permission, I'll just give you the usual brief overall examination." And he took the old stetho out of his right carman. "We must make sure you're quite fit, mustn't we? Yes indeed, we must." So while I lay there with my pyjama top off and he did this, that and the other, I said:

"What exactly is it, sir, that you're going to do?"

"Oh," said Dr Branom, his cold stetho going all down my back, "it's quite simple, really. We just show you some films."

"Films?" I said. I could hardly believe my ookos, brothers, as you may well understand. "You mean," I said, "it will be just like going to the pictures?"

"They'll be special films," said this Dr Branom. "Very special films. You'll be having your first session this afternoon. Yes," he said, getting up from bending over me, "you seem to be quite a fit young boy. A bit under-nourished, perhaps. That will be the fault of the prison food. Put your pyjama top back on. After every meal," he said, sitting on the edge of the bed, we shall be giving you a shot in the

1 **to cop** (slang): ,erwischen'. | 4 **mag:** Kurzform von *magazine.* |
11 **stetho:** Kurzform von *stethoscope:* Stethoskop, Hörrohr. | 21 **pictures** (pl., coll.): Kino(vorstellung).

arm. That should help." I felt really grateful to this very nice Dr Branom. I said:

"Vitamins, sir, will it be?"

"Something like that," he said, smiling real horrorshow and friendly. "Just a jab in the arm after every meal." Then he went out. I lay on the bed thinking this was like real heaven, and I read some of the mags they'd given me – *Worldsport*, *Sinny* (this being a film mag) and *Goal*. Then I lay back on the bed and shut my glazzies and thought how nice it was going to be out there again, Alex with perhaps a nice easy job during the day, me being now too old for the old skolliwoll, and then perhaps getting a new like gang together for the nochy, and the first rabbit would be to get old Dim and Pete, if they had not been got already by the millicents. This time I would be very careful not to get loveted. They were giving another like chance, me having done murder and all, and it would not be like fair to get loveted again, after going to all this trouble to show me films that were going to make me a real good malchick. I had a real horrorshow smeck at everybody's like innocence, and I was smecking my gulliver off when they brought in my lunch on a tray. The veck who brought it was the one who'd led me to this malenky bedroom when I came into the mesto, and he said:

"It's nice to know somebody's happy." It was really a very nice appetising bit of pishcha they'd laid out on the tray – two or three lomticks of like hot roastbeef with mashed kartoffel and vedge, then there was also ice cream

---

28 **mashed kartoffel** (N.): *mashed potatoes* (pl.): Kartoffelbrei. | **vedge** (N.): Gemüse (von *vegetable*).

and a nice hot chasha of chai. And there was even a cancer to smoke and a matchbox with one match in. So this looked like it was the life, O my brothers. Then, about half an hour after while I was lying a bit sleepy on the bed, a woman nurse came in, a real nice young devotchka with real horrorshow groodies (I had not seen such for two years) and she had a tray and a hypodermic. I said:

"Ah, the old vitamins, eh?" And I clickclicked at her but she took no notice. All she did was to slam the needle into my left arm, and then swishhhh in went the vitamin stuff. Then she went out again, clack clack on her high-heeled nogas. Then the white-coated veck who was like a male nurse came in with a wheel-chair. I was a malenky bit surprised to viddy that. I said:

"What giveth then, brother? I can walk, surely, to wherever we have to itty to." But he said:

"Best I push you there." And indeed, O my brothers, when I got off the bed I found myself a malenky bit weak. It was the under-nourishment like Dr Branom had said, all that horrible prison pishcha. But the vitamins in the after-meal injection would put me right. No doubt at all about that, I thought.

9 to slam: ,knallen'. | 11 high-heeled: hochhackig, mit hohen Absätzen. | 13 wheel-chair: Rollstuhl.

Four

Where I was wheeled to, brothers, was like no sinny I had ever viddied before. True enough, one wall was all covered with silver screen, and direct opposite was a wall with square holes in for the projector to project through, and there were stereo speakers stuck all over the mesto. But against the right-hand one of the other walls was a bank of all like little meters, and in the middle of the floor facing the screen was like a dentist's chair with all lengths of wire running from it, and I had to like crawl from the wheel-chair to this, being given some help by another like male nurse veck in a white coat. Then I noticed that underneath the projection holes was like all frosted glass and I thought I viddied shadows of like people moving behind it and I thought I slooshied somebody cough kashl kashl kashl. But then all I could like notice was how weak I seemed to be, and I put that down to changing over from prison pishcha to this new rich pishcha and the vitamins injected into me. "Right," said the wheelchair-wheeling veck, "now I'll leave you. The show will commence as soon as Dr Brodsky arrives. Hope you enjoy it." To be truthful, brothers, I did not really feel that I wanted to viddy any film-show this afternoon. I was just not in the mood. I would have liked much better to have a nice quiet spachka on the bed, nice and quiet and all on my oddy knocky. I felt very limp.

What happened now was that one white-coated veck

7 **right-hand:** recht, zur Rechten. | 8 **meter:** Meter, Messgerät. | 13 **frosted glass:** Mattglas. | 21 **truthful:** wahr(haftig), ehrlich. | 26 **limp:** schlaff, schlapp.

strapped my gulliver to a like head-rest, singing to himself all the time some vonny cally pop-song. "What's this for?" I said. And this veck replied, interrupting his like song an instant, that it was to keep my gulliver still and make me look at the screen. "But," I said, I *want* to look at the screen. I've been brought here to viddy films and viddy films I shall." And then the other white-coat veck (there were three altogether, one of them a devotchka who was like sitting at the bank of meters and twiddling with knobs) had a bit of a smeck at that. He said:

"You never know. Oh, you never know. Trust us, friend. It's better this way." And then I found they were strapping my rookers to the chair-arms and my nogas were like stuck to a foot-rest. It seemed a bit bezoomny to me but I let them get on with what they wanted to get on with. If I was to be a free young malchick again in a fortnight's time I would put up with much in the meantime, O my brothers. One veshch I did not like, though, was when they put like clips on the skin of my forehead, so that my top glaz-lids were pulled up and up and up and I could not shut my glaz-zies no matter how I tried. I tried to smeck and said: "This must be a real horrorshow film if you're so keen on my vid-dying it." And one of the white-coat vecks said, smecking:

"Horrorshow is right, friend. A real show of horrors." And then I had a cap stuck on my gulliver and I could viddy all wires running away from it, and they stuck a little suction pad on my belly and one on the old tick-tocker, and I could just about viddy wires running away from those.

1 **to strap:** mit einem Riemen befestigen, schnallen. | **head-rest:** Kopf-stütze. | 9 **to twiddle:** herumdrehen, herumspielen. | **knob:** Knopf. | 19 **clip:** Klammer, Klemme. | 26 f. **suction pad:** Saugkissen, -fuß.

Then there was the shoom of a door opening and you could tell some very important chelloveck was coming in by the way the white-coated under-vecks went all stiff. And then I viddied this Dr Brodsky. He was a malenky veck, very fat, with all curly hair curling all over his gulliver, and on his spuddy nose he had very thick otchkies. I could just viddy that he had a real horrorshow suit on, absolutely the heighth of fashion, and he had a like very delicate and subtle von of operating theatres coming from him. With him was Dr Branom, all smiling as though to give me confidence. "Everything ready?" said Dr Brodsky in a very breathy goloss. Then I could slooshy voices saying Right right right from like a distance, then nearer to, then there was a quiet like humming shoom as though things had been switched on. And then the lights went out and there was Your Humble Narrator and Friend sitting alone in the dark, all on his frightened oddy knocky, not able to move nor shut his glazzies nor anything. And then, O my brothers, the film-show started off with some very gromky atmosphere music coming from the speakers, very fierce and full of discord. And then on the screen the picture came on, but there was no title and no credits. What came on was a street, as it might have been any street in any town, and it was a real dark nochy and the lamps were lit. It was a very good like professional piece of sinny, and there were none of these flickers and blobs you get, say, when you viddy one of these dirty films in somebody's house in a back street.

6 **spuddy nose:** Kartoffelnase. | 9 **operating theatre:** Operationssaal. | 12 **breathy:** hauchig, gehaucht. | 21 **discord:** Missklang. | 22 **credits** (pl.): Vor-, Nachspann (Liste der an einem Film Beteiligten). | 26 **flicker:** Flackern, Flimmern. | **blob:** Tropfen, Klecks.

All the time the music bumped out, very like sinister. And then you could viddy an old man coming down the street very starry, and then there leaped out on this starry veck two malchicks dressed in the heighth of fashion, as it was at this time (still thin trousers but no like cravat anymore, more of a real tie), and they started to filly with him. You could slooshy his screams and moans, very realistic, and you could even get the like heavy breathing and panting of the two tolchocking malchicks. They made a real pudding out of this starry veck, going crack crack crack at him with their fisty rookers, tearing his platties off and then finishing up by booting his nagoy plott (this lay all krovvy-red in the grahzny mud of the gutter) and then running off very skorry. Then there was a close-up gulliver of this beaten-up starry veck, and the krovvy flowed beautiful red. It's funny how the colours of the like real world only seem really real when you viddy them on the screen.

Now all the time I was watching this I was beginning to get very aware of a like not feeling all that well, and this I put down to the under-nourishment and my stomach not quite ready for the rich pishcha and vitamins I was getting here. But I tried to forget this, concentrating on the next film which came on at once, my brothers, without any break at all. This time the film like jumped right away on a young devotchka who was being given the old in-out by first one malchick then another then another then another, she creeching away very gromky through the speakers and like very pathetic and tragic music going on at the same

---

1 **sinister**: unheilvoll, böse. | 7 **moan**: Stöhnen. | 12 **to boot**: mit Stiefeln, mit Füßen treten. | 14 **close-up**: Nahaufnahme. | 20 **to put down**: zuschreiben.

time. This was real, very real, though if you thought about it properly you couldn't imagine lewdies actually agreeing to having all this done to them in a film, and if these films were made by the Good or the State you couldn't imagine them being allowed to take these films without like interfering with what was going on. So it must have been very clever what they called cutting or editing or some such veshch. For it was very real. And when it came to the sixth or seventh malchick leering and smecking and then going into it and the devotchka creeching on the sound-track like bezoomny, then I began to feel sick. I had like pains all over and felt I could sick up and at the same time not sick up, and I began to feel like in distress, O my brothers, being fixed rigid too on this chair. When this bit of film was over I could slooshy the goloss of this Dr Brodsky from over by the switchboard saying, "Reaction about twelve point five? Promising, promising."

Then we shot straight into another lomtick of film, and this time it was of just a human litso, a very like pale human face held still and having different nasty veshches done to it. I was sweating a malenky bit with the pain in my guts and a horrible thirst and my gulliver going throb throb throb, and it seemed to me that if I could not viddy this bit of film I would perhaps be not so sick. But I could not shut my glazzies, and even if I tried to move my glaz-balls about I still could not get like out of the line of fire of this picture. So I had to go on viddying what was being done and hear-

---

7 **to edit:** (Film) schneiden. | 10 **sound-track:** Tonspur. | 16 **switchboard:** Schaltbrett, Regiepult. | 22 **to throb:** pochen, schlagen. | 25 **glazball** (N.): Augapfel. | 26 **line of fire:** Schusslinie.

ing the most ghastly creechings coming from this litso. I knew it could not really be *real*, but that made no difference. I was heaving away but could not be sick, viddying first a britva cut out an eye, then slice down the cheek, then go rip rip rip all over, while red krovvy shot on to the camera lens. Then all the teeth were like wrenched out with a pair of pliers, and the creeching and the blood were terrific. Then I slooshied this very pleased goloss of Dr Brodsky going, "Excellent, excellent, excellent."

The next lomtick of film was of an old woman who kept a shop being kicked about amid very gromky laughter by a lot of malchicks, and these malchicks broke up the shop and then set fire to it. You could viddy this poor starry ptitsa trying to crawl out of the flames, screaming and creeching, but having had her leg broke by these malchicks kicking her she could not move. So then all the flames went roaring round her, and you could viddy her agonised litso like appealing through the flames and then disappearing into the flames, and then you could slooshy the most gromky and agonised and agonising screams that ever came from a human goloss. So this time I knew I had to sick up, so I creeched:

"I want to be sick. Please let me be sick. Please bring something for me to be sick into." But this Dr Brodsky called back:

"Imagination only. You've nothing to worry about. Next film coming up." That was perhaps meant to be a joke, for I

---

3 **to heave:** keuchen. | 4 **to slice:** in Scheiben schneiden, aufschlitzen. | 6 **lens:** (Glas-)Linse. | 7 **pliers** (pl.): Zange. | 20 **agonised:** qualerfüllt, von Todesangst gezeichnet.

heard a like smeck coming from the dark. And then I was forced to viddy a most nasty film about Japanese torture. It was the 1939–45 War, and there were soldiers being fixed to trees with nails and having fires lit under them and having their yarbles cut off, and you even viddied a gulliver being sliced off a soldier with a sword, and then with his head rolling about and the rot and the glazzies looking alive still, the plott of this soldier actually ran about, krovvy like a fountain out of the neck, and then it dropped, and all the time there was very very loud laughter from the Japanese. The pains I felt now in my belly and the headache and the thirst were terrible, and they all seemed to be coming out of the screen. So I creeched:

"Stop the film! Please, please stop it! I can't stand any more." And then the goloss of this Dr Brodsky said:

"Stop it? *Stop it*, did you say? Why, we've hardly started." And he and the others smecked quite loud.

Five

I do not wish to describe, brothers, what other horrible veshches I was like forced to viddy that afternoon. The like minds of this Dr Brodsky and Dr Branom and the others in white coats, and remember there was this devotchka twiddling with the knobs and watching the meters, they must have been more cally and filthy than any prestoopnick in the Staja itself. Because I did not think it was possible for any veck to even think of making films of what I was forced to viddy, all tied to this chair and my glazzies made to be wide open. All I could do was to creech very gromky for them to turn it off, and that like part drowned the noise of dratsing and fillying and also the music that went with it all. You can imagine it was like a terrible relief when I'd viddied the last bit of film and this Dr Brodsky said, in a very yawny and bored like goloss, "I think that should be enough for Day One, don't you, Branom?" And there I was with the lights switched on, my gulliver throbbing like a bolshy big engine that makes pain, and my rot all dry and cally inside, and feeling I could like sick up every bit of pishcha I had ever eaten, O my brothers, from the day I was like weaned. "All right," said this Dr Brodsky, "he can be taken back to his bed." Then he like patted me on the pletcho and said, "Good, good. A very promising start," grinning all over his litso, then he like waddled out, Dr Branom after him, but Dr Branom gave me a like very droogy and sympathetic type smile as though he had nothing to do with all this veshch but was like forced into it as I was.

22 **to wean:** (Kind) entwöhnen. | 25 **to waddle:** watscheln.

Anyhow, they freed my plott from the chair and they let go the skin above my glazzies so that I could open and shut them again, and I shut them, O my brothers, with the pain and throb in my gulliver, and then I was like carried to the old wheelchair and taken back to my malenky bedroom, the under-veck who wheeled me singing away at some hound-and-horny popsong so that I like snarled, "Shut it, thou," but he only smecked and said: "Never mind, friend," and then sang louder. So I was put into the bed and still felt bolnoy but could not sleep, but soon I started to feel that soon I might start to feel that I might soon start feeling just a malenky bit better, and then I was brought some nice hot chai with plenty of moloko and sakar and, peeting that, I knew that that like horrible nightmare was in the past and all over. And then Dr Branom came in, all nice and smiling. He said:

"Well, by my calculations you should be starting to feel all right again. Yes?"

"Sir," I said, like wary. I did not quite kopat what he was getting at govoreeting about calculations, seeing that getting better from feeling bolnoy is like your own affair and nothing to do with calculations. He sat down, all nice and droogy, on the bed's edge and said:

"Dr Brodsky is pleased with you. You had a very positive response. Tomorrow, of course, there'll be two sessions, morning and afternoon, and I should imagine that you'll be feeling a bit limp at the end of the day. But we have to be hard on you, you have to be cured." I said:

10 **bolnoy** (N.): krank. | 13 **sakar** (N.): Zucker. | 19 f. **what he was getting at**: worauf er hinauswollte.

"You mean I have to sit through –? You mean I have to look at –? Oh, no," I said. "It was horrible."

"Of course it was horrible," smiled Dr Branom. Violence is a very horrible thing. That's what you're learning now. Your body is learning it."

"But," I said, "I don't understand. I don't understand about feeling sick like I did. I never used to feel sick before. I used to feel like very the opposite. I mean, doing it or watching it I used to feel real horrorshow. I just don't understand why or how or what –"

"Life is a very wonderful thing," said Dr Branom in a very like holy goloss. "The processes of life, the make-up of the human organism, who can fully understand these miracles? Dr Brodsky is, of course, a remarkable man. What is happening to you now is what should happen to any normal healthy human organism contemplating the actions of the forces of evil, the workings of the principle of destruction. You are being made sane, you are being made healthy."

"That I will not have," I said, "nor can understand it at all. What you've been doing is to make me feel very very ill."

"Do you feel ill now?" he said, still with the old droogy smile on his litso. "Drinking tea, resting, having a quiet chat with a friend – surely you're not feeling anything but well?"

I like listened and felt for pain and sickness in my gulliver and plott, in a like cautious way, but it was true, brothers,

12 **make-up:** Machart, Zusammensetzung. | 16 **to contemplate s. th.:** etwas betrachten, ins Auge fassen, über etwas nachsinnen.

that I felt real horrorshow and even wanting my dinner. "I don't get it," I said. "You must be doing something to me to make me feel ill." And I sort of frowned about that, thinking.

"You felt ill this afternoon," he said, "because you're getting better. When we're healthy we respond to the presence of the hateful with fear and nausea. You're becoming healthy, that's all. You'll be healthier still this time tomorrow." Then he patted me on the noga and went out, and I tried to puzzle the whole veshch out as best I could. What it seemed to me was that the wires and other veshches that were fixed to my plott perhaps were making me feel ill, and that it was all a trick really. I was still puzzling out all this and wondering whether I should refuse to be strapped down to this chair tomorrow and start a real bit of dratsing with them all, because I had my rights, when another chelloveck came in to see me. He was a like smiling starry veck who said he was called the Discharge Officer, and he carried a lot of bits of paper with him. He said:

"Where will you go when you leave here?" I hadn't really thought about that sort of veshch at all, and it only now really began to dawn on me that I'd be a fine free malchick very soon, and then I viddied that would only be if I played it everybody's way and did not start any dratsing and creeching and refusing and so on. I said:

"Oh, I shall go home. Back to my pee and em."

"Your –?" He didn't get nadsat talk at all, so I said:

2 **to get** (coll.): kapieren. | 7 **nausea**: Übelkeit, Brechreiz. | 10 **to puzzle out**: austüfteln, ausknobeln. | 18 f. **discharge officer**: Entlassungsbeamter.

"To my parents in the dear old flatblock."

"I see," he said. "And when did you last have a visit from your parents?"

"A month," I said, "very near. They like suspended visiting-day for a bit because of one prestoopnick getting some blasting-powder smuggled in across the wires from his ptitsa. A real cally trick to play on the innocent, like punishing them as well. So it's like near a month since I had a visit."

"I see," said this veck. "And have your parents been informed of your transfer and impending release?" That had a real lovely zvook that did, that slovo *release*. I said:

"No." Then I said, "It will be a nice surprise for them, that, won't it? Me just walking through the door and saying, 'Here I am, back, a free veck again.' Yes, real horrorshow."

"Right," said the Discharge Officer veck, "we'll leave it at that. So long as you have somewhere to live. Now, there's the question of your having a job, isn't there?" And he showed me this long list of jobs I could have, but I thought, well, there would be time enough for that. A nice malenky holiday first. I could do a crasting job soon as I got out and fill the old carmans with pretty polly, but I would have to be very careful and I would have to do the job all on my oddy knocky. I did not trust so-called droogs any more. So I told this veck to leave it a bit and we would govoreet about it again. He said right right right, then got ready to leave. He showed himself to be a very queer sort of a veck, be-

6 **blasting-powder:** Sprengstoff. | 11 **transfer:** Verlegung. | **impending:** nahe bevorstehend.

cause what he did now was to like giggle and then say, "Would you like to punch me in the face before I go?" I did not think I could possibly have slooshied that right, so I said:

"Eh?"

"Would you," he giggled, "like to punch me in the face before I go?" I frowned like at that, very puzzled, and said:

"Why?"

"Oh," he said, "just to see how you're getting on." And he brought his litso real near, a fat grin all over his rot. So I fisted up and went smack at his litso, but he pulled himself away real skorry, grinning still, and my rooker just punched air. Very puzzling, this was, and I frowned as he left, smecking his gulliver off. And then, my brothers, I felt real sick again, just like in the afternoon, just for a couple of minootas. It then passed off skorry, and when they brought my dinner in I found I had a fair appetite and was ready to crunch away at the roast chicken. But it was funny that starry chelloveck asking for a tolchock in the litso. And it was funny feeling sick like that.

What was even funnier was when I went to sleep that night, O my brothers. I had a nightmare, and, as you might expect, it was one of those bits of film I'd viddied in the afternoon. A dream or nightmare is really only like a film inside your gulliver, except that it is as though you could walk into it and be part of it. And this is what happened to me. It was a nightmare of one of the bits of film they showed me near the end of the afternoon like session, all of smecking malchicks doing the ultra-violent on a young ptitsa who was creeching away in her red red krovvy, her platties all razrezzed real horrorshow. I was in this fillying about, smecking away and being like the ringleader, dressed in the heighth of nadsat fashion. And then at the heighth of all this dratsing and tolchocking I felt like paralysed and wanting to be very sick, and all the other malchicks had a real gromky smeck at me. Then I was dratsing my way back to being awake all through my own krovvy, pints and quarts and gallons of it, and then I found myself in my bed in this room. I wanted to be sick, so I got out of the bed all trembly so as to go off down the corridor to the old vaysay. But, behold, brothers, the door was locked. And turning round I viddied for like the first raz that there were bars on the window. And so, as I reached for the like pot in the malenky cupboard beside the bed, I viddied that there would be no escaping from any of all this. Worse, I did not dare to go back into my own sleeping gulliver. I soon found I did not want to be sick after all, but then I was poogly of getting back into bed to sleep. But soon I fell smack into sleep and did not dream any more.

---

1 **ringleader**: Rädelsführer. | 3 **paralysed**: gelähmt. | 6 **pint**: Pinte (englisches Hohlmaß; 1 pt = 0,568 l). | **quart**: Quarte (englisches Hohlmaß; 1 qt = 1,1365 dm³). | 7 **gallon**: Gallone (englisches Hohlmaß; 1 g = 4,54 l). | 8 **trembly** (coll.): zitternd, bebend. | 9 **vaysay** (N.): WC, Toilette. | 9 f. **behold**: sieh da!

Six

"Stop it, stop it, stop it," I kept on creeching out. "Turn it off, you grahzny bastards, for I can stand no more." It was the next day, brothers, and I had truly done my best morning and afternoon to play it their way and sit like a horror-show smiling cooperative malchick in the chair of torture while they flashed nasty bits of ultra-violence on the screen, my glazzies clipped open to viddy all, my plott and rookers and nogas fixed to the chair so I could not get away. What I was being made to viddy now was not really a veshch I would have thought to be too bad before, it being only three or four malchicks crasting in a shop and filling their carmans with cutter, at the same time fillying about with the creeching starry ptitsa running the shop, tolchocking her and letting the red red krovvy flow. But the throb and like crash crash crash crash in my gulliver and the wanting to sick and the terrible dry rasping thirstiness in my rot, all were worse than yesterday. "Oh, I've had enough," I cried. "It's not fair, you vonny sods," and I tried to struggle out of the chair but it was not possible, me being good as stuck to it.

"First-class," creeched out this Dr Brodsky. "You're doing really well. Just one more and then we're finished."

"What it was now was the starry 1939–45 War again, and it was a very blobby and liny and crackly film you could viddy had been made by the Germans. It opened with German eagles and the Nazi flag with that like crooked cross

---

6 **cooperative**: mitwirkend, zusammenarbeitend. | 17 **thirstiness**: Durst. | 24 **blobby**: bekleckst. | **crackly**: 1. knisternd; 2. grobkörnig. | 26 **eagle** (Air Force slang): Stuka (im Zweiten Weltkrieg verwendetes deutsches Sturzkampfflugzeug).

that all malchicks at school love to draw, and then there were very haughty and nadmenny like German officers walking through streets that were all dust and bomb-holes and broken buildings. Then you were allowed to viddy lewdies being shot against walls, officers giving the orders, and also horrible nagoy plotts left lying in gutters, all like cages of bare ribs and white thin nogas. Then there were lewdies being dragged off creeching, though not on the sound-track, my brothers, the only sound being music, and being tolchocked while they were dragged off. Then I noticed, in all my pain and sickness, what music it was that like crackled and boomed on the sound-track, and it was Ludwig van, the last movement of the Fifth Symphony, and I creeched like bezoomny at that. "Stop!" I creeched. "Stop, you grahzny vonny disgusting sods. It's a sin, that's what it is, a filthy unforgivable sin, you bratchnies!" They didn't stop right away, because there was only a minute or two more to go – lewdies being beaten up and all blood, then more firing squads, then the old Nazi flag and THE END. But when the lights came on this Dr Brodsky and also Dr Branom were standing in front of me, and Dr Brodsky said:

"What's all this about sin, eh?"

"That," I said, very sick. "Using Ludwig van like that. He did no harm to anyone. Beethoven just wrote music." And then I was really sick and they had to bring a bowl that was in the shape of like a kidney.

"Music," said Dr Brodsky, like musing. So you're keen

2 **nadmenny** (N.): arrogant. | 12 **to crackle**: knistern, prasseln, knattern. | **to boom**: dröhnen, brausen, brummen. | 16 **unforgivable**: unverzeihlich. | 19 **firing squad**: Exekutionskommando. | 26 **kidney**: Niere.

on music. I know nothing about it myself. It's a useful emotional heightener, that's all I know. Well, well. What do you think about that, eh, Branom?"

"It can't be helped," said Dr Branom. "Each man kills the thing he loves, as the poet-prisoner said. Here's the punishment element, perhaps. The Governor ought to be pleased."

"Give me a drink," I said, "for Bog's sake."

"Loosen him," ordered Dr Brodsky. "Fetch him a carafe of ice-cold water." So then these under-vecks got to work and soon I was peeting gallons and gallons of water and it was like heaven, O my brothers. Dr Brodsky said:

"You seem a sufficiently intelligent young man. You seem, too, to be not without taste. You've just got this violence thing, haven't you? Violence and theft, theft being an aspect of violence." I didn't govoreet a single slovo, brothers. I was still feeling sick, though getting a malenky bit better now. But it had been a terrible day. "Now, then," said Dr Brodsky, "how did you think this is done? Tell me, what do you think we're doing to you?"

"You're making me feel ill," I said. "I'm ill when I look at those filthy pervert films of yours. But it's not really the films that's doing it. But I feel that if you'll stop these films I'll stop feeling ill."

"Right," said Dr Brodsky. "It's association, the oldest educational method in the world. And what really causes you to feel ill?"

---

2 **emotional heightener:** gefühlsmäßiger, auf das Gefühl wirkender Verstärker. | 4 f. **Each man kills the thing he loves:** Zitat aus »The Ballad of Reading Gaol« von Oscar Wilde (1856–1900), geschrieben 1897 kurz nach seiner Entlassung aus dem Gefängnis von Reading.

"These grahzny sodding veshches that come out of my gulliver and my plott," I said, "that's what it is."

"Quaint," said Dr Brodsky, like smiling, "the dialect of the tribe. Do you know anything of its provenance, Branom?"

"Odd bits of old rhyming slang," said Dr Branom, who did not look quite so much like a friend anymore. "A bit of gypsy talk, too. But most of the roots are Slav. Propaganda. Subliminal penetration."

"All right, all right, all right," said Dr Brodsky, like impatient and not interested any more. "Well," he said to me, "it isn't the wires. It's nothing to do with what's fastened to you. Those are just for measuring your reactions. What is it, then?"

I viddied then, of course, what a bezoomny shoot I was not to notice that it was the hypodermic needle shots in the rooker. "Oh," I creeched, "oh, I viddy all now. A filthy cally vonny trick. An act of treachery, sod you, and you won't do it again."

"I'm glad you've raised your objections now," said Dr Brodsky. "Now we can be perfectly clear about it. We can get this stuff of Ludovico's into your system in many

3f. **the dialect of the tribe:** Anspielung auf den zweiten Teil von T. S. Eliots *Little Gidding* (1942). Eliot zitiert wiederum aus »Le Tombeau d'Edgar Poe« des französischen Dichters Stéphane Mallarmé (1842–1898). | 4 **provenance:** Herkunft, Ursprung. | 6 **rhyming slang:** Eigenart des Cockney, bei der das gemeinte Wort durch sich darauf reimende Worte oder Phrasen ersetzt wird (z. B. *plates of meat: feet*). | 8 **gypsy talk:** Zigeunersprache. | **Slav:** slawisch. | 9 **subliminal:** unterbewusst, unterschwellig. | **penetration:** Durch-, Eindringen. | 18 **sod you** (taboo slang): etwa: sei verdammt. | 22 **system:** Körper, Organismus.

different ways. Orally, for instance. But the subcutaneous method is the best. Don't fight against it, please. There's no point in your fighting. You can't get the better of us."

"Grahzny bratchnies," I said, like snivelling. Then I said, "I don't mind about the ultra-violence and all that cal. I can put up with that. But it's not fair on the music. It's not fair I should feel ill when I'm slooshying lovely Ludwig van and G. F. Handel and others. All that shows you're an evil lot of bastards and I shall never forgive you, sods."

They both looked a bit like thoughtful. Then Dr Brodsky said: "Delimitation is always difficult. The world is one, life is one. The sweetest and most heavenly of activities partake in some measure of violence – the act of love, for instance; music, for instance. You must take your chance, boy. The choice has been all yours." I didn't understand all these slovos, but now I said:

"You needn't take it any further, sir." I'd changed my tune a malenky bit in a cunning way. "You've proved to me that all the dratsing and ultra-violence and killing is wrong wrong and terribly wrong. I've learned my lesson, sirs. I see now what I've never seen before. I'm cured, praise God." And I raised my glazzies in a like holy way to the ceiling. But both these doctors shook their gullivers like sadly and Dr Brodsky said:

"You're not cured yet. There's still a lot to be done. Only when your body reacts promptly and violently to violence,

---

1 **orally:** mündlich, durch den Mund. | **subcutaneous:** subkutan, unter die, der Haut. | 3 **to get the better of s.o.:** die Oberhand über jdn. gewinnen, jdn. überwinden. | 4 **snivelling:** wehleidig, weinerlich; triefnäsig. | 11 **delimitation:** Abgrenzung.

as to a snake, without further help from us, without medication, only then – " I said:

"But, sir, sirs, I *see* that it's wrong. It's wrong because it's against like society, it's wrong because every veck on earth has the right to live and be happy without being beaten and tolchocked and knifed. I've learned a lot, oh really I have." But Dr Brodsky had a loud long smeck at that, showing all his white zoobies, and said:

"The heresy of an age of reason," or some such slovos. "I see what is right and approve, but I do what is wrong. No, no, my boy, you must leave it all to us. But be cheerful about it. It will soon be all over. In less than a fortnight now you'll be a free man." Then he patted me on the pletcho.

Less than a fortnight, O my brothers and friends, it was like an age. It was like from the beginning of the world to the end of it. To finish the fourteen years with remission in the Staja would have been nothing to it. Every day it was the same. When the devotchka with the hypodermic came round, though, four days after this govoreeting with Dr Brodsky and Dr Branom, I said, "Oh, no you won't," and tolchocked her on the rooker, and the syringe went tinkle clatter on to the floor. That was like to viddy what they would do. What they did was to get four or five real bolshy white-coated bastards of under-vecks to hold me down on the bed, tolchocking me with grinny litsos close to mine, and then this nurse ptitsa said, "You wicked naughty little devil, you," while she jabbed my rooker with another syringe and squirted this stuff in real brutal and nasty. And

1 f. **medication:** Beimischung von Arzneistoffen; Verordnung, medizinische Behandlung. | 9 **heresy:** Ketzerei. | 22 **to clatter:** klappern, rasseln. | 27 **to jab:** piksen.

then I was wheeled off exhausted to this like hell sinny as before.

Every day, my brothers, these films were like the same, all kicking and tolchocking and red red krovvy dripping off of litsos and plotts and spattering all over the camera lenses. It was usually grinning and smecking malchicks in the heighth of nadsat fashion, or else teeheeing Jap torturers or brutal Nazi kickers and shooters. And each day the feeling of wanting to die with the sickness and gulliver pains and aches in the zoobies and horrible horrible thirst grew really worse. Until one morning I tried to defeat the bastards by crash crash crashing my gulliver against the wall so that I should tolchock myself unconscious, but all that happened was I felt sick with viddying that this kind of violence was like the violence in the films, so I was just exhausted and was given the injection and was wheeled off like before.

And then there came a morning where I woke up and had my breakfast off eggs and toast and jam and very hot milky chai, and then I thought: It can't be much longer now. Now must be very near the end of the time. I have suffered to the heighth and cannot suffer any more. And I waited and waited, brothers, for this nurse ptitsa to bring in the syringe, but she did not come. And then the white-coated under-veck came and said:

"Today, old friend, we are letting you walk."

"Walk?" I said. "Where?"

"To the usual place," he said. "Yes, yes, look not so as-

---

7 **to teehee:** leicht auflachen. | **Jap** (pej.): Kurzform von *Japanese*. | **torturer:** Folterer. | 8 **kicker** (coll.): Treter. | **shooter:** Schütze.

tonished. You are to walk to the films, me with you of course. You are no longer to be carried in a wheelchair."

"But," I said, "how about my horrible morning injection?" For I was really surprised at this, brothers, they being so keen on pushing this Ludovico veshch into me, as they said. "Don't I get that horrible sicky stuff rammed into my poor suffering rooker any more?"

"All over," like smecked this veck. "For ever and ever amen. You're on your own now, boy. Walking and all to the chamber of horrors. But you're still to be strapped down and made to see. Come on then, my little tiger." And I had to put my over-gown and toofles on and walk down the corridor to the like sinny mesto.

Now this time, O my brothers, I was not only very sick but very puzzled. There it was again, all the old ultra-violence and vecks with their gullivers smashed and torn krovvy-dripping ptitsas creeching for mercy, the like private and individual fillying and nastiness. Then there were the prison-camps and the Jews and the grey like foreign streets full of tanks and uniforms and vecks going down in withering rifle-fire, this being the public side of it. And this time I could blame nothing for me feeling sick and thirsty and full of aches except what I was forced to viddy, my glazzies still being clipped open and my nogas and plott fixed to the chair but this set of wires and other veshches no longer coming out of my plott and gulliver. So what could it be but the films I was viddying that were doing

6 **sicky** (N.): *sickening:* ekelhaft, widerlich, Übelkeit erregend. | **to ram:** rammen, stopfen. | 9 **on one's own:** selbständig, unabhängig; sich selbst überlassen. | 19 **prison-camp:** Gefangenenlager. | 20 f. **withering:** vernichtend. | 21 **rifle-fire:** Gewehrfeuer, Kugelhagel.

this to me? Except, of course, brothers, that this Ludovico stuff was like a vaccination and there it was cruising about in my krovvy, so that I would be sick always for ever and ever amen whenever I viddied any of this ultra-violence. So now I squared my rot and went boo hoo hoo, and the tears like blotted out what I was forced to viddy in like all blessed runny silvery dewdrops. But these white-coat bratchnies were skorry with their tashtooks to wipe the tears away, saying, "There, there, wazzums all weepy-weepy den?" And there it was again all clear before my glazzies, these Germans prodding like beseeching and weeping Jews – vecks and cheenas and malchicks and devotchkas – into mestos where they would all snuff it of poison gas. Boo hoo hoo I had to go again, and along they came to wipe the tears off, very skorry, so I should not miss one solitary veshch of what they were showing. It was a terrible and horrible day, O my brothers and only friends.

I was lying on the bed all alone that nochy after my dinner of fat thick mutton stew and fruit pie and ice cream, and I thought to myself: "Hell hell hell, there might be a chance for me if I get out now." I had no weapon, though. I was allowed no britva here, and I had been shaved every other day by a fat bald-headed veck who came to my bed before breakfast, two white-coated bratchnies standing by to viddy I was a good non-violent malchick. The nails on my rookers

2 **vaccination:** Impfung. | **to cruise:** kreuzen, herumfahren; hier: zirkulieren. | 6 **to blot out:** auslöschen; verdecken. | 7 **runny:** laufend (Nase). | **dewdrops** (pl.): Tautropfen. | 9 f. **wazzums all weepy-weepy den:** etwa: wer wird denn gleich weinen? | 11 **to beseech:** dringend bitten, anflehen. | 24 **bald-headed:** kahlköpfig.

had been scissored and filed real short so I could not scratch. But I was still skorry on the attack, though they had weakened me down, brothers, to a like shadow of what I had been in the old free days. So now I got off the bed and went to the locked door and began to fist it real horrorshow and hard, creeching at the same time, "Oh help, help. I'm sick, I'm dying. Doctor doctor doctor, quick. Please. Oh, I'll die, I know I shall. Help." My gorlo was real dry and sore before anyone came. Then I heard nogas coming down the corridor and a like grumbling goloss, and then I recognised the goloss of the white-coated veck who brought my pishcha and like escorted me to my daily doom. He like grumbled:

"What is it? What goes on? What's your little nasty game in there?"

"Oh, I'm dying," I like moaned. "Oh, I have a ghastly pain in my side. Appendicitis, it is. Ooooooh."

"Appendy shitehouse," grumbled this veck, and then to my joy, brothers, I could slooshy the like clank of keys. "If you're trying it, little friend, my friends and me will beat and kick you all through the night." Then he opened up and brought in like the sweet air of the promise of my freedom. Now I was like behind the door when he pushed it open, and I could viddy him in the corridor light looking round for me puzzled. Then I raised my two fisties to tolchock him on the neck nasty, and then, I swear, as I sort of viddied him in advance lying moaning or out out out and felt the like joy rise in my guts, it was then that this sickness rose in me as it might be a wave and I felt a horrible fear as if I was

---

1 **to scissor**: (mit der Schere) schneiden. | **to file**: feilen. | 16 **appendicitis**: Blinddarmentzündung. | 17 **shitehouse** (slang): Scheißhaus. | 18 **clank**: Rasseln.

really going to die. I like tottered over to the bed going urgh urgh urgh, and the veck, who was not in his white coat but an over-gown, viddied clear enough what I had in my mind for he said:

"Well, everything's a lesson, isn't it? Learning all the time, as you could say. Come on, little friend, get up from that bed and hit me. I want you to, yes, really. A real good crack across the jaw. Oh I'm dying for it, really I am." But all I could do, brothers, was to just lay there sobbing boo hoo hoo. "Scum," like sneered this veck now. "Filth." And he pulled me up by like the scruff of my pyjama-top, me being very weak and limp, and he raised and swung his right rooker so that I got a fair old tolchock clean on the litso. "That," he said, "is for getting me out of my bed, you young dirt." And he wiped his rookers against each other swish swish and went out. Crunch crunch went the key in the lock.

And what, brothers, I had to escape into sleep from them was the horrible and wrong feeling that it was better to get the hit than give it. If that veck had stayed I might even have like presented the other cheek.

8 **to be dying for s. th.** (coll.): sich nach etwas sehnen. | 20 f. **I might even have like presented the other cheek:** Anspielung auf Matthäus 5,39: »Ich aber sage euch, dass ihr nicht widerstreben sollt dem Übel; sondern, wenn dir jemand einen Streich gibt auf deine rechte Backe, dem biete die andere auch dar.«

Seven

I could not believe, brothers, what I was told. It seemed that I had been in that vonny mesto for near ever and would be there for near ever more. But it had always been a fortnight and now they said the fortnight was near up. They said:

"Tomorrow, little friend, out out out." And they made with the old thumb, like pointing to freedom. And then the white-coated veck who had tolchocked me and who had still brought me my trays of pishcha and like escorted me to my everyday torture said: "But you still have one really big day in front of you. It's to be your passing-out day." And he had a leery smeck at that.

I expected this morning that I would be ittying as usual to the sinny mesto in my pyjamas and toofles and overgown. But no. This morning I was given my shirt and undervesshches and my platties of the night and my horror-show kick-boots, all lovely and washed or ironed or polished. And I was even given my cut-throat britva that I had used in the old happy days for fillying and dratsing. So I gave with the puzzled frown at this as I got dressed, but the white-coated under-veck just like grinned and would govoreet nothing, O my brothers.

I was led quite kindly to the same old mesto, but there were changes there. Curtains had been drawn in front of the sinny screen and the frosted glass under the projection holes was no longer there, it having perhaps been pushed up or folded to the sides like blind or shutters. And where

12 **passing-out day:** Entlassungstag. | 21 **to give with s.th.:** etwas machen, zum Einsatz bringen. | 28 **blind:** Rollo.

there had been just the noise of coughing kashl kashl kashl
and like shadows of lewdies was now a real audience, and in
this audience there were litsos I knew. There was the Staja
Governor and the holy man, the charlie or charles as he was
called, and the Chief Chasso and this very important and
well-dressed chelloveck who was the Minister of the Interi-
or or Inferior. All the rest I did not know. Dr Brodsky and
Dr Branom were there, although now not white-coated,
instead they were dressed as doctors would dress who were
big enough to want to dress in the heighth of fashion. Dr
Branom just stood, but Dr Brodsky stood and govoreeted
in a like learned manner to all the lewdies assembled.
When he viddied me coming in he said, "Aha. At this stage,
gentlemen, we introduce the subject himself. He is, as you
will perceive, fit and well-nourished. He comes straight
from a night's sleep and a good breakfast, undrugged, un-
hypnotised. Tomorrow we send him with confidence out
into the world again, as decent a lad as you would meet on a
May morning, unvicious, unviolent, if anything – as you
will observe – inclined to the kindly word and the helpful
act. What a change is here, gentlemen, from the wretched
hoodlum the State committed to unprofitable punishment
some two years ago, unchanged after two years. Unchanged, do I say? Not quite. Prison taught him the false
smile, the rubbed hands of hypocrisy, the fawning greased
obsequious leer. Other vices it taught him, as well as con-

---

16 **undrugged:** ohne Arznei, Drogen oder Schlafmittel. | 22 **unprofit-
able:** unrentabel, nutzlos. | 25 **hypocrisy:** Heuchelei. | **fawning:** krieche-
risch, schmeichlerisch. | **greased:** (fig.) schmierig. | 26 **obsequious:**
willfährig, gefügig, knechtisch. | **leer:** (lüsterner, boshafter, gehässiger)
Seitenblick.

firming him in those he had long practised before. But, gentlemen, enough of words. Actions speak louder than. Action now. Observe, all."

I was a bit dazed by all this govoreeting and I was trying to grasp in my mind that like this was all about me. Then all the lights went out and there came on two like spotlights shining from the projection-squares, and one of them was full on Your Humble and Suffering Narrator. And into the other spotlight there walked a bolshy big chelloveck I had never viddied before. He had a lardy like litso and like strips of hair pasted over his near-bald gulliver. He was about thirty or forty or fifty, some old age like that, starry. He it-tied up to me and the spotlight ittied with him, and soon the two spotlights had made like one big pool. He said to me, very sneery, "Hello, heap of dirt. Pooh, you don't wash much, judging from the horrible smell." Then, as if he was like dancing, he stamped on my nogas, left, right, then he gave me a finger-nail flick on the nose that hurt like bezoomny and brought the old tears to my glazzies, then he twisted at my left ooko like it was a radio dial. I could slooshy titters and a couple of real horrorshow hawhaw-haws coming from like the audience. My nose and nogas and earhole stung and pained like bezoomny, so I said:

"What do you do that to me for? I've never done any wrong to you, brother."

"Oh," this veck said, "I do this" – flickflicked nose again – "and that" – twisted smarting earhole – "and the other" –

10 **lardy:** speckartig, speckig. | 11 **to paste:** kleben, kleistern, pappen. | 15 **pooh:** Ausruf des Ekels; etwa: pfui! | 18 **flick:** Schnipsen, leichter, schneller Hieb oder Schlag. | 20 **radio dial:** Senderwahlknopf am Radio. | 21 **titter:** Kichern, Gekicher.

stamped nasty on right noga – "because I don't care for your horrible type. And if you want to do anything about it, start, start, please do." Now I knew that I'd have to be real skorry and get my cut-throat britva out before this horrible killing sickness whooshed up and turned the like joy of battle into feeling I was going to snuff it. But, O brothers, as my rooker reached for the britva in my inside carman I got this like picture in my mind's glazzy of this insulting chelloveck howling for mercy with the red red krovvy all streaming out of his rot, and hot after this picture the sickness and dryness and pains were rushing to overtake, and I viddied that I'd have to change the way I felt about this rotten veck very very very skorry indeed, so I felt in my carmans for cigarettes or for pretty polly, and, O my brothers, there was not either of these veshches. I said, all howly and blubbery:

"I'd like to give you a cigarette, brother, but I don't seem to have any." This veck went:

"Wah wah. Boohoohoo. Cry, baby." Then he flickflickflicked with his bolshy horny nail at my nose again, and I could slooshy very loud smecks of like mirth coming from the dark audience. I said, real desperate, trying to be nice to this insulting and hurtful veck to stop the pains and sickness coming up:

"Please let me do something for you, please." And I felt in my carmans but could only find my cut-throat britva, so I took this out and handed it to him and said, "Please take this, please. A little present. Please have it." But he said:

16 **blubbery** (N.): heulend, weinend (von *to blubber* ›heulen‹). | 23 **hurtful**: verletzend.

"Keep your stinking bribes to yourself. You can't get round me that way." And he banged at my rooker and cut-throat britva fell on the floor. So I said:

"Please, I must do something. Shall I clean your boots? Look, I'll get down and lick them." And, my brothers, believe it or kiss my sharries, I got down on my knees and pushed my red yahzick out a mile and a half to lick his grahzny vonny boots. But all this veck did was to kick me not too hard on the rot. So then it seemed to me that it would not bring on the sickness and pain if I just gripped his ankles with my rookers tight around them and brought this grahzny bratchny down to the floor. So I did this and he got a real bolshy surprise, coming down crack amid loud laughter from the vonny audience. But viddying him on the floor I could feel the whole horrible feeling coming over me, so I gave him my rooker to lift him up skorry and up he came. Then just as he was going to give me a real nasty and earnest tolchock on the litso Dr Brodsky said:

"All right, that will do very well." Then this horrible veck sort of bowed and danced off like an actor while the lights came up on me blinking and with my rot square for howling. Dr Brodsky said to the audience: "Our subject is, you see, impelled towards the good by, paradoxically, being impelled towards evil. The intention to act violently is accompanied by strong feelings of physical distress. To counter these the subject has to switch to a diametrically opposed attitude. Any questions?"

1 **bribe:** Bestechung(sgeschenk). | 1f. **to get round s.o.:** jdn. herumkriegen, beschwatzen. | 23 **to impel:** antreiben. | **paradoxically:** paradoxerweise. | 25 **to counter:** entgegenwirken, entgegnen. | 26 **diametrically:** diametral, genau entgegengesetzt.

"Choice," rumbled a rich deep goloss. I viddied it belonged to the prison charlie. "He has no real choice, has he? Self-interest, fear of physical pain, drove him to that grotesque act of self-abasement. Its insincerity was clearly to be seen. He ceases to be a wrongdoer. He ceases also to be a creature capable of moral choice."

"These are subtleties," like smiled Dr Brodsky. "We are not concerned with motive, with the higher ethics. We are concerned only with cutting down crime –"

"And," chipped in this bolshy well-dressed Minister, "with relieving the ghastly congestion in our prisons."

"Hear hear," said somebody.

There was a lot of govoreeting and arguing then and I just stood there, brothers, like completely ignored by all these ignorant bratchnies, so I creeched out:

"Me, me, me. How about me? Where do I come into all of this? Am I like just some animal or dog?" And that started them off govoreeting real loud and throwing slovos at me. So I creeched louder still, creeching: "Am I just to be like a clockwork orange?" I didn't know what made me use those slovos, brothers, which just came like without asking into my gulliver. And that shut all those vecks up for some reason for a minoota or two. Then one very thin starry professor type chelloveck stood up, his neck like all cables carrying like power from his gulliver to his plott, and he said:

1 **to rumble:** rumpeln, poltern. | 3 **self-interest:** Eigennutz. | 4 **self-abasement:** Selbsterniedrigung. | **insincerity:** Unaufrichtigkeit. | 5 **wrongdoer:** Übel-, Missetäter, Sünder. | 7 **subtlety:** Feinheit, Spitzfindigkeit. | 8 **ethics** (pl.): Ethik, Sittenlehre. | 10 **to chip in:** ins Gespräch fallen, beisteuern. | 11 **congestion:** Überfüllung, Andrang. | 12 **hear hear:** 1. hört! hört!; 2. sehr richtig!

"You have no cause to grumble, boy. You made your choice and all this is a consequence of your choice. Whatever now ensues is what you yourself have chosen." And the prison charlie creeched out:

"Oh, if only I could believe that." And you could viddy the Governor give him a look like meaning that he would not climb so high in like Prison Religion as he thought he would. Then loud arguing started again, and then I could slooshy the slovo Love being thrown around, the prison charles himself creeching as loud as any about Perfect Love Casteth Out Fear and all that cal. And now Dr Brodsky said, smiling all over his litso:

"I am glad, gentlemen, this question of Love has been raised. Now we shall see in action a manner of Love that was thought to be dead with the Middle Ages." And then the lights went down and the spotlights came on again, one on your poor and suffering Friend and Narrator, and into the other there like rolled or sidled the most lovely young devotchka you could ever hope in all your jeezny, O my brothers, to viddy. That is to say, she had real horrorshow groodies all of which you could like viddy, she having on platties which came down down down off her pletchoes. And her nogas were like Bog in His Heaven, and she walked like to make you groan in your keeshkas, and yet her litso was a sweet smiling young like innocent litso. She came up towards me with the light like it was the light of heavenly grace and all that cal coming with her, and the first thing that flashed into my gulliver was that I would like to have

10 f. **perfect love casteth out fear:** 1. Johannesbrief 4,18: »[...] die vollendete Liebe treibt die Furcht aus«.

her right down there on the floor with the old in-out real savage, but skorry as a shot came the sickness, like a like detective that had been watching round a corner and now followed to make his grahzny arrest. And now the von of lovely perfume that came off her made me want to think of starting to like heave in my keeshkas, so I knew I had to think of some new like way of thinking about her before all the pain and thirstiness and horrible sickness came over me real horrorshow and proper. So I creeched out:

"O most beautiful and beauteous of devotchkas, I throw like my heart at your feet for you to like trample all over. If I had a rose I would give it to you. If it was all rainy and cally now on the ground you could have my platties to walk on so as not to cover your dainty nogas with filth and cal." And as I was saying all this, O my brothers, I could feel the sickness like slinking back. "Let me," I creeched out, "worship you and be like your helper and protector from the wicked little world." Then I thought of the right slovo and felt better for it, saying, "Let me be like your true knight," and down I went again on the old knees, bowing and like scraping.

And then I felt real shooty and dim, it having been like an act again, for this devotchka smiled and bowed to the audience and like danced off, the lights coming up to a bit of applause. And the glazzies of some of these starry vecks in the audience were like popping out at this young devotchka with dirty and like unholy desire, O my brothers.

"He will be your true Christian," Dr Brodsky was creech-

---

10 **beauteous** (poet.): schön. | 16 **to slink**: schleichen. | 22 **shooty** (N.): dumm, töricht. | 26 **to pop out**: aus den Höhlen treten (Augen).

ing out, "ready to turn the other cheek, ready to be cruci-
fied rather than crucify, sick to the very heart at the thought
even of killing a fly." And that was right, brothers, because
when he said that I thought of killing a fly and felt just that
tiny bit sick, but I pushed the sickness and pain back by
thinking of the fly being fed with bits of sugar and looked
after like a bleeding pet and all that cal. "Reclamation," he
creeched. "Joy before the Angels of God."

"The point is," this Minister of the Inferior was saying
real gromky, "that it works."

"Oh," the prison charlie said, like sighing, "it works all
right, God help the lot of us."

1 f. **to crucify s.o.:** jdn. kreuzigen. | 8 **joy before the angels of God:**
Anspielung auf Lukas 15,10.

Part Three

One

"What's it going to be then, eh?"

That, my brothers, was me asking myself the next morning, standing outside this white building that was like
tacked on to the old Staja, in my platties of the night of two
years back in the grey light of dawn, with a malenky bit of a
bag with my few personal veshches in and a bit of cutter
kindly donated by the vonny Authorities to like start me
off in my new life.

The rest of the day before had been very tiring, what
with interviews to go on tape for the telenews and photographs being took flash flash flash and more like demon-
strations of me folding in the face of ultra-violence and all
that embarassing cal. And then I had like fallen into the bed
and then, as it looked to me, been wakened up to be told to
get off out, to itty off home, they did not want to viddy
Your Humble Narrator never not no more, O my brothers.
So there I was, very very early in the morning, with just
this bit of pretty polly in my left carman, jinglejangling it
and wondering:

"What's it going to be then, eh?"

Some breakfast some mesto, I thought, me not having
eaten at all that morning, every veck being so anxious to

6 **to tack on:** anheften, anhängen. | 9 **to donate:** schenken, spenden,
stiften. | 12 **tape:** (Ton-)Band. | 13 **took:** *taken.* | 14 **to fold:** hier: ein-
knicken, kapitulieren. | 16 **wakened:** *woken.* | 20 **to jinglejangle:** Zu-
sammensetzung aus *to jingle* ›klimpern‹, ›klingeln lassen‹ und *to jangle*
›misstönend klingen‹, ›poltern‹.

tolchock me off out to freedom. A chasha of chai only had I peeted. This Staja was in a very like gloomy part of the town, but there were malenky workers' caffs all around and I soon found one of those, my brothers. It was very cally and vonny, with one bulb in the ceiling with fly-dirt like obscuring its bits of light, and there were early rabbiters slurping away at chai and horrible-looking sausages and slices of kleb which they like wolfed, going wolf wolf wolf and then creeching for more. They were served by a very cally devotchka but with very bolshy groodies on her, and some of the eating vecks tried to grab her, going haw haw haw while she went he he he, and the sight of them near made me want to sick, brothers. But I asked for some toast and jam and chai very politely and with my gentleman's goloss, then I sat in a dark corner to eat and peet.

While I was doing this, a malenky like dwarf of a veck it-tied in, selling the morning's gazettas, a twisted and grahzny prestoopnick type with thick glasses on with steel rims, his platties like the colour of a very starry decaying currant pudding. I kupetted a gazetta, my idea being to get ready for plunging back into normal jeezny again by viddying what was ittying on in the world. This gazetta I had seemed to be like a Government gazetta, for the only news that was on the front page was about the need for every veck to make sure he put the Government back in again on the next General Election, which seemed to be about two or three weeks

---

3 **caff** (N.): vermutl.: Café, Cafeteria. | 6 **to obscure**: verdunkeln. | **rabbiter** (N.): Arbeiter. | 8 **to wolf** (coll.): (gierig) verschlingen. | 18 **rims** (pl.): (Brillen-)Gestell. | 19 **currant**: Korinthe. | 25 **to put back in**: wiedereinsetzen, wiederwählen. | 25 f. **general election**: allgemeine Parlamentswahlen.

off. There were very boastful slovos about what the Government had done, brothers, in the last year or so, what with increased exports and a real horrorshow foreign policy and improved social services and all that cal. But that the Government was really most boastful about was the way in which they reckoned the streets had been made safer for all peace-loving night-walking lewdies in the last six months, what with better pay for the police and the police getting like tougher with young hooligans and perverts and burglars and all that cal. Which interessovatted Your Humble Narrator some deal. And on the second page of the gazetta there was a blurry like photograph of somebody who looked very familiar, and it turned out to be none other than me me me. I looked very gloomy and like scared, but that was really with the flashbulbs going pop pop pop all the time. What it said underneath my picture was that here was the first graduate of the new State Institute of Criminal Types, cured of his criminal instincts in a fortnight only, now a good law-fearing citizen and all that cal. Then I viddied there was a very boastful article about this Ludovico's Technique and how clever the Government was and all that cal. Then there was another picture of some veck I thought I knew, and it was this Minister of the Inferior or Interior. It seemed that he had been doing a bit of boasting, looking forward to a nice crime-free era in which there would be no more fear of cowardly attacks from young hooligans and perverts and burglers and all that cal. So I went arghhhhhh

3 f. **foreign policy:** Außenpolitik. | 4 **social services:** Sozialeinrichtungen. | 9 f. **burglar:** Einbrecher. | 12 **blurry:** verschwommen, unklar. | 15 **flashbulb:** Blitzlicht. | **pop:** paff! | 17 **graduate:** Absolvent. | 25 **era:** Ära, Zeitalter, Epoche.

and threw this gazetta on the floor, so that it covered up stains of spilled chai and horrible spat gobs from the cally animals that used this caff.

"What's it going to be then, eh?"

What it was going to be now, brothers, was homeways and a nice surprise for dadada and mum, their only son and heir back in the family bosom. Then I could lay back on the bed in my own malenky den and slooshy some lovely music, and at the same time I could think over what to do now with my jeezny. The Discharge Officer had given me a long list the day before of jobs I could try for, and he had telephoned to different vecks about me, but I had no intention, my brothers, of going off to rabbit right away. A malenky bit of rest first, yes, and a quiet think on the bed to the sound of lovely music.

And so the autobus to Center, and then the autobus to Kingsley Avenue, the flats of Flatblock 18A being just near. You will believe me, my brothers, when I say my heart was going clopclopclop with the like excitement. All was very quiet, it still being early winter morning, and when I ittied into the vestibule of the flatblock there was no veck about, only the nagoy vecks and cheenas of the Dignity of Labour. What surprised me, brothers, was the way that had been cleaned up, there being no longer any dirty ballooning slovos from the rots of the Dignified Labourers, not any dirty parts of the body added to their naked plotts by dirty-minded pencilling malchicks. And what also surprised me was that the lift was working. It came purring down when I

2 **gob** (coll.): (Schleim-)Klumpen, Spucke. | 7 **family bosom** (fig.): Schoß der Familie. | 21 **vestibule:** Vor-, Eingangshalle. | 28 **to purr:** schnurren.

pressed the electric knopka, and when I got in I was surprised again to viddy all was clean inside the like cage.

So up I went to the tenth floor, and there I saw 10-8 as it had been before, and my rooker trembled and shook as I took out of my carman the little klootch I had for opening up. But I very firmly fitted the klootch in the lock and turned, then opened up then went in, and there I met three pairs of surprised and almost frightened glazzies looking at me, and it was pee and em having their breakfast, but it was also another veck that I had never viddied in my jeezny before, a bolshy thick veck in his shirt and braces, quite at home, brothers, slurping away at the milky chai and munchmunching at his eggiweg and toast. And it was this stranger veck who spoke first, saying:

"Who are you, friend? Where did you get hold of a key? Out, before I push your face in. Get out there and knock. Explain your business, quick."

My dad and mum sat like petrified, and I could viddy they had not yet read the gazetta, then I remembered that the gazetta did not arrive till papapa had gone off to his work. But then mum said, "Oh, you've broken out. You've escaped. Whatever shall we do? We shall have the police here, oh oh oh. Oh you bad and wicked boy, disgracing us all like this." And, believe it or kiss my sharries, she started to go boo hoo. So I started to try and explain, they could ring up the Staja if they wanted, and all this time this stranger veck sat there like frowning and looking as if he could push my litso in with his hairy bolshy beefy fist. So I said:

18 **to petrify:** (fig.) versteinern, erstarren (lassen).

"How about you answering a few, brother? What are you doing here and for how long? I didn't like the tone of what you just said just then. Watch it. Come on, speak up." He was a working-man type veck, very ugly, about thirty or forty, and he sat now with his rot open at me, not govoreeting one single slovo. Then my dad said:

"This is all a bit bewildering, son. You should have let us know you were coming. We thought it would be at least another five or six years before they let you out. Not," he said, and he said it very like gloomy, "that we're not very pleased to see you again and a free man, too."

"Who is this?" I said. "Why can't he speak up? What's going on in here?"

"This is Joe," said my mum. "He lives here now. The lodger, that's what he is. Oh, dear dear dear," she went.

"You," said this Joe. "I've heard all about you, boy. I know what you've done, breaking the hearts of your poor grieving parents. So you're back, eh? Back to make life a misery for them once more, is that it? Over my dead corpse you will, because they've let me be more like a son to them than like a lodger." I could nearly have smecked loud at that if the old razdraz within me hadn't started to wake up the feeling of wanting to be sick, because this veck looked about the same age as my pee and em, and there he was like trying to put a son's protecting rooker round my crying mum, O my brothers.

"So," I said, and I near felt like collapsing in all tears myself. "So that's it, then. Well, I give you five large minootas to clear all your horrible cally veshches out of my room."

3 **speak up:** sprich lauter.

And I made for this room, this veck being a malenky bit too slow to stop me. When I opened the door my heart cracked to the carpet, because I viddied it was no longer like my room at all, brothers. All my flags had gone off the walls and this veck had put up pictures of boxers, also like a team sitting smug with folded rookers and a silver like shield in front. And then I viddied what else was missing. My stereo and my disc-cupboard were no longer there, nor was my locked treasure chest that contained bottles and drugs and two shining clean syringes. "There's been some filthy vonny work going on here," I creeched. "What have you done with my own personal veshches, you horrible bastard?" This was to this Joe, but it was my dad that answered, saying:

"That was all took away, son, by the police. This new regulation, see, about compensation for the victims."

I found it very hard not to be very ill, but my gulliver was aching shocking and my rot was so dry that I had to take a skorry swig from the milk-bottle on the table, so that this Joe said, "Filthy piggish manners." I said:

"But she died. That one died."

"It was the cats, son," said my dad like sorrowful, "that were left with nobody to look after them till the will was read, so they had to have somebody in to feed them. So the police sold your things, clothes and all, to help with the looking after of them. That's the law, son. But you were never much of a one for following the law."

I had to sit down then, and this Joe said, "Ask permission

6 **smug**: schmuck, geschniegelt und gebügelt; selbstgefällig. | 19 **swig**: (kräftiger) Schluck. | 20 **piggish**: schweinisch, unflätig; gierig.

before you sit, you mannerless young swine," so I cracked back skorry with a "Shut your dirty big fat hole, you," feeling sick. Then I tried to be all reasonable and smiling for my health's sake like, so I said, "Well, that's my room, there's no denying that. This is my home also. What suggestions have you, my pee and em, to make?" But they just looked very glum, my mum shaking a bit, her litso all lines and wet with like tears, and then my dad said:

"All this needs thinking about, son. We can't very well just kick Joe out, not just like that, can we? I mean, Joe's here doing a job, a contract it is, two years, and we made like an arrangement, didn't we, Joe? I mean, son, thinking you were going to stay in prison a long time and that room going begging." He was a bit ashamed, you could viddy that from his litso. So I just smiled and like nodded, saying:

"I viddy all. You got used to a bit of peace and you got used to a bit of extra pretty polly. That's the way it goes. And your son has been nothing but a terrible nuisance." And then, O my brothers, believe it or kiss my sharries, I started to like cry, feeling very like sorry for myself. So my dad said:

"Well, you see, son, Joe's paid next month's rent already. I mean, whatever we do in the future we can't say to Joe to get out, can we, Joe?" This Joe said:

"It's you two I've got to think of, who've been like a father and mother to me. Would it be right or fair to go off and leave you to the tender mercies of this young monster

---

7 **glum:** verdrießlich, mürrisch, finster. | 10 **to kick out** (coll.): rausschmeißen. | **just like that:** einfach so. | 14 **to go begging:** leer, zur Verfügung stehen. | 18 **nuisance:** Ärgernis, Plage. | 27 **tender mercies** (iron.): sanfte Gnadenerweise.

who has been like no real son at all? He's weeping now, but that's his craft and artfulness. Let him go off and find a room somewhere. Let him learn the error of his ways and that a bad boy like he's been doesn't deserve such a good mum and dad as what he's had."

"All right," I said, standing up in all like tears still. "I know how things are now. Nobody wants or loves me. I've suffered and suffered and suffered and everybody wants me to go on suffering. I know."

"You've made others suffer," said this Joe. "It's only right you should suffer proper. I've been told everything that you've done, sitting here at night round the family table, and pretty shocking it was to listen to. Made me real sick a lot of it did."

"I wish," I said, "I was back in the prison. Dear old Staja as it was. I'm ittying off now," I said. "You won't ever viddy me no more. I'll make my own way, thank you very much. Let it lie heavy on your consciences." My dad said:

"Don't take it like that, son," and my mum just went boo hoo hoo, her litso all screwed up real ugly, and this Joe put his rooker round her again, patting her and going there there like bezoomny. And so I just sort of staggered to the door and went out, leaving them to their horrible guilt, O my brothers.

2 **artfulness:** Verschlagenheit.

Two

Ittying down the street in a like aimless sort of a way, brothers, in these night platties which lewdies like stared at as I went by, cold too, it being a bastard cold winter day, all I felt I wanted was to be away from all this and not have to think any more about any sort of veshch at all. So I got the autobus to Center, then I walked back to Taylor Place, and there was the disc-bootick MELODIA I had used to favour with my inestimable custom, O my brothers, and it looked much the same sort of mesto as it always had, and walking in I expected to viddy old Andy there, that bald and very very thin helpful like veck from whom I had kupetted discs in the old days. But there was no Andy there now, brothers, only a scream and a creech of nadsat (teenage, that is) malchicks and ptitsas slooshying some new horrible popsong and dancing to it as well, and the veck behind the counter not much more than a nadsat himself, clicking his rooker bones and smecking like bezoomny. So I went up and waited till he like deigned to notice me, then I said:

"I'd like to hear a disc of Mozart Number Forty." I don't know why that should have come into my gulliver, but it did. The counter-veck said:

"Forty what, friend?" I said:

"Symphony. Symphony Number Forty in G Minor."

"Ooooh," went one of the dancing nadsats, a malchick with his hair all over his glazzies, "seemfunnah. Don't it seem funny? He wants a seemfunnah."

14 nadsat (N.): im Teenageralter. | 19 to deign: geruhen. | 20 Number Forty: Mozarts Sinfonie Nr. 40 g-Moll (KV 550). | 24 G minor: g-Moll.

I could feel myself growing all razdraz within, but I had to watch that, so I like smiled at the veck who had taken over Andy's place and at all the creeching nadsats. This counter-veck said, "You go into that listen-booth over there, friend, and I'll pipe something through."

So I went over to the malenky box where you could slooshy the discs you wanted to buy, and then this veck put a disc on for me, but it wasn't the Mozart Forty, it was the Mozart "Prague" – he seemingly having just picked any Mozart he could find on the shelf – and that should have started making me real razdraz and I had to watch that for fear of the pain and sickness, but what I'd forgotten was something I shouldn't have forgotten and now made me want to snuff it. It was that these doctor bratchnies had so fixed things that any music that was like for the emotions would make me sick just like viddying or wanting to do violence. It was because all those violence films had music with them. And I remembered especially that horrible Nazi film with the Beethoven Fifth, last movement. And now here was lovely Mozart made horrible. I dashed out of the box like bezoomny to get away from the sickness and pain that were coming on, and I dashed out of the shop with these nadsats smecking after me and the counter-veck creeching, "Eh eh eh!" But I took no notice and went staggering almost like blind across the road and round the corner to the Korova Milkbar. I knew what I wanted.

The mesto was near empty, it being still morning. It looked strange too, having been painted with all red moo-

4 **listen-booth:** *listening-booth:* Vorspielkabine. | 9 **Prague:** Mozarts Sinfonie Nr. 38 D-Dur »Prager Sinfonie« (KV 504). | 28 f. **to moo:** muhen.

ing cows, and behind the counter was no veck I knew. But when I said, "Milk, plus, large," the veck with a like lean litso very newly shaved knew what I wanted. I took the large moloko plus to one of the little cubies that were all around this mesto, there being like curtains to shut them off from the main mesto, and there I sat down in the plushy chair and sipped and sipped. When I'd finished the whole lot I began to feel that things were happening. I had my glazzies like fixed on a malenky bit of silver paper from a cancer packet that was on the floor, the sweeping-up of this mesto not being all that horrorshow, brothers. This scrap of silver began to grow and grow and grow and it was so like bright and fiery that I had to squint my glazzies at it. It got so big that it became not only this whole cubie I was lolling in but like the whole Korova, the whole street, the whole city. Then it was the whole world, then it was the whole everything, brothers, and it was like a sea washing over every veshch that had ever been made or thought of even. I could sort of slooshy myself making special sort of shooms and govoreeting slovos like "Dear dead idlewilds, rot not in variform guises" and all that cal. Then I could like feel the vision beating up in all this silver, and then there were colours like nobody had ever viddied before, and then I could viddy like a group of statues a long long long way off that was like being pushed nearer and nearer and nearer, all lit up by very bright light from below and above alike, O my brothers. This group of statues was of God or Bog and all

---

2 **lean:** mager, hager. | 7 **to sip:** nippen, schlürfen. | 10 **sweeping-up:** Aufkehren. | 14 **to loll:** sich lümmeln. | 20 **idlewild:** Nonsens-Wort. | 21 **variform:** vielgestaltig. | 22 **to beat up** (coll.): hier: sich verbreiten, aufquellen.

His Holy Angels and Saints, all very bright like bronze, with beards and bolshy great wings that waved about in a kind of wind, so that they could not really be of stone or bronze, really, and the eyes or glazzies like moved and were alive. These bolshy big figures came nearer and nearer and nearer till they were like going to crush me down, and I could slooshy my goloss going "Eeeeee." And I felt I had got rid of everything – platties, plott, brain, eemya, the lot – and felt real horrorshow, like in heaven. Then there was the shoom of like crumbling and crumpling, and Bog and the Angels and Saints sort of shook their gullivers at me, as though to govoreet that there wasn't quite time now but I must try again, and then everything like leered and smecked and collapsed and the big warm light grew cold, and then there I was as I was before, the empty glass on the table and wanting to cry and feeling like death was the only answer to everything.

And that was it, that was what I viddied quite clear was the thing to do, but how to do it I did not properly know, never having thought of that before, O my brothers. In my little bag of personal veshches I had my cut-throat britva, but I at once felt very sick as I thought of myself going swishhhh at myself and all my own red red krovvy flowing. What I wanted was not something violent but something that would make me like just go off gentle to sleep and that be the end of Your Humble Narrator, no more trouble to anybody no more. Perhaps, I thought, if I ittied off to the Public Biblio round the corner I might find some book on

8 **eemya** (N.): Name. | 10 **to crumble:** zerkrümeln, zerbröckeln. | **to crumple:** zerknittern, zusammenknüllen.

the best way of snuffing it with no pain. I thought of myself dead and how sorry everyone was going to be, pee and em and that cally vonny Joe who was like a usurper, and also Dr Brodsky and Dr Branom and that Inferior Interior Minister and every veck else. And the boastful vonny Government too. So out I scatted into the winter, and it was afternoon now, near two o'clock, as I could viddy from the bolshy Center timepiece, so that me being in the land with the old moloko plus must have took like longer than I thought. I walked down Marghanita Boulevard and then turned into Boothby Avenue, then round the corner again, and there was the Public Biblio.

It was a starry cally sort of mesto that I could not remember going into since I was a very malenky malchick, no more than about six years old, and there were two parts to it – one part to borrow books and one part to read in, full of gazettas and mags and like the von of very starry old men with their plotts stinking of like old age and poverty. These were standing at the gazetta stands all round the room, snuffling and belching and govoreeting to themselves and turning over the pages to read the news very sadly, or else they were sitting at the tables looking at the mags or pretending to, some of them asleep and one or two of them snoring real gromky. I couldn't like remember what it was I wanted at first, then I remembered with a bit of shock that I had ittied here to find out how to snuff it without pain, so I goolied over to the shelf full of reference veshches. There were a lot of books, but there was none

3 **usurper:** Usurpator, unrechtmäßiger Besitzer. | 8 **timepiece:** Chronometer, Uhr. | 20 **to snuffle:** schnüffeln, schniefen; schnauben. | 27 **reference:** Nachschlage…

with a title, brothers, that would really do. There was a medical book that I took down, but when I opened it it was full of drawings and photographs of horrible wounds and diseases, and that made me want to sick just a bit. So I put that back and then took down the big book or Bible, as it was called, thinking that might give me like comfort as it had done in the old Staja days (not so old really, but it seemed a very very long time ago), and I staggered over to a chair to read in it. But all I found was about smiting seventy times seven and a lot of yahoodies cursing and tolchocking each other, and that made me want to be sick, too. So then I near cried, so that a very starry ragged moodge opposite me said:

"What is it, son? What's the trouble?"

"I want to snuff it," I said. "I've had it, that's what it is. Life's become too much for me."

A starry reading veck next to me said, "Shhhh," without looking up from some bezoomny mag he had full of drawings of like bolshy geometrical veshches. That rang a bell somehow. This other moodge said:

"You're too young for that, son. Why, you've got everything in front of you."

"Yes," I said, bitter. "Like a pair of false groodies." This mag-reading veck said, "Shhhh" again, looking up this

9 **to smite**: schlagen; erneute Anspielung auf Matthäus 5,39. | 9 f. **seventy times seven**: Anspielung auf Matthäus 18,21 f.: »Da trat Petrus zu ihm und sprach: Herr, wie oft muss ich dann meinem Bruder, der an mir sündigt, vergeben? Jesus sprach zu ihm: Ich sage dir: nicht siebenmal, sondern siebenzigmal siebenmal.« Alex verdreht also den Sinn, indem er beide Anspielungen verbindet. | 15 **to have had it** (slang): erledigt sein, sein Fett weg haben.

time, and something clicked for both of us. I viddied who it was. He said, real gromky:

"I never forget a shape, by God. I never forget the shape of anything. By God, you young swine, I've got you now." Crystallography, that was it. That was what he'd been taking away from the Biblio that time. False teeth crunched up real horrorshow. Platties torn off. His books razrezzed, all about Crystallography. I thought I had best get out of here real skorry, brothers. But this starry old moodge was on his feet, creeching like bezoomny to all the starry old coughers at the gazettas round the walls and to them dozing over mags at the tables. "We have him," he creeched. "The poisonous young swine who ruined the books on Crystallography, rare books, books not to be obtained ever again, anywhere." This had a terrible mad shoom about it, as though this veck was really off his gulliver. "A prize specimen of the cowardly brutal young," he creeched. "Here in our midst and at our mercy. He and his friends beat me and kicked me and thumped me. They stripped me and tore out my teeth. They kicked me home, dazed and naked." All this wasn't quite true, as you know, brothers. He had some platties on, he hadn't been completely nagoy. I creeched back:

"That was over two years ago. I've been punished since then. I've learned my lesson. See over there – my picture's in the papers."

"Punishment, eh?" said one starry like ex-soldier type.

---

1 **something clicked for both of us** (coll.): etwas kam uns beiden bekannt vor. | 10 **cougher:** Huster (von *to cough*). | 16 **specimen:** Exemplar. | 19 **to thump:** (mit aller Wucht) schlagen.

"You lot should be exterminated. Like so many noisome pests. Punishment, indeed."

"All right, all right," I said. "Everybody's entitled to his opinion. Forgive me, all. I must go now." And I started to itty out of this mesto of bezoomny old men. Aspirin, that was it. You could snuff it on a hundred aspirin. Aspirin from the old drugstore. But the crystallography veck creeched:

"Don't let him go. We'll teach him all about punishment, the murderous young pig. Get him." And believe it, brothers, or do the other veshch, two or three starry dodderers, about ninety years old apiece, grabbed me with their trembly old rookers, and I was made sick by the von of old age and disease which came from these near-dead moodges. The crystal veck was on to me now, starting to deal me malenky weak tolchocks on my litso, and I tried to get away and itty out, but these starry rookers that held me were stronger than I had thought. Then other starry vecks came hobbling from the gazettas to have a go at Your Humble Narrator. They were creeching veshches like: "Kill him, stamp on him, murder him, kick his teeth in," and all that cal, and I could viddy what it was clear enough. It was old age having a go at youth, that's what it was. But some of them were saying, "Poor old Jack, near killed poor Jack he did, this is the young swine" and so on, as though it had all happened yesterday. Which to them I suppose it had. There was now like a sea of vonny runny dirty old men trying to

1 **to exterminate:** ausrotten. | **noisome:** schädlich, ungesund; widerlich. | 2 **pests** (pl.): Ungeziefer. | 7 **drugstore** (AE): Drogerie. | 10 f. **dodderer** (N.): Schlotterer, Tattergreis (von *to dodder* ›schlottern‹). | 18 **to hobble:** humpeln, hinken, hoppeln. | **to have a go at s.o.** (coll.): jdn. angreifen.

get at me with their like feeble rookers and horny old claws, creeching and panting on to me, but our crystal droog was there in front, dealing out tolchock after tolchock. And I daren't do a solitary single veshch, O my brothers, it being better to be hit at like that than to want to sick and feel that horrible pain, but of course the fact that there was violence going on made me feel that the sickness was peeping round the corner to viddy whether to come out into the open and roar away.

Then an attendant veck came along, a youngish veck, and he creeched, "What goes on here? Stop it at once. This is a reading room." But nobody took any notice. So the attendant veck said, "Right, I shall phone the police." So I creeched, and I never thought I would ever do that in all my jeezny:

"Yes yes yes, do that, protect me from these old madmen." I noticed that the attendant veck was not too anxious to join in the dratsing and rescue me from the rage and madness of these starry vecks' claws; he just scatted off to his like office or wherever the telephone was. Now these old men were panting a lot now, and I felt I could just flick at them and they would all fall over, but I just let myself be held, very patient, by these starry rookers, my glazzies closed, and feel the feeble tolchocks on my litso, also slooshy the panting breathy old golosses creeching, "Young swine, young murderer, hooligan, thug, kill him." Then I got such a real painful tolchock on the nose that I said to myself to hell to hell, and I opened my glazzies up and

1 **horny:** hornig, verhornt. | 7 **to peep:** (verstohlen) gucken. | 21 f. **to flick at s.o.:** jdm. einen ganz leichten Schlag versetzen. | 26 **thug:** Verbrecher, Rowdy, Schläger.

started to struggle to get free, which was not hard, brothers, and I tore off creeching to the sort of hallway outside the reading room. But these starry avengers still came after me, panting like dying, with their animal claws all trembling to get at your friend and Humble Narrator. Then I was tripped up and was on the floor and was being kicked at, then I slooshied golosses of young vecks creeching, "All right, all right, stop it now," and I knew the police had arrived.

---

2 **to tear off:** davonrasen. | 3 **avenger:** Rächer.

Three

I was like dazed, O my brothers, and could not viddy
very clear, but I was sure I had met these millicents some
mesto before. The one who had hold of me, going, "There
there there," just by the front door of the Public Biblio, him
I did not know at all, but it seemed to me he was like very
young to be a rozz. But the other two backs that I was sure I
had viddied before. They were lashing into these starry
old vecks with great bolshy glee and joy, swishing with
malenky whips, creeching, "There, you naughty boys. That
should teach you to stop rioting and breaking the State's
peace, you wicked villains, you." So they drove these panting and wheezing and near dying starry avengers back into
the reading room, then they turned round, smecking with
the fun they'd had, to viddy me. The older one of the two
said:

"Well well well well well well well. If it isn't little Alex.
Very long time no viddy, droog. How goes?" I was like
dazed, the uniform and the shlem or helmet making it very
hard to viddy who this was, though litso and goloss very familiar. Then I looked at the other one, and about him, with
his grinny bezoomny litso, there was no doubt. Then, all
numb and growing number, I looked back at the well well
welling one. This one was then fatty old Billyboy, my old
enemy. The other was, of course, Dim, who had used to be
my droog and also the enemy of stinking fatty goaty Billy-

9 **glee:** Fröhlichkeit, Frohsinn. | 11 **to riot:** Aufruhr erregen, Krawall
machen. | 13 **to wheeze:** keuchen, schnaufen. | 23 **numb:** starr, erstarrt. |
26 **goaty** (N.): etwa: bockig. (Billyboy ist von Alex bei der ersten geschil-
derten Begegnung als *billygoat* bezeichnet worden, vgl. S. 27, Z. 12.)

boy, but was now a Millicent with uniform and shlem and whip to keep order. I said:

"Oh, no."

"Surprise, eh?" And old Dim came out with the old guff I remembered so horrorshow: "Huh huh huh."

"It's impossible," I said. "It can't be so. I don't believe it."

"Evidence of the old glazzies," grinned Billyboy. "Nothing up our sleeves. No magic, droog. A job for two who are now of job age. The police."

"You're too young," I said. "Much too young. They don't make rozzes of malchicks of your age."

"Was young," went old millicent Dim. I could not get over it, brothers, I really could not. "That's what we was, young droogie. And you it was that was always the youngest. And here now we are."

"I still can't believe it," I said. Then Billyboy, rozz Billyboy that I couldn't get over, said to this young millicent that was like holding on to me and that I did not know:

"More good would be done, I think, Rex, if we doled out a bit of the old summary. Boys will be boys, as always was. No need to go through the old station routine. This one here has been up to his old tricks, as we can well remember though you, of course, can't. He has been attacking the aged and defenceless, and they properly have been retaliating. But we must have our say in the State's name."

"What is all this?" I said, not able hardly to believe my ookos. "It was them that went for me, brothers. You're not

8 **(to have) s.th. up one's sleeve:** etwas in petto, auf Lager haben, im Schilde führen. | 20 **summary (punishment):** summarische, unverzügliche Bestrafung. | **Boys will be boys** (prov.): etwa: Jugend hat keine Tugend. | 24 **to retaliate:** Vergeltung üben.

on their side and can't be. You can't be, Dim. It was a veck we fillied with once in the old days trying to get his own malenky bit of revenge after all this long time."

"Long time is right," said Dim. "I don't remember them days too horrorshow. Don't call me Dim no more, either. Officer call me."

"Enough is remembered, though," Billyboy kept nodding. He was not so fatty as he had been. "Naughty little malchicks handy with cut-throat britvas – these must be kept under." And they took me in a real strong grip and like walked me out of the Biblio. There was a Millicent patrol-car waiting outside, and this veck they called Rex was the driver. They like tolchocked me into the back of this auto, and I couldn't help feeling it was all really like a joke, and that Dim anyway would pull his shlem off his gulliver and go haw haw haw. But he didn't. I said, trying to fight the strack inside me:

"And old Pete, what happened to old Pete? It was sad about Georgie," I said. "I slooshied all about that."

"Pete, oh yes, Pete," said Dim. "I seem to remember like the name." I could viddy we were driving out of town. I said:

"Where are we supposed to be going?"

Billyboy turned round from the front to say, "It's light still. A little drive into the country, all winter-bare but lonely and lovely. It's not right, not always, for lewdies in the town to viddy too much of our summary punishment. Streets must be kept clean in more than one way." And he

---

10 **to keep under:** unterdrücken, niederhalten. | 11 f. **patrol-car:** Streifenwagen.

turned to the front again. "Come," I said. "I just don't get this at all. The old days are dead and gone days. For what I did in the past I have been punished. I have been cured."

"That was read out to us," said Dim. "The Super read all that out to us. He said it was a very good way."

"Read to you," I said, a malenky bit nasty. "You still too dim to read for yourself, O brother?"

"Ah, no," said Dim, very like gentle and like regretful. "Not to speak like that. Not no more, droogie." And he launched a bolshy tolchock right on my cluve, so that all red red nose-krovvy started to drip drip drip.

"There was never any trust," I said, bitter, wiping off the krovvy with my rooker. "I was always on my oddy knocky."

"This will do," said Billyboy. We were now in the country and it was all bare trees and a few odd distant like twitters, and in the distance there was some like farm machine making a whirring shoom. It was getting all dusk now, this being the heighth of winter. There were no lewdies about, nor no animals. There was just the four. "Get out, Alex boy," said Dim. "Just a malenky bit of summary."

All through what they did this driver veck just sat at the wheel of the auto, smoking a cancer, reading a malenky bit of a book. He had the light on in the auto to viddy by. He took no notice of what Billyboy and Dim did to your Humble Narrator. I will not go into what they did, but it was all like panting and thudding against this like background of whirring farm engines and the twittwittwittering in the

4 **super:** Kurzform von *superintendent*: Polizeichef. | 8 **regretful:** voll Bedauern, betrübt. | 10 **cluve** (N.): ‚Schnabel'. | 15 f. **twitter:** Gezwitscher. | 17 **to whirr:** schwirren, surren. | 26 **to thud:** dumpf (auf)schlagen, bumsen, dröhnen.

bare or nagoy branches. You could viddy a bit of smoky breath in the auto light, this driver turning the pages over quite calm. And they were on to me all the time, O my brothers. Then Billyboy or Dim, I couldn't say which one, said, "About enough, droogie, I should think, shouldn't you?" Then they gave one final tolchock on the litso each and I fell over and just laid there on the grass. It was cold but I was not feeling the cold. Then they dusted their rookers and put back on their shlems and tunics which they had taken off, and then they got back into the auto. "Be viddying you some more sometime, Alex," said Billyboy, and Dim just gave one of his old clowny guffs. The driver finished the page he was reading and put his book away, then he started the auto and they were off townwards, my ex-droog and ex-enemy waving. But I just laid there, fagged and shagged.

After a bit I was hurting bad, and then the rain started, all icy. I could viddy no lewdies in sight, nor no lights of houses. Where was I to go, who had no home and not much cutter in my carmans? I cried for myself boo hoo hoo. Then I got up and began walking.

Four

Home, home home, it was home I was wanting, and it was HOME I came to, brothers. I walked through the dark and followed not the town way but the way where the shoom of a like farm machine had been coming from. This brought me to a sort of village I felt I had viddied before, but was perhaps because all villages look the same, in the dark especially. Here were houses and there was a like drinking mesto, and right at the end of the village there was a malenky cottage on its oddy knock, and I could viddy its name shining white on the gate. HOME, it said. I was all dripping wet with this icy rain, so that my platties were no longer in the heighth of fashion but real miserable and like pathetic, and my luscious glory was a wet tangled cally mess all spread over my gulliver, and I was sure there were cuts and bruises all over my litso, and a couple of my zoobies sort of joggled loose when I touched them with my tongue or yahzick. And I was sore all over my plott and very thirsty, so that I kept opening my rot to the cold rain, and my stomach growled grrrrr all the time with not having had any pishcha since morning and then not very much, O my brothers.

HOME, it said, and perhaps here would be some veck to help. I opened the gate and sort of slithered down the path, the rain like turning to ice, and then I knocked gentle and pathetic on the door. No veck came, so I knocked a malenky bit longer and louder, and then I heard the shoom of nogas

11f. **dripping wet:** tropfnass. | 14 **tangled:** wirr. | 16 **bruise:** Quetschung, Beule, blauer Fleck. | 17 **to joggle loose:** sich losrütteln. | 24 **to slither:** schlittern, rutschen.

coming to the door. Then the door opened and a male go-loss said, "Yes, what is it?"

"Oh," I said, "please help. I've been beaten up by the police and just left to die on the road. Oh, please give me a drink of something and a sit by the fire, please, sir."

The door opened full then, and I could viddy like warm light and a fire going crackle crackle within. "Come in," said this veck, "whoever you are. God help you, you poor victim, come in and let's have a look at you." So I like staggered in, and it was no big act I was putting on, brothers, I really felt done and finished. This kind veck put his rookers round my pletchoes and pulled me into this room where the fire was, and of course I knew right away where it was and why HOME on the gate looked so familiar. I looked at this veck and he looked at me in a kind sort of way, and I remembered him well now. Of course he would not remember me, for in those carefree days I and my so-called droogs did our bolshy dratsing and filling and crasting in maskies which were real horrorshow disguises. He was a shortish veck in middle age, thirty, forty, fifty, and he had otchkies on. "Sit down by the fire," he said, "and I'll get you some whisky and warm water. Dear dear dear, somebody *has* been beating you up." And he gave a like tender look at my gulliver and litso.

"The police," I said. "The horrible ghastly police."

"Another victim," he said, like sighing. "A victim of the modern age. I'll go and get you that whisky and then I must clean up your wounds a little." And off he went. I had a look

---

10 **to put on an act** (coll.): eine Schau abziehen. | 17 **carefree:** sorgenfrei, unbeschwert. | 19 **shortish:** ziemlich kurz; etwas kurz.

round this malenky comfortable room. It was nearly all books now and a fire and a couple of chairs, and you could viddy somehow that there wasn't a woman living there. On the table was a typewriter and a lot of like tumbled papers, and I remembered that this veck was a writer veck. *A Clockwork Orange*, that had been it. It was funny that that stuck in my mind. I must not let on, though, for I needed help and kindness now. Those horrible grahzny bratchnies in that terrible white mesto had done that to me, making me need help and kindness and forcing me to want to give help and kindness myself, if anybody would take it.

"Here we are, then," said this veck returning. He gave me this hot stimulating glassful to peet, and it made me feel better, and he cleaned up these cuts on my litso. Then he said, "You have a nice hot bath, I'll draw it for you, and then you can tell me all about it over a nice hot supper which I'll get ready while you're having the bath." O my brothers, I could have wept at his kindness, and I think he must have viddied the old tears in my glazzies, for he said, "There there there", patting me on the pletcho.

Anyway, I went up and had this hot bath, and he brought in pyjamas and an over-gown for me to put on, all warmed by the fire, also a very worn pair of toofles. And now, brother, though I was aching and full of pains all over, I felt I would soon feel a lot better. I ittied downstairs and viddied that in the kitchen he had set the table with knives and forks and a fine big loaf of kleb, also a bottle of PRIMA SAUCE, and soon he served out a nice fry of eggiwegs and

---

4 **to tumble:** hier: durchwühlen, durcheinanderwerfen. | 7 **to let on:** hier: sich (etwas) anmerken lassen. | 13 **stimulating:** anregend. | 28 **fry of eggiwegs** (N.): Spiegeleier.

lomticks of ham and bursting sausages and big bolshy mugs of hot sweet milky chai. It was nice sitting there in the warm, eating, and I found I was very hungry, so that after the fry I had to eat lomtick after lomtick of kleb and butter spread with strawberry jam out of a bolshy great pot. "A lot better," I said. "How can I ever repay?"

"I think I know who you are," he said. "If you are who I think you are, then you've come, my friend, to the right place. Wasn't that your picture in the papers this morning? Are you the poor victim of this horrible new technique? If so, then you have been sent here by Providence. Tortured in prison, then thrown out to be tortured by the police. My heart goes out to you, poor poor boy." Brothers, I could not get a slovo in, though I had my rot wide open to answer his questions. "You are not the first to come here in distress," he said. "The police are fond of bringing their victims to the outskirts of this village. But it is providential that you, who are also another kind of victim, should come here. Perhaps, then, you have heard of me?"

I had to be very careful, brothers. I said, "I have heard of *A Clockwork Orange*. I have not read it, but I have heard of it."

"Ah," he said, and his litso shone like the sun in its flaming morning glory. "Now tell me about yourself."

"Little enough to tell, sir," I said, all humble. "There was a foolish and boyish prank, my so-called friends persuading or rather forcing me to break into the house of an old ptitsa – lady, I mean. There was no real harm meant. Unfor-

6 **to repay:** zurückzahlen, vergelten. | 17 **outskirts** (pl.): Grenze, Rand, Umgebung. | **providential:** schicksalhaft. | 26 **boyish:** kindisch. | **prank:** Posse, Streich.

tunately the lady strained her good heart in trying to throw me out, though I was quite ready to go of my own accord, and then she died. I was accused of being the cause of her death. So I was sent to prison, sir."

"Yes yes yes, go on."

"Then I was picked out by the Minister of the Inferior or Interior to have this Ludovico's veshch tried out on me."

"Tell me all about it," he said, leaning forward eager, his pullover elbows with all strawberry jam on them from the plate I'd pushed to one side. So I told him all about it. I told him the lot, all, my brothers. He was very eager to hear all, his glazzies like shining and his goobers apart, while the grease on the plates grew harder harder harder. When I had finished he got up from the table, nodding a lot and going hm hm hm, picking up the plates and other veshches from the table and taking them to the sink for washing up. I said:

"I will do that, sir, and gladly."

"Rest, rest, poor lad," he said, turning the tap on so that all steam came burping out. "You've sinned, I suppose, but your punishment has been out of all proportion. They have turned you into something other than a human being. You have no power of choice any longer. You are committed to socially acceptable acts, a little machine capable only of good. And I see that clearly – that business about the marginal conditionings. Music and the sexual act, literature and art, all must be a source now not of pleasure but of pain."

2 **of one's own accord:** freiwillig. | 25 **marginal:** auf der Grenze liegend, in den unsicheren Bereich zwischen zwei Entscheidungsmöglichkeiten fallend. | **conditioning:** Konditionierung (Ausbilden bedingter Reaktionen).

"That's right, sir," I said, smoking one of this kind man's cork-tipped cancers.

"They always bite off too much," he said, drying a plate like absent-mindedly. "But the essential intention is the real sin. A man who cannot choose ceases to be a man."

"That's what the charles said, sir," I said. "The prison chaplain, I mean."

"Did he, did he? Of course he did. He'd have to, wouldn't he, being a Christian? Well, now then," he said, still wiping the same plate he'd been wiping ten minutes ago, "we shall have a few people in to see you tomorrow. I think you can be used, poor boy. I think you can help dislodge this overbearing Government. To turn a decent young man into a piece of clockwork should not, surely, be seen as any triumph for any government, save one that boasts of its repressiveness." He was still wiping this same plate. I said:

"Sir, you're still wiping that same plate. I agree with you, sir, about boasting. This Government seems to be very boastful."

"Oh," he said, viddying this plate for the first time and then putting it down. "I'm still not too handy," he said, "with domestic chores. My wife used to do them all and leave me to my writing."

"Your wife, sir?" I said. "Has she gone and left you?" I really wanted to know about his wife, remembering very

2 **cork-tipped**: mit einem Mundstück aus Kork versehen. | 3 **to bite off too much** (fig.): sich übernehmen. | 12 f. **to dislodge**: vertreiben. | 13 **overbearing**: anmaßend, herrisch. | 16 **repressiveness**: Repressivität, Unterdrückung. | 23 **chore**: regelmäßige und notwendige (Haus-)Arbeit, Pflicht.

well. "Yes, left me," he said, in a like loud and bitter goloss. "She died, you see. She was brutally raped and beaten. The shock was very great. It was in this house," his rookers were trembling, holding a wiping-up cloth, "in that room next door. I have had to steel myself to continue to live here, but she would have wished me to stay where her fragrant memory still lingers. Yes yes yes. Poor little girl." I viddied all clearly, my brothers, what had happened that far-off nochy, and viddying myself on that job, I began to feel I wanted to sick and the pain started up in my gulliver. This veck viddied this, because my litso felt it was all drained of red red krovvy, very pale, and he would be able to viddy this. "You go to bed now," he said kindly. "I've got the spare room ready. Poor poor boy, you must have had a terrible time. A victim of the modern age, just as she was. Poor poor poor girl."

---

2 **to rape:** vergewaltigen. | 5 **to steel o.s.:** sich härten, wappnen. |
6 **fragrant:** angenehm.

Five

I had a real horrorshow night's sleep, brothers, with no dreams at all, and the morning was very clear and like frosty, and there was the very pleasant like von of breakfast frying away down below. It took me some little time to remember where I was, as it always does, but it soon came back to me and then I felt like warmed and protected. But, as I laid there in the bed, waiting to be called down to breakfast, it struck me that I ought to get to know the name of this kind protecting and like motherly veck, so I had a pad round in my nagoy nogas looking for *A Clockwork Orange*, which would be bound to have his eemya in, he being the author. There was nothing in my bedroom except a bed and a chair and a light, so I ittied next door to this veck's own room, and there I viddied his wife on the wall, a bolshy blown-up photo, so I felt a malenky bit sick remembering. But there were two or three shelves of books there too, and there was, as I thought there must be, a copy of *A Clockwork Orange*, and on the back of the book, like on the spine, was the author's eemya – F. Alexander. Good Bog, I thought, he is another Alex. Then I leafed through, standing in my pyjamas and bare nogas but not feeling one malenky bit cold, the cottage being warm all through, and I could not viddy what the book was about. It seemed written in very bezoomny like style, full of Ah and Oh and all that cal, but what seemed to come out of it was that all lewdies nowadays were being turned into machines and

11 **pad:** Substantivbildung zu *to pad (along)* ›(dahin)trotten‹, ›latschen‹. |
16 **to blow up:** (Foto) vergrößern. | 20 **spine:** Buchrücken.

that they were really – you and me and him and kiss-my-sharries – more like natural growth like a fruit. F. Alexander seemed to think that we all like grow on what he called the world-tree in the world-orchard that like Bog or God planted, and we were there because Bog or God had need of us to quench his thirsty love, or some such cal. I didn't like the shoom of this at all, O my brothers, and wondered how bezoomny this F. Alexander really was, perhaps driven bezoomny by his wife's snuffing it. But then he called me down in a like sane veck's goloss, full of joy and love and all that cal, so down Your Humble Narrator went.

"You've slept long," he said, ladling out boiled eggs and pulling black toast from under the grill. "It's nearly ten already. I've been up hours, working."

"Writing another book, sir?" I said.

"No no, not that now," he said, and we sat down nice and droogy to the old crack crack crack of eggs and crackle crunch crunch of this black toast, very milky chai standing by in bolshy great morning mugs. "No, I've been on the phone to various people."

"I thought you didn't have a phone," I said, spooning egg in and not watching what I was saying.

"Why?" he said, very alert like some skorry animal with an egg-spoon in its rooker. "Why shouldn't you think I have a phone?"

"Nothing," I said, "nothing, nothing." And I wondered, brothers, how much he remembered of the earlier part of that distant nochy, me coming to the door with the old tale

6 **to quench:** löschen, stillen. | 12 **to ladle out:** austeilen. | 21 **to spoon:** löffeln. | 23 **alert:** wachsam.

and saying to phone the doctor and she saying no phone. He took a very close smot at me but then went back to being like kind and cheerful and spooning up the old eggiweg. Munching away, he said:

"Yes, I've rung up various people who will be interested in your case. You can be a very potent weapon, you see, in ensuring that this present evil and wicked Government is not returned in the forthcoming election. The Government's big boast, you see, is the way it has dealt with crime in these last months." He looked at me very close again over his steaming egg, and I wondered again if he was viddying what part I had so far played in his jeezny. But he said, "Recruiting brutal young roughs for the police. Proposing debilitating and will-sapping techniques of conditioning." All these long slovos, brothers, and a like mad or bezoomny look in his glazzies. "We've seen it all before," he said. "in other countries. The thin end of the wedge. Before we know where we are we shall have the full apparatus of totalitarianism." 'Dear dear dear,' I thought, egging away and toast-crunching. I said:

"Where do I come into all this, sir?"

"You," he said, still with this bezoomny look, "are a living witness to these diabolical proposals. The people, the common people must know, must see." He got up from his breakfast and started to walk up and down the kitchen,

---

2 **smot** (N.): Blick. | 6 **potent:** mächtig, stark. | 7 **to ensure:** sichern, sicherstellen. | 8 **forthcoming:** bevorstehend. | 9 **boast:** Prahlerei. | 12 f. **to recruit:** rekrutieren, anwerben. | 13 **rough:** Schläger, Rowdy. | 13 f. **to debilitate:** schwächen, entkräften. | 14 **will-sapping:** den Willen untergrabend. | 17 **wedge:** Keil. | 18 f. **totalitarianism:** Totalitarismus. | 19 **to egg away** (N.): weiter Eier essen. | 23 **diabolical:** teuflisch.

from the sink to the like larder, saying very gromky, "Would they like their sons to become what you, poor victim, have become? Will not the Government itself now decide what is and what is not crime and pump out the life and guts and will of whoever sees fit to displease the Government?" He became quieter but did not go back to his egg. "I've written an article," he said, "this morning, while you were sleeping. That will be out in a day or so, together with your unhappy picture. You shall sign it, poor boy, a record of what they have done to you." I said:

"And what do you get out of all of this, sir? I mean, besides the pretty polly you'll get for the article, as you call it? I mean, why are you so hot and strong against this Government, if I may make like so bold as to ask?"

He gripped the edge of the table and said, gritting his zoobies, which were very cally and all stained with cancer-smoke, "Some of us have to fight. There are great traditions of liberty to defend. I am no partisan man. Where I see the infamy I seek to erase it. Party names mean nothing. The tradition of liberty means all. The common people will let it go, oh yes. They will sell liberty for a quieter life. That is why they must be prodded, *prodded* –" And here, brothers, he picked up a fork and stuck it two or three razzes into the wall, so that it all got bent. Then he threw it on the floor. Very kindly he said, "Eat well, poor boy, poor victim of the

---

5 **to see fit to do s.th.**: beschließen, für richtig halten, etwas zu tun. | 15f. **to grit one's zoobies**: mit den Zähnen knirschen. | 18 **partisan**: Partei… | 19 **infamy**: Ehrlosigkeit, Schändlichkeit, Niedertracht. | **to erase**: auslöschen, tilgen; Anspielung auf eine Äußerung des französischen Philosophen Voltaire in einem Brief an den Mathematiker, Philosophen und Schriftsteller Jean Le Rond d'Alembert vom 28. November 1762.

modern world," and I could viddy quite clear he was going off his gulliver. "Eat, eat. Eat my egg as well." But I said:

"And what do I get out of this? Do I get cured of the way I am? Do I find myself able to slooshy the old Choral Symphony without being sick once more? Can I live a normal jeezny again? What, sir, happens to me?"

He looked at me, brothers, as if he hadn't thought of that before and, anyway, it didn't matter compared with Liberty and all that cal, and he had a look of surprise at me saying what I said, as though I was being like selfish in wanting something for myself. Then he said, "Oh, as I say, you're a living witness, poor boy. Eat up all your breakfast and then come and see what I've written, for it's going into *The Weekly Trumpet* under your name, you unfortunate victim."

Well, brothers, what he had written was a very long and very weepy piece of writing, and as I read it I felt very sorry for the poor malchick who was govoreeting about his sufferings and how the Government had sapped his will and how it was up to all lewdies to not let such a rotten and evil Government rule them again, and then of course I realised that the poor suffering malchick was none other than Y.H.N. "Very good," I said. "Real horrorshow. Written well thou hast, O sir." And then he looked at me very narrow and said:

"What?"

"Oh, that," I said, "is what we call nadsat talk. All the teens use that, sir." So then he ittied off to the kitchen to wash up the dishes, and I was left in these borrowed night platties and toofles, waiting to have done to me what was

1 f. **to go off one's gulliver** (N.): den Kopf verlieren, verrückt werden, überschnappen.

going to be done to me, because I had no plans for myself,
O my brothers.

While the great F. Alexander was in the kitchen a dinga-
lingaling came at the door. "Ah," he creeched, coming out
wiping his rookers, "it will be these people. I'll go." So he
went and let them in, a kind of rumbling hahaha of talk and
hallo and filthy weather and how are things in the hallway,
then they ittied into the room with the fire and the books
and the article about how I had suffered, viddying me and
going Aaaaah as they did it. There were three lewdies, and
F. Alex gave me their eemyas. Z. Dolin was a very wheezy
smoky kind of a veck, coughing kashl kashl kashl with the
end of a cancer at his rot, spilling ash all down his platties
and then brushing it away with like very impatient rookers.
He was a malenky round veck, fat, with big thick-framed
otchkies on. Then there was Something Something Rubinstein, a very tall and polite chelloveck with a real gentleman's goloss, very starry with a like eggy beard. And lastly
there was D. B. da Silva who was like skorry in his movements and had this strong von of scent coming from him.
They all had a real horrorshow look at me and seemed like
overjoyed with what they viddied. Z. Dolin said:

"All right, all right, eh? What a superb device he can be,
this boy. If anything, of course, he could for preference look
even iller and more zombyish than he does. Anything for
the cause. No doubt we can think of something."

11 **wheezy:** keuchend, asthmatisch. | 16 f. **Rubinstein:** vermutl. An-
spielung auf Harold R., Rechtsanwalt von Burgess' Verleger William
Heinemann. | 18 **eggy** (N.): mit Ei verschmiert. | 22 **overjoyed:** über-
glücklich. | 23 **superb:** prächtig, herrlich. | 25 **zombyish** (N.): zombiehaft
(von *zombie* ›wiederbeseelter Leichnam‹).

I did not like that crack about zombyish, brothers, and so I said, "What goes on, bratties? What dost thou in mind for thy little droog have?" And then F. Alexander swooshed in with:

"Strange, strange, that manner of voice pricks me. We've come into contact before, I'm sure we have." And he brooded, like frowning. I would have to watch this, O my brothers. D. B. da Silva said:

"Public meetings, mainly. To exhibit you at public meetings will be a tremendous help. And, of course, the newspaper angle is all tied up. A ruined life is the approach. We must inflame all hearts." He showed his thirty-odd zoobies, very white against his dark-coloured litso, he looking a malenky bit like some foreigner. I said:

"Nobody will tell me what I will get out of this. Tortured in jail, thrown out of my home by my own parents and their filthy overbearing lodger, beaten by old men and nearly killed by the millicents – what is to become of me?" The Rubinstein veck came in with:

"You will see, boy, that the Party will not be ungrateful. Oh, no. At the end of it all there will be some very acceptable little surprise for you. Just you wait and see."

"There's only one veshch I require," I creeched out, "and that's to be normal and healthy as I was in the starry days, having my malenky bit of fun with *real* droogs and not those who just call themselves that and are really more like traitors. Can you do that, eh? Can any veck restore me to

1 **crack:** Witz, Seitenhieb. | 3 **to swoosh:** eigtl.: rauschen; hier etwa: schnell ins Wort fallen. | 5 **to prick** (fig.): keine Ruhe lassen, quälen. | 11 **angle:** Standpunkt; Blickwinkel; Methode, Vorgehensweise. | 13 **to inflame:** entflammen. | **thirty-odd:** über dreißig.

what I was? That's what I want and that's what I want to know."

Kashl kashl kashl coughed this Z. Dolin. "A martyr to the cause of Liberty," he said. "You have your part to play and don't forget it. Meanwhile, we shall look after you." And he began to stroke my left rooker as if I was like an idiot, grinning in a bezoomny way. I creeched:

"Stop treating me like a thing that's like got to be just used. I'm not an idiot you can impose on, you stupid bratchnies. Ordinary prestoopnicks are stupid, but I'm not ordinary and nor am I dim. Do you slooshy?"

"Dim," said F. Alexander, like musing. "Dim. That was a name somewhere. Dim."

"Eh?" I said. "What's Dim got to do with it? What do *you* know about Dim?" And then I said, "Oh, Bog help us." I didn't like the like look in F. Alexander's glazzies. I made for the door, wanting to go upstairs and get my platties and then itty off.

"I could almost believe," said F. Alexander, showing his stained zoobies, his glazzies mad. "But such things are impossible. For, by Christ, if he were I'd tear him. I'd split him, by God, yes, yes, so I would."

"There," said D. B. da Silva, stroking his chest like he was a doggie to calm him down. "It's all in the past. It was other people altogether. We must help this poor victim. That's what we must do now, remembering the Future and our Cause."

"I'll just get my platties," I said, at the stair-foot, "that is

---

3 **martyr:** Märtyrer. | 9 **to impose on s.o.:** jdm. imponieren. | 28 **stair-foot:** unterer Treppenabsatz.

to say clothes, and then I'll be ittying off all on my oddy knocky. I mean, my gratitude for all, but I have my own jeezny to live." Because, brothers, I wanted to get out of here real skorry. But Z. Dolin said:

"Ah, no. We have you, friend, and we keep you. You come with us. Everything will be all right, you'll see." And he came up to me to like grab hold of my rooker again. Then, brothers, I thought of fight, but thinking of fighting made me like want to collapse and sick, so I just stood. And then I saw this like madness in F. Alexander's glazzies and said:

"Whatever you say. I am in your rookers. But let's get it started and all over, brothers." Because what I wanted now was to get out of this mesto called HOME. I was beginning not to like the like look of the glazzies of F. Alexander one malenky bit.

"Good," said this Rubinstein. "Get dressed and let's get started."

"Dim dim dim," F. Alexander kept saying in a like low mutter. "What or who was this Dim?" I ittied upstairs real skorry and dressed in near two seconds flat. Then I was out with these three and into an auto, Rubinstein one side of me and Z. Dolin coughing kashl kashl kashl the other side, D.B. da Silva doing the driving, into the town and to a flat-block not really all that distant from what had used to be my own flatblock or home. "Come, boy, out," said Z. Dolin, coughing to make the cancer-end in his rot glow red like some malenky furnace. "This is where you shall be in-

20 **mutter:** Gemurmel. | 21 **two seconds flat** (coll.): genau zwei Sekunden.

stalled." So we ittied in, and there was like another of these Dignity of Labour veshches on the wall of the vestibule, and we upped in the lift, brothers, and then went into a flat like all the flats of all the flatblocks of the town. Very very malenky, with two bedrooms and one live-eat-work-room, the table of this all covered with books and papers and ink and bottles and all that cal. "Here is your new home," said D.B. da Silva. "Settle here, boy. Food is in the food-cup-board. Pyjamas are in a drawer. Rest, rest, perturbed spirit."

"Eh," I said, not quite ponying that.

"All right," said Rubinstein, with his starry goloss. "We are now leaving you. Work has to be done. We'll be with you later. Occupy yourself as best you can."

"One thing," coughed Z. Dolin kashl kashl kashl. "You saw what stirred in the tortured memory of our friend F. Alexander. Was it, by any chance – ? That is to say, did you –? I think you know what I mean. We won't let it go any further."

"I've paid," I said. "Bog knows I've paid for what I did. I've paid not only like for myself but for those bratchnies too that called themselves my droogs." I felt violent so then I felt a bit sick. "I'll lay down a bit," I said. "I've been through terrible terrible times."

"You have," said D.B. da Silva, showing all his thirty zoobies. "You do that."

So they left me, brothers. They ittied off about their businesses, which I took to be about politics and all that cal, and I was on the bed, all on my oddy knocky with every-

---

3 **to up** (N.): hinauffahren. | 9 **Rest, rest, perturbed spirit:** Shakespeare, *Hamlet* I,5,182 (*to perturb:* beunruhigen, verwirren).

thing very very quiet. I just laid there with my sabogs kicked off my nogas and my tie loose, like all bewildered and not knowing what sort of a jeezny I was going to live now. And all sorts of like pictures kept like passing through my gulliver, of the different chellovecks I'd met at school and in the Staja, and the different veshches that had happened to me, and how there was not one veck you could trust in the whole bolshy world. And then I like dozed off, brothers.

When I woke up I could slooshy music coming out of the wall, real gromky, and it was that that had dragged me out of my bit of like sleep. It was a symphony that I knew real horrorshow but had not slooshied for many a year, namely the Symphony Number Three of the Danish veck Otto Skadelig, a very gromky and violent piece, especially in the first movement, which was what was playing now. I slooshied for two seconds in like interest and joy, but then it all came over me, the start of the pain and the sickness, and I began to groan deep down in my keeshkas. And then there I was, me who had loved music so much, crawling off the bed and going oh oh oh to myself, and then bang bang banging on the wall creeching, "Stop, stop it, turn it off!" But it went on and it seemed to be like louder. So I crashed at the wall till my knuckles were all red red krovvy and torn skin, creeching and creeching, but the music did not stop. Then I thought I had to get away from it, so I lurched out of the malenky bedroom and ittied skorry to the front door of the flat, but this had been locked from the outside and I could not get out. And all the time the music got more and

15 **Skadelig:** fiktiver Komponist. | 24 **knuckle:** Fingergelenk, Knöchel.

more gromky, like it was all a deliberate torture, O my brothers. So I stuck my little fingers real deep in my ookos, but the trombones and kettledrums blasted through gromky enough. So I creeched again for them to stop and went hammer hammer hammer on the wall, but it made not one malenky bit of difference. "Oh, what am I to do?" I boohooed to myself. "Oh, Bog in heaven Help me." I was like wandering all over the flat in pain and sickness, trying to shut out the music and like groaning deep out of my guts, and then on top of the pile of books and papers and all that cal that was on the table in the living-room I viddied what I had to do and what I had wanted to do until those old men in the Public Biblio and then Dim and Billyboy disguised as rozzes stopped me, and that was to do myself in, to snuff it, to blast off for ever out of this wicked and cruel world. What I viddied was the slovo DEATH on the cover of a like pamphlet, even though it was only DEATH TO THE GOVERNMENT. And like it was Fate there was another like malenky booklet which had an open window on the cover, and it said, "Open the window to fresh air, fresh ideas, a new way of living." And so I knew that it was like telling me to finish it all off by jumping out. One moment of pain, perhaps, and then sleep for ever and ever and ever.

The music was still pouring in all brass and drums and the violins miles up through the wall. The window in the room where I had laid down was open. I ittied to it and viddied a fair drop to the autos and buses and walking chell-

---

3 kettledrum: Pauke. | to blast: schmettern, donnern. | 15 to blast off: abheben (Flugzeug, Rakete). | 17 pamphlet: Flugschrift, Broschüre. | 19 booklet: Büchlein, Broschüre. | 25 brass: Blechbläser.

ovecks below. I creeched out to the world: "Goodbye, goodbye, may Bog forgive you for a ruined life." Then I got on to the sill, the music blasting away to my left, and I shut my glazzies and felt the cold wind on my litso, then I jumped.

3 **sill:** Fensterbrett.

Six

I jumped, O my brothers, and I fell on the sidewalk hard,
but I did not snuff it, oh no. If I had snuffed it I would not
be here to write what I written have. It seems that the jump
was not from a big enough heighth to kill. But I cracked my
back and my wrists and nogas and felt very bolshy pain before I passed out, brothers, with astonished and surprised
litsos of chellovecks in the streets looking at me from
above. And just before I passed out I viddied clear that not
one chelloveck in the whole horrid world was for me and
that that music through the wall had all been like arranged
by those who were supposed to be like my new droogs and
that it was some veshch like this that they wanted for their
horrible selfish and boastful politics. All that was in like a
million millionth part of one minoota before I threw over
the world and the sky and the litsos of the staring chellovecks that were above me.

Where I was when I came back to jeezny after a long
black black gap of it might have been a million years was a
hospital, all white and with this von of hospitals you get, all
like sour and smug and clean. These antiseptic veshches
you get in hospitals should have a real horrorshow von of
like frying onions or of flowers. I came very slow back to
knowing who I was and I was all bound up in white and I
could not feel anything in my plott, pain nor sensation nor
any veshch at all. All round my gulliver was a bandage and
there were bits of stuff like stuck to my litso, and my rookers were all in bandages and bits of stick were like fixed to

15 **to throw s.th. over** (coll.): die Beziehung zu etwas beenden.

my fingers like on it might be flowers to make them grow straight, and my poor old nogas were all straightened out too, and it was all bandages and wire cages and into my right rooker, near the pletcho, was red red krovvy dripping from a jar upside down. But I could not feel anything, O my brothers. There was a nurse sitting by my bed and she was reading some book that was all like very dim print and you could viddy it was a story because of a lot of inverted commas, and she was like breathing hard uh uh uh over it, so it must have been a story about the old in-out in-out. She was a real horrorshow devotchka, this nurse, with a very red rot and like long lashes over her glazzies, and under her like very stiff uniform you could viddy she had very horrorshow groodies. So I said to her, "What gives, O my little sister? Come thou and have a nice lay-down with your malenky droog in this bed." But the slovos didn't come out horrorshow at all, it being as though my rot was all stiffened up, and I could feel with my yahzick that some of my zoobies were no longer there. But this nurse like jumped and dropped her book on the floor and said:

"Oh, you've recovered consciousness."

That was like a big rotful for a malenky ptitsa like her, and I tried to say so, but the slovos came out only like er er er. She ittied off and left me on my oddy knocky, and I could viddy now that I was in a malenky room of my own, not in one of these long wards like I had been in as a very little malchick, full of coughing dying starry vecks all round

8 f. **inverted commas** (pl.): Anführungszeichen. | 12 **lash:** Wimper. | 22 **big rotful** (N.): große Worte. | 26 **ward:** (Krankenhaus-)Abteilung, Station.

to make you want to get well and fit again. It had been like diphtheria I had had then, O my brothers.

It was like now as though I could not hold to being conscious all that long, because I was like asleep again almost right away, very skorry, but in a minoota or two I was sure that this nurse ptitsa had come back and brought chellovecks in white coats with her and they were viddying me very frowning and going hm hm hm at Your Humble Narrator. And with them I was sure there was the old charles from the Staja govoreeting, "Oh my son, my son," breathing a like very stale von of whisky on to me and then saying, "But I would not stay, oh no. I could not in no wise subscribe to what those bratchnies are going to do to other poor prestoopnicks. So I got out and am preaching sermons now about it all, my little beloved son in J. C."

I woke up again later on and who should I viddy there round the bed but the three from whose flat I had jumped out, namely D. B. da Silva and Something Something Rubinstein and Z. Dolin. "Friend," one of these vecks was saying, but I could not viddy or slooshy horrorshow which one, "friend, little friend," this goloss was saying, "the people are on fire with indignation. You have killed those horrible boastful villains' chances of re-election. They will go and will go for ever and ever. You have served Liberty well."

I tried to say:

"If I had died it would have been even better for you political bratchnies, would it not, pretending and treacherous

12 **no wise** (obs.): in keiner Weise. | 13 **to subscribe to s.th.**: sich etwas anschließen, bei etwas mitmachen. | 15 **J. C.**: Abk. für *Jesus Christ*. | 23 **re-election**: Wiederwahl.

droogs as you are." But all that came out was er er er. Then one of these three seemed to hold out a lot of bits cut from gazettas and what I could viddy was a horrible picture of me all krovvy on a stretcher being carried off and I seemed to like remember a kind of a popping of lights which must have been photographer vecks. Out of one glazz I could read like headlines which were sort of trembling in the rooker of the chelloveck that held them, like BOY VICTIM OF CRIMINAL REFORM SCHEME and GOVERNMENT AS MURDERER and then there was like a picture of a veck that looked familiar to me and it said OUT OUT OUT, and that would be the Minister of the Inferior or Interior. Then the nurse ptitsa said:

"You shouldn't be exciting him like that. You shouldn't be doing anything that will make him upset. Now come on, let's have you out." I tried to say:

"Out out out," but it was er er er again. Anyway, these three political vecks went. And I went, too, only back to the land, back to all blackness lit up by like odd dreams which I didn't know whether they were dreams or not, O my brothers. Like for instance I had this idea of my whole plott or body being like emptied of as it might be dirty water and then filled up again with clean. And then there were really lovely and horrorshow dreams of being in some veck's auto that had been crasted by me and driving up and down the world all on my oddy knocky running lewdies down and hearing them creech they were dying, and in me no pain and no sickness. And also there were dreams of doing the

---

4 **stretcher:** Tragbahre. | 5 **popping:** Knall, Puff. | 7 **headline:** Schlagzeile.

old in-out in-out with devotchkas, forcing like them down on the ground and making them have it and everybody standing round clapping their rookers and cheering like bezoomny. And then I woke up again and it was my pee and em come to viddy their ill son, my em boohooing real horrorshow. I could govoreet a lot better now and could say:

"Well well well well well, what gives? What makes you think you are like welcome?" My papapa said, in a like ashamed way:

"You were in the papers, son. It said they had done great wrong to you. It said how the Government drove you to try and do yourself in. And it was our fault too, in a way, son. Your home's your home, when all's said and done, son." And my mum kept on going boohoohoo and looking ugly as kiss-my-sharries. So I said:

"And how beeth thy new son Joe? Well and healthy and prosperous, I trust and pray." My mum said:

"Oh, Alex Alex. Owwwwwwwww." My papapa said:

"A very awkward thing, son. He got into a bit of trouble with the police and was done by the police."

"Really?" I said. "Really? Such a good sort of chelloveck and all. Amazed proper I am, honest."

"Minding his own business, he was," said my pee. "And the police told him to move on. Waiting at a corner he was, son, to see a girl he was going to meet. And they told him to move on and he said he had rights like everybody else, and then they sort of fell on top of him and hit him about cruel."

16 **beeth:** *is.* | 19 **awkward:** peinlich. | 22 **Amazed proper I am:** *I am properly amazed.*

"Terrible," I said. "Really terrible. And where is the poor boy now?"

"Owwwww," boohooed my mum. "Gone back owww-wwwme."

"Yes," said dad. "He's gone back to his home town to get better. They've had to give his job here to somebody else."

"So now," I said, "you're willing for me to move back in again and things be like they were before."

"Yes, son," said my papapa. "Please, son."

"I'll consider it," I said. "I'll think about it real careful."

"Owwwww," went my mum.

"Ah, shut it," I said, "or I'll give you something proper to yowl and creech about. Kick your zoobies in I will." And, O my brothers, saying that made me feel a malenky bit better, as if all like fresh red red krovvy was flowing all through my plott. That was something I had to think about. It was like as though to get better I had had to get worse.

"That's no way to speak to your mother, son," said my papapa. "After all, she brought you into the world."

"Yes," I said, "and a right grahzny vonny world too." I shut my glazzies tight in like pain and said, "Go away now. I'll think about coming back. But things will have to be very different."

"Yes, son," said my pee. "Anything you say."

"You'll have to make up your mind," I said, "who's to be boss."

"Owwwwww," my mum went on.

"Very good, son," said my papapa. "Things will be as you like. Only get well."

When they had gone I laid and thought a bit about different veshches, like all different pictures passing through my gulliver, and when the nurse ptitsa came back in and like straightened the sheets on the bed I said to her:

"How long is it I've been in here?"

"A week or so," she said.

"And what have they been doing to me?"

"Well," she said, "you were all broken up and bruised and had sustained severe concussion and had lost a lot of blood. They've had to put all that right, haven't they?"

"But," I said, "has anyone been doing anything with my gulliver? What I mean is, have they been playing around with inside like my brain?"

"Whatever they've done," she said, "it'll all be for the best."

But a couple of days later a couple of like doctor vecks came in, both youngish vecks with these very sladky smiles, and they had like a picture book with them. One of them said, "We want you to have a look at these and to tell us what you think about them. All right?"

"What giveth, O little droogies?" I said. "What new bezoomny idea dost thou in mind have?" So they both had a like embarassed smeck at that and then they sat down either side of the bed and opened up this book. On the first page there was like a photograph of a bird-nest full of eggs.

"Yes?" one of these doctor vecks said.

"A bird-nest," I said, "full of like eggs. Very very nice."

"And what would you like to do about it?" the other one said.

"Oh," I said, "smash them. Pick up the lot and like throw

2 **to straighten:** glätten. | 7 **to sustain:** erleiden. | **concussion:** Gehirnerschütterung.

them against a wall or a cliff or something and then viddy them all smash up real horrorshow."

"Good, good," they both said, and then the page was turned. It was like a picture of one of these bolshy great birds called peacocks with all its tail spread out in all colours in a very boastful way. "Yes?" said one of these vecks.

"I would like," I said, "to pull out like all those feathers in its tail and slooshy it creech blue murder. For being so like boastful."

"Good," they both said, "good good good." And they went on turning the pages. There were like pictures of real horrorshow devotchkas, and I said I would like to give them the old in-out in-out with lots of ultra-violence. There were like pictures of chellovecks being given the boot straight in the litso and all red red krovvy everywhere and I said I would like to be in on that. And there was a picture of the old nagoy droog of the prison charlie carrying his cross up a hill, and I said I would like to have the old hammer and nails. Good good good. I said:

"What is all this?"

"Deep hypnopaedia," or some such slovo, said one of these two vecks. "You seem to be cured."

"Cured?" I said. "Me tied down to this bed like this and you say cured? Kiss my sharries is what I say."

"Wait," the other said. "It won't be long now."

So I waited and, O my brothers, I got a lot better, munching away at eggiwegs and lomticks of toast and peeting bol-

---

5 **peacock**: Pfau. | 16 **to be on s.th.** (coll.): bei etwas dabeisein. | 21 **hypnopaedia**: in Aldous Huxleys Roman *Brave New World* (1932) verwendete, dort auch als »sleep-teaching« bezeichnete Konditionierungstechnik.

shy great mugs of milky chai, and then one day they said I was going to have a very very very special visitor.

"Who?" I said, while they straightened the bed and combed my luscious glory for me, me having the bandage off now from my gulliver and the hair growing again.

"You'll see, you'll see," they said. And I viddied all right. At two-thirty in the afternoon there were like all photographers and men from gazettas with notebooks and pencils and all that cal. And, brothers, they near trumpeted a bolshy fanfare for this great and important veck who was coming to viddy Your Humble Narrator. And in he came, and of course it was none other than the Minister of the Interior or Inferior, dressed in the heighth of fashion and with this very upper-class haw haw haw goloss. Flash flash bang went the cameras when he put out his rooker to me to shake it. I said:

"Well well well well well. What giveth then, old droogie?"

Nobody seemed to quite pony that, but somebody said in a like harsh goloss:

"Be more respectful, boy, in addressing the Minister."

"Yarbles," I said, like snarling like a doggie. "Bolshy great yarblockos to thee and thine."

"All right, all right," said the Interior Inferior one very skorry. "He speaks to me as a friend, don't you, son?"

"I am everyone's friend," I said. "Except to my enemies."

"And who are your enemies?" said the Minister, while all the gazetta vecks went scribble scribble scribble. "Tell us that, my boy."

---

14 **bang:** paff!, bum(s)!, peng! | 28 **to scribble:** kritzeln.

"All who do me wrong," I said, "are my enemies."

"Well," said the Int Inf Min, sitting down by my bed. "I and the Government of which I am a member want to you regard us as friends. Yes, friends. We have put you right, yes? You are getting the best of treatment. We never wished you harm, but there are some who did and do. And I think you know who those are."

"All who do me wrong," I said, "are my enemies."

"Yes yes yes," he said. "There are certain men who wanted to use you, yes, use you for political ends. They would have been glad, yes, glad for you to be dead, for they thought that they could then blame it all on the Government. I think you know who those men are."

"I did not," I said, "like the look of them."

"There is a man," said the Intinfmin, "called F. Alexander, a writer of subversive literature, who has been howling for your blood. He has been mad with desire to stick a knife in you. But you're safe from him now. We put him away."

"He was supposed to be like a droogie," I said. "Like a mother to me was what he was."

"He found out that you had done wrong to him. At least," said the Min very very skorry, "he believed you had done wrong. He formed this idea in his mind that you had been responsible for the death of someone near and dear to him."

"What you mean," I said, "is that he was told."

"He had this idea," said the Min. "He was a menace. We put him away for his own protection. And also," he said, "for yours."

16 **subversive:** umstürzlerisch, staatsgefährdend.

"Kind," I said. "Most kind of thou."

"When you leave here," said the Min, "you will have no worries. We shall see to everything. A good job on a good salary. Because you are helping us."

"Am I?" I said.

"We always help our friends, don't we?" And then he took my rooker and some veck creeched, "Smile!" and I smiled like bezoomny without thinking, and then flash flash crack flash bang there were pictures being taken of me and the Intinfmin all droogy together. "Good boy," said this great chelloveck. "Good good boy. And now, see, a present."

What was brought in now, brothers, was a big shiny box, and I viddied clear what sort of a veshch it was. It was a stereo. It was put down next to the bed and opened up and some veck plugged its lead into the wall-socket. "What shall it be?" asked a veck with otchkies on his nose, and he had in his rookers lovely shiny sleeves full of music. "Mozart, Beethoven, Schoenberg? Carl Orff?"

"The Ninth," I said. "The glorious Ninth."

And the ninth it was, O my brothers. Everybody began to leave nice and quiet while I laid there with my glazzies closed, slooshying the lovely music. The Min said, "Good good boy," patting me on the pletcho, then he ittied off. Only one veck was left, saying, "Sign here, please." I opened my glazzies up to sign, not knowing what I was signing and not, O my brothers, caring either. Then I was left alone with the glorious Ninth of Ludwig van.

15 **to plug:** anschließen, einstöpseln. | **wall-socket:** Wandsteckdose. | 18 **Schoenberg:** Arnold Schönberg (1874–1951), österreichischer Komponist, Erfinder der Zwölftontechnik. | **Orff:** Carl O. (1895–1982), deutscher Komponist.

Oh, it was gorgeosity and yumyumyum. When it came on to the Scherzo I could viddy myself very clear running and running on like very light and mysterious nogas, carving the whole litso of the creeching world with my cutthroat britva. And there was the slow movement and the lovely last singing movement still to come. I was cured all right.

Seven

"What's it going to be then, eh?"

There was me, Your Humble Narrator, and my three droogs, that is Len, Rick, and Bully, Bully being called Bully because of his bolshy big neck and very gromky goloss which was just like some bolshy great bull bellowing auuuuuuuh. We were sitting in the Korova Milkbar making up our rassoodocks what to do with the evening, a flip dark chill winter bastard though dry. All round were chellovecks well away on milk plus vellocet and synthemesc and drencrom and other veshches which take you far far far away from this wicked and real world into the land to viddy Bog And All His Holy Angels And Saints in your left sabog with lights bursting and spurting all over your mozg. What we were peeting was the old moloko with knives in it, as we used to say, to sharpen you up and make you ready for a bit of dirty twenty-to-one, but I've told you all that before.

We were dressed in the heighth of fashion, which in those days was these very wide trousers and a very loose black shiny leather like jerkin over an open-necked shirt with a like scarf tucked in. At this time too it was the heighth of fashion to use the old britva on the gulliver, so that most of the gulliver was like bald and there was hair only on the sides. But it was always the same on the old nogas – real horrorshow bolshy big boots for kicking litsos in.

"What's it going to be then, eh?"

I was like the oldest of we four, and they all looked up to

6 **to bellow:** brüllen. | 14 **to spurt:** (heraus)spritzen. | 20 **jerkin:** (Leder-) Wams. | **open-necked:** mit offenem Kragen. | 21 **to tuck in:** einschlagen, einstecken.

me as their leader, but I got the idea sometimes that Bully had the thought in his gulliver that he would like to take over, this being because of his bigness and the gromky goloss that bellowed out of him when he was on the warpath. But all the ideas came from Your Humble, O my brothers, and also there was this veshch that I had been famous and had had my picture and articles and all that cal in the gazettas. Also I had by far the best job of all we four, being in the National Gramodisc Archives on the music side with a real horrorshow carman full of pretty polly at the week's end and a lot of nice free discs for my own malenky self on the side.

This evening in the Korova there was a fair number of vecks and ptitsas and devotchkas and malchicks smecking and peeting away, and cutting through their govoreeting and the burbling of the in-the-landers with their "Gorgor fallatuke and the worm sprays in filltip slaughterballs" and all that cal you could slooshy a popdisc on the stereo, this being Ned Achimota singing "That Day, Yeah, That Day". At the counter were three devotchkas dressed in the heighth of nadsat fashion, that is to say long uncombed hair dyed white and false groodies sticking out a metre or more and very very tight short skirts with all like frothy white underneath, and Bully kept saying, "Hey, get in there we could, three of us. Old Len is not like interested. Leave old Len alone with his God." And Len kept saying, "Yarbles, yarbles. Where is the spirit for all for one and one for all, eh

4 **warpath:** Kriegspfad. | 9 **National Gramodisc Archives** (pl.): Nationales Schallplattenarchiv. | 16 **in-the-lander** (N.): jd., der einen Rausch hat, sich auf einem Trip befindet. | 16 f. **Gorgor fallatuke … slaughterballs:** Nonsens-Satz. | 23 **frothy:** schaumig, schäumend.

boy?" Suddenly I felt both very very tired and also full of tingly energy, and I said:

"Out out out out out."

"Where to?" said Rick, who had a litso like a frog's.

"Oh, just to viddy what's doing in the great outside," I said. But somehow, my brothers, I felt very bored and a bit hopeless, and I had been feeling that a lot these days. So I turned to the chelloveck nearest me on the big plush seat that ran right round the whole mesto, a chelloveck, that is, who was burbling away under the influence, and I fisted him real skorry ack ack ack in the belly. But he felt it not, brothers, only burbling away with his "Cart cart virtue, where in toptails lieth the poppoppicorns?" So we scatted out into the big winter nochy.

We walked down Marghanita Boulevard and there were no millicents patrolling that way, so when we met a starry veck coming away from a news-kiosk where he had been kupetting a gazetta I said to Bully, "All right, Bully boy, thou canst if thou like wishest." More and more these days I had been just giving the orders and standing back to viddy them being carried out. So Bully cracked into him er er er, and the other two tripped him and kicked at him, smecking away, while he was down and then let him crawl off to where he lived, like whimpering to himself. Bully said:

"How about a nice yummy glass of something to keep out the cold, O Alex?" For we were not too far from the Duke of New York. The other two nodded yes yes yes but

---

2 **tingly:** prickelnd, kribbelnd. | 10 **under the influence:** betrunken; bekifft. | 12 f. **Cart cart … poppoppicorns?:** Nonsens-Satz. | 16 **to patrol:** patrouillieren, auf Streife gehen. | 25 **yummy** (coll.): lecker.

all looked at me to viddy whether that was all right. I nodded too and so off we ittied. Inside the snug there were these starry ptitsas or sharps or baboochkas you will remember from the beginning and they all started on their, "Evening, lads, God bless you, boys, best lads living, that's what you are," waiting for us to say, "What's it going to be, girls?" Bully rang the collocoll and a waiter came in rubbing his rookers on his grazzy apron. "Cutter on the table, droogies," said Bully, pulling out his own rattling and chinking mound of deng. "Scotchmen for us and the same for the old baboochkas, eh?" And then I said:

"Ah, to hell. Let them buy their own." I didn't know what it was, but these last days I had become like mean. There had come into my gulliver a like desire to keep all my pretty polly to myself, to like hoard it up for some reason. Bully said:

"What gives, bratty? What's coming over old Alex?"

"Ah, to hell," I said. "I don't know. I don't know. What it is is I don't like just throwing away my hard-earned pretty polly, that's what it is."

"Earned?" said Rick. "Earned? It doesn't have to be earned, as well thou knowest, old droogie. Took, that's all, just took, like." And he smecked real gromky and I viddied one or two of his zoobies weren't all that horrorshow.

"Ah," I said, "I've got some thinking to do." But viddying these baboochkas looking all eager like for some free alc, I like shrugged my pletchoes and pulled out my own cutter from my trouser carman, notes and coin all mixed together, and plonked it tinkle crackle on the table.

9 **to chink:** klirren, klimpern. | 10 **mound:** Hügel, Haufen. | 15 **to hoard s.th. up:** etwas aufhäufen, hamstern. | 26 **alc:** Kurzform von *alcohol*.

"Scotchmen all round, right," said the waiter. But for some reason I said:

"No, boy, for me make it one small beer, right." Len said:

"This I do not much go for," and he began to put his rooker on my gulliver like kidding I must have fever, but I like snarled doggy-wise for him to give over skorry. "All right, all right droog," he said. "As thou like sayest." But Bully was having a smot with his rot open at something that had come out of my carman with the pretty polly I'd put on the table. He said:

"Well well well. And we never knew."

"Give me that," I snarled and grabbed it skorry. I couldn't explain how it had got there, brothers, but it was a photograph I had scissored out of the old gazetta and it was of a baby. It was of a baby gurgling goo goo goo with all like moloko dribbling from its rot and looking up and like smecking at everybody, and it was all nagoy and its flesh was like in all folds with being a very fat baby. There was then like a bit of haw haw haw struggling to get hold of this bit of paper from me, so I had to snarl again at them and I grabbed the photo and tore it up into tiny teeny pieces and let it fall like a bit of snow onto the floor. The whisky came in then and the starry baboochkas said, "Good health, lads, God bless you, boys, the best lads living, that's what you are," and all that cal. And one of them who was all lines and wrinkles and no zoobies in her shrunken old rot said, "Don't tear up money, son. If you don't need it give it to them as does," which was very bold and forward of her. But Rick said:

5 **to kid:** hier: so tun als ob. | 6 **doggy-wise** (N.): wie ein Hund. | **to give over:** aufhören, ablassen. | 15 **to gurgle:** gurgeln, glucksen. | 21 **teeny:** *teeny-weeny:* klitzeklein. | 28 **forward:** vorwitzig.

"Money that was not, O baboochka. It was a picture of a dear little itsy witsy bitsy bit of a baby." I said:

"I'm getting just that bit tired, that I am. It's you who's the babies, you lot. Scoffing and grinning and all you can do is smeck and give people bolshy cowardly tolchocks when they can't give them back." Bully said:

"Well now, we always thought it was you who was the king of that and also the teacher. Not well, that's the trouble with thou, old droogie."

I viddied this sloppy glass of beer I had on the table in front of me and felt like all vomity within, so I went "Aaaaah" and poured all the frothy vonny cal all over the floor. One of the starry ptitsas said:

"Waste not want not." I said:

"Look, droogies. Listen. Tonight I am somehow just not in the mood. I know not why or how it is, but there it is. You three go your own ways this nightwise, leaving me out. Tomorrow we shall meet same place same time, me hoping to be like a lot better."

"Oh," said Bully, "right sorry I am." But you could viddy a like gleam in his glazzies, becaue now he would be taking over for this nochy. Power, power, everybody like wants power. "We can postpone till tomorrow," said Bully, "what we in mind had. Namely, that bit of shop-crasting in Gagarin Street. Flip horrorshow taking there, droog, for the having."

---

2 **itsy witsy bitsy:** Ansammlung von Diminutiven. | 4 **to scoff:** spotten. | 10 **sloppy:** labberig, abgestanden. | 11 **vomity** (N.): zum Kotzen (von *vomit*). | 17 **nightwise** (N.): Nacht. | 23 **to postpone:** auf-, verschieben. | 25 **Gagarin:** Juri G. (1934–1968), russischer Kosmonaut; umkreiste als erster Mensch die Erde.

"No," I said. "You postpone nothing. You just carry on in your own like style. Now," I said, "I itty off." And I got up from my chair.

"Where to, then?" asked Rick.

5 "That know I not," I said. "Just to be on like my own and sort things out." You could viddy the old baboochkas were real puzzled at me going out like that and like all morose and not the bright and smecking malchickiwick you will remember. But I said, "Ah, to hell, to hell," and scatted out all 10 on my oddy knocky into the street.

It was dark and there was a wind sharp as a nozh getting up, and there were very very few lewdies about. There were these patrol cars with brutal rozzes inside them like cruising about, and now and then on the corner you could 15 viddy a couple of very young millicents stamping against the bitchy cold and letting out steam breath on the winter air, O my brothers. I suppose really a lot of the old ultra-violence and crasting was dying out now, the rozzes being so brutal with who they caught, though it had become like 20 a fight between naughty nadsats and the rozzes who could be more skorry with the nozh and britva and the stick and even the gun. But what was the matter with me these days was that I didn't care much. It was like something soft getting into me and I could not pony why. What I wanted 25 these days I did not know. Even the music I liked to slooshy in my own malenky den was what I would have smecked at before, brothers. I was slooshying more like malenky romantic songs, what they call *Lieder*, just a goloss and a pia-

---

7 **morose**: mürrisch, verdrießlich. | 16 **bitchy cold**: Hundekälte, mordsmäßige Kälte.

no, very quiet and like yearny, different from when it had been all bolshy orchestras and me lying on the bed between the violins and the trombones and the kettledrums. There was something happening inside me, and I wondered if it was like some disease or if it was what they had done to me that time upsetting my gulliver and perhaps going to make me real bezoomny.

So thinking like this with my gulliver bent and my rookers stuck in my trouser carmans I walked the town, brothers, and at last I began to feel very tired and also in great need of a nice bolshy chasha of milky chai. Thinking about this chai, I got a sudden like picture of me sitting before a bolshy fire in an armchair peeting away at this chai, and what was funny and very very strange was that I seemed to have turned into a very starry chelloveck, about seventy years old, because I could viddy my own volosss, which was very grey, and I also had whiskers, and these were very grey too. I could viddy myself as an old man, sitting by a fire, and then the like picture vanished. But it was very like strange.

I came to one of those tea-and-coffee mestos, brothers, and I could viddy through the long long window that it was full of very dull lewdies, like ordinary, who had these very patient and expressionless litsos and would do no harm to no one, all sitting there and govoreeting like quietly and peeting away at their nice harmless chai and coffee. I ittied inside and went up to the counter and bought me a nice hot chai with plenty of moloko, then I ittied to one of these ta-

---

1 **yearny** (N.): sehnsüchtig, verlangend (von *to yearn* ›sich sehnen‹, ›verlangen‹). | 13 **armchair**: Lehnstuhl.

bles and sat down to peet it. There was like a young couple at this table, peeting and smoking filter-tip cancers, and govoreeting and smecking very quietly between themselves, but I took no notice of them and just went on peeting away and like dreaming and wondering what it was in me that was like changing and what was going to happen to me. But I viddied that the devotchka at this table who was with this chelloveck was real horrorshow, not the sort you would want to like throw down and give the old in-out in-out to, but with a horrorshow plott and litso and a smiling rot and very very fair voloss and all that cal. And then the veck with her, who had a hat on his gulliver and had his litso like turned away from me, swivelled round to viddy the bolshy big clock they had on the wall in this metsto, and then I viddied who he was and then he viddied who I was. It was Pete, one of my three droogs from those days when it was Georgie and Dim and him and me. It was Pete like looking a lot older though he could not now be more than nineteen and a bit, and he had a bit of a moustache and an ordinary day-suit and this hat on. I said:

"Well well well droogie, what gives? Very very long time no viddy." He said:

"It's little Alex, isn't it?"

"None other," I said. "A long long long time since those dead and gone good days. And now poor Georgie, they told me, is underground and old Dim is a brutal millicent, and here is thou and here is I, and what news hast thou, old droogie?"

---

13 **to swivel:** (sich) drehen. | 19 **moustache:** Schnurrbart. | 22 **long time no viddy** (N.): lange nicht gesehen. | 26 **underground:** ,unter der Erde'.

"He talks funny, doesn't he?" said this devotchka, like giggling.

"This," said Pete to the devotchka, "is an old friend. His name is Alex. May I," he said to me, "introduce my wife?"

My rot fell wide open then. "Wife?" I like gaped. "Wife wife wife? Ah no, that cannot be. Too young art thou to be married, old droog. Impossible impossible."

This devotchka who was like Pete's wife (impossible impossible) giggled again and said to Pete, "Did you used to talk like that too?"

"Well," said Pete, and he like smiled. "I'm nearly twenty. Old enough to be hitched, and it's been two months already. You were very young and very forward, remember."

"Well," I like gaped still. "Over this get can I not, old droogie. Pete married. Well well well."

"We have a small flat," said Pete. "I am earning very small money at State Marine Insurance, but things will get better, that I know. And Georgina here –"

"What again is that name?" I said, rot still open like bezoomny. Pete's wife (wife, brothers) like giggled again.

"Georgina," said Pete. "Georgina works too. Typing, you know. We manage, we manage." I could not, brothers, take my glazzies off him, really. He was like grown up now, with a grown up goloss and all. "You must," said Pete, "come and see us sometime. You still," he said, "look very young, despite all your terrible experiences. Yes yes yes, we've read all about them. But, of course, you *are* very young still."

---

5 **to gape:** gaffen, glotzen. | 12 **to be hitched** (coll.): verheiratet sein (Abwandlung von *to get hitched* ›heiraten‹). | 17 **State Marine Insurance:** Staatliche See-Versicherung.

"Eighteen," I said, "just gone."

"Eighteen, eh? As old as that. Well well well. Now," he said, "we have to be going." And he like gave this Georgina of his a like loving look and pressed one of her rookers between his and she gave him one of those looks back, O my brothers. "Yes," said Pete, turning back to me, "we're off to a little party at Greg's."

"Greg?" I said.

"Oh, of course," said Pete, "you wouldn't know Greg, would you? Greg is after your time. While you were away Greg came into the picture. He runs little parties, you know. Mostly wine-cup and word-games. But very nice, very pleasant, you know. Harmless, if you see what I mean."

"Yes," I said. "Harmless. Yes yes, I viddy that real horror-show." And this Georgina devotchka giggled again at my slovos. And then these two ittied off to their vonny word-games at this Greg's, whoever he was. I was left all on my oddy knocky with my milky chai, which was getting cold now, like thinking and wondering.

Perhaps that was it, I kept thinking. Perhaps I was getting too old for this sort of jeezny I had been leading, brothers. I was eighteen now, just gone. Eighteen was not a young age. At eighteen old Wolfgang Amadeus had written concertos and symphonies and operas and oratorios and all that cal, no, not cal, heavenly music. And then there was old Felix M. with his *Midsummer Night's Dream* overture. And

---

12 **wine-cup:** Weinbowle. | 25 **oratorio:** Oratorium (opernartiges Musikwerk). | 27 **"Midsummer Night's Dream" overture:** Konzertouvertüre zu Shakespeares *Ein Sommernachtstraum*, op. 21 (1826) von Felix Mendelssohn-Bartholdy (1809–1847).

there were others. And there was this like French poet set by old Benjy Britt, who had done all his best poetry by the age of fifteen, O my brothers. Arthur, his first name. Eighteen was not all that young an age, then. But what was I going to do?

Walking the dark chill bastards of winter streets after itying off from this chai and coffee mesto, I kept viddying like visions, like these cartoons in the gazettas. There was Your Humble Narrator Alex coming home from work to a good hot plate of dinner, and there was this ptitsa all welcoming and greeting like loving. But I could not viddy her all that horrorshow, brothers, I could not think who it might be. But I had this sudden very strong idea that if I walked into the room next to this room where the fire was burning away and my hot dinner laid on the table, there I should find what I really wanted, and now it all tied up, that picture scissored out of the gazetta and meeting old Pete like that. For in that other room in a cot was laying gurgling goo goo goo my son. Yes yes yes, brothers, my son. And now I felt this bolshy big hollow inside my plott, feeling very surprised too at myself. I knew what was happening, O my brothers. I was like growing up.

Yes yes yes, there it was. Youth must go, ah yes. But youth is only being in a way like it might be an animal. No, it is not just like being an animal so much as being like one of these malenky toys you viddy being sold in the streets, like little chellovecks made out of tin and with a spring in-

1 **French poet:** Gemeint ist Arthur Rimbaud (1854–1891), Begründer des rhythmischen Prosagedichts (*vers libre*), dessen *Illuminations* 1939 von dem englischen Komponisten Benjamin Britten (1913–1976) vertont wurden. | 18 **cot:** Kinderbett.

side and then a winding handle on the outside and you wind it up grrr grrr grrr and off it itties, like walking, O my brothers. But it itties in a straight line and bangs straight into things bang bang and it cannot help what it is doing. Being young is like being like one of these malenky machines.

My son, my son. When I had my son I would explain all that to him when he was starry enough to like understand. But then I knew he would not understand or would not want to understand at all and would do all the veshches I had done, yes perhaps even killing some poor starry forella surrounded with mewing kots and koshkas, and I would not be able to really stop him. And nor would he be able to stop his own son, brothers. And so it would itty on to like the end of the world, round and round and round, like some bolshy gigantic like chelloveck, like old Bog Himself (by courtesy of Korova Milkbar) turning and turning and turning a vonny grahzny orange in his gigantic rookers.

But first of all, brothers, there was this veshch of finding some devotchka or other who would be a mother to this son. I would have to start on that tomorrow, I kept thinking. That was something like new to do. That was something I would have to get started on, a new like chapter beginning.

That's what it's going to be then, brothers, as I come to the like end of this tale. You have been everywhere with your little droog Alex, suffering with him, and you have viddied some of the most grahzny bratchnies old Bog ever made, all on to your old droog Alex. And all it was was that

---

1 **winding handle:** Aufziehgriff. | 16 **by courtesy of:** mit freundlicher Genehmigung. | 28 **(to be) on to s.o.:** hinter jdm. her sein.

I was young. But now as I end this story, brothers, I am not young, not no longer, oh no. Alex like groweth up, oh yes.

But where I itty now, O my brothers, is all on my oddy knocky, where you cannot go. Tomorrow is all like sweet flowers and the turning vonny earth and the stars and the old Luna up there and your old droog Alex all on his oddy knocky seeking like a mate. And all that cal. A terrible grahzny vonny world, really, O my brothers. And so farewell from your little droog. And to all others in this story profound shooms of lip-music, brrrrrr. And they can kiss my sharries. But you, O my brothers, remember sometimes thy little Alex that was. Amen. And all that cal.

Etchingham, Sussex
August 1961

13 **Etchingham, Sussex:** Wohnort von A. Burgess nach seiner Rückkehr aus Leningrad (heute: Sankt Petersburg).

Editorische Notiz

Der englische Text folgt der Ausgabe: Anthony Burgess, *A Clockwork Orange. The Restored Edition*, edited with an introduction and notes by Andrew Biswell, London: Penguin, 2013.

Grundlage der vorgenommenen »Restaurierungen« ist ein von Burgess korrigiertes Typoskript aus dem Jahre 1961. Leider macht Biswell nur wenige Angaben zu den ihn leitenden editorischen Prinzipien. Die augenfälligste Veränderung ist die Einfügung von Noten für den Gesang der Gefangenen im ersten Kapitel des zweiten Teils (S. 107). Das Fehlen der Noten in den Erstausgaben des Romans erklärt Biswell mit der plausiblen Vermutung, angesichts des Stands der Drucktechnik in den frühen 1960er Jahren (vor Einführung der preiswerteren Offsetlithographie) hätte die Einfügung von Noten zusätzliche Kosten verursacht, die die Verlage nicht auf sich nehmen wollten.

Das wesentliche von Biswell klar benannte Prinzip ist es, so viel Nadsat wie möglich in den Text aufzunehmen. Auch dies erscheint insoweit plausibel, als die neuen Wörter dem Text größere Lebhaftigkeit und Originalität verleihen dürften. Außerdem sind etliche orthographische Varianten vereinheitlicht. Dennoch fehlt eine Aussage darüber, ob der Auswahl der in die neue Textfassung eingegangenen Lesarten rein subjektive Kriterien zugrunde liegen oder ob sie auf der Basis eines editorischen Grundprinzips erfolgt, das aus einer stringenten Analyse des Druckvorgangs hervorgegangen ist.

Um eine streng wissenschaftliche Edition handelt es sich bei Biswells *Restored Edition* sicherlich nicht, allein schon wegen des Fehlens einer Varianzliste und eines editorischen Apparats. Möglicherweise wird sie also nicht das letzte Wort in Sachen Textkonstituierung von *A Clockwork Orange* bleiben.

Das Glossar erklärt in der Regel alle Wörter, die im *Thematischen Grund- und Aufbauwortschatz Englisch* von Gernot Häublein und Recs Jenkins (Stuttgart: Ernst Klett Sprachen GmbH, 2009) nicht enthalten sind. Im Zweifelsfall wurde großzügig verfahren, d. h. eher eine Vokabel mehr aufgenommen.

Wörter der vom Erzähler verwendeten Kunstsprache »Nadsat« (die Bezeichnung wird von Burgess wiederholt verwendet und ist in die Sekundärliteratur eingegangen) sind als solche gekennzeichnet. Die Lektüre von *A Clockwork Orange* verlangt auch vom muttersprachlichen Leser einen gewissen Einsatz bei der Entschlüsselung der Erzählersprache. Dem wurde insoweit Rechnung getragen, als nicht jede ungewöhnliche Wortwahl oder Phrase des Englischen kommentiert wurde, solange die Erschließung im Rahmen einer allgemeinen Kenntnis von Vokabular, Grammatik und Wortbildung der englischen Sprache durch den fremdsprachlichen Leser angenommen werden kann.

Im Glossar verwendete englische Abkürzungen

adv.	adverb
AE	American English
arch.	archaic (veraltet)
BE	British English
coll.	colloquial (umgangssprachlich)
dial.	dialectal (mundartlich)
fig.	figuratively (übertragen)
Fr.	French
iron.	ironical
Ital.	Italian
N.	Nadsat
obs.	obsolete (nicht mehr gebräuchlich)
o.s.	oneself
pej.	pejorative (abschätzig)
pl.	plural
poet.	poetical (dichterisch, gehoben)
prov.	proverbial (sprichwörtlich)
Russ.	Russian
s.o.	someone
s.th.	something

Literaturhinweise

I. Bibliographien

Boytinck, Paul, *Anthony Burgess: An Annotated Bibliography and Reference Guide*, New York 1985.

Brewer, Jeutonne, *Anthony Burgess: A Bibliography. With a Foreword by Anthony Burgess*, Metuchen (N.J.) 1980.

II. Interviews mit Anthony Burgess

Ingersoll, Earl G. / Ingersoll, Mary C. (Hrsg.), *Conversations with Anthony Burgess*, Jackson 2008.

III. Kommentare von Anthony Burgess zu *A Clockwork Orange*

»The Manicheans«, in: *Times Literary Supplement*, 3. März 1966, S. 153 f.

»Clockwork Marmalade«, in: *Listener*, 17. Februar 1972, S. 197–199.

»You've Had Your Time«, in: *Malahat Review* Nr. 44 (1977) S. 10–16.

»Clockwork Oranges«, in: A. B., *1985*, Boston 1978, S. 84–99.

»Introduction«, in: A. B., *A Clockwork Orange*, New York 1988, S. V–XI.

IV. Sekundärliteratur

Aggeler, Geoffrey, »Pelagius and Augustine in the Novels of Anthony Burgess«, in: *English Studies* 55 (1974) S. 43–55.

– *Anthony Burgess: The Artist as Novelist*, Tuscaloosa 1979.

Aggeler, Geoffrey, (Hrsg.), *Critical Essays on Anthony Burgess*, Boston 1986.

Anderson, Ken, »A Note on *A Clockwork Orange*«, in: *Notes on Contemporary Literature* 2 (1972) S. 5–7.

Biswell, Andrew, *The Real Life of Anthony Burgess*, London 2005.

Bloom, Harold (Hrsg.), *Anthony Burgess*, New York 1987.

Bowie, Robert, »Freedom and Art in *A Clockwork Orange:* Anthony Burgess and the Christian Premises of Dostoevsky«, in: *Thought* 56 (1981) S. 402–416.

Brophy, Elizabeth, *A Clockwork Orange:* English and Nadsat«, in: *Notes on Contemporary Literature* 2 (1972) S. 4f.

Carson, Julie, »Pronomilization in *A Clockwork Orange*«, in: *Papers on Language and Literature* 12 (1976) S. 200–205.

Coale, Samuel, *Anthony Burgess*, New York 1981.

Coleman, Julian, »Burgess' *A Clockwork Orange*«, in: *Explicator* 42 (1983) S. 62f.

Connelly, Wayne C., »Optimism in Burgess' *A Clockwork Orange*«, in: *Extrapolation: A Science-Fiction Newsletter* 14 (1972) S. 25–29.

Cullinan, John, »Anthony Burgess' *A Clockwork Orange:* Two Versions«, in: *English Language Notes* 9 (1972) S. 287–292.

Derrick, Christopher, »This Our Exile: The Novels of Anthony Burgess«, in: *Triumph* 2 (1967) S. 28–33.

De Vitis, A. A., *Anthony Burgess*, New York 1972.

Dix, Carol M., *Anthony Burgess*, London 1971.

Evans, Robert O., »*Nadsat:* The Argot and Its Implications in Anthony Burgess' *A Clockwork Orange*«, in: *Journal of Modern Literature* 1 (1971) S. 406–410.

– »The *nouveau roman*, Russian Dystopias and Anthony Burgess«, in: *Studies in the Literary Imagination* 6 (1973) S. 27–37.

Ghosh-Schellhorn, Martina, *Anthony Burgess: A Study in Character*, Frankfurt a. M. 1986.

Guetti, James, »Voiced Narrative: *A Clockwork Orange*«, in: J. G., *Word-Music: The Aesthetic Aspect of Narrative Fiction*, New Brunswick (N. J.) 1980, S. 54–76.

Hanselmann, Gottfried, *Die Zukunftsromane von Anthony Burgess*, Pfaffenweiler 1985.

Hartveit, Lars, »Anthony Burgess, *A Clockwork Orange.* Impact and Form: The Limits of Persuasion«, in: L. H., *The Art of Persuasion: A Study of Six Novels*, Bergen 1977, S. 117–131.

Ingersoll, Earl, »Burgess' A Clockwork Orange, in: Explicator 45
(1986) S. 60–62.

LeClair, Thomas, »Essential Opposition: The Novels of Anthony
Burgess«, in: Critique: Studies in Modern Fiction 12 (1971) S. 77–94.

Lewis, Roger, Anthony Burgess: A Biography, London 2002.

Matthews, Richard, The Clockwork Universe of Anthony Burgess,
San Bernardino (Cal.) 1978.

Mentzer, Thomas L., »The Ethics of Behavior Modification: A Clockwork Orange Revisited«, in: Essays in Arts and Sciences 9 (1980)
S. 93–105.

Morris, Robert K., The Consolations of Philosophy: An Essay on the
Novels of Anthony Burgess, Columbia (Mo.) 1971.

Petrix, Esther, »Linguistics, Mechanics, and Metaphysics: Anthony
Burgess's A Clockwork Orange (1962)«, in: Old Lines, New Forces:
Essays on the Contemporary British Novel, 1960–1970, hrsg. von
Robert K. Morris, Rutherford (N.J.) 1976, S. 38–52.

Petzold, Dieter, »Der Moralist als Provokateur: Anthony Burgess's
Erfolgsroman A Clockwork Orange«, in: Anglistik und Englisch-
unterricht 19 (1983) S. 7–20.

Pritchard, William H., »The Novels of Anthony Burgess«, in:
Massachussetts Review (1966) S. 525–539.

Rabinovitz, Rubin, »Mechanism vs. Organism: Anthony Burgess'
A Clockwork Orange«, in: Modern Fiction Studies 24 (1978/79)
S. 538–541.

– »Ethical Values in Anthony Burgess' A Clockwork Orange«, in:
Studies in the Novel 11 (1979) S. 43–50.

Ray, Philip E., »Alex before and after: A New Approach to Burgess'
A Clockwork Orange«, in: Modern Fiction Studies 27 (1981)
S. 479–487.

Roughley, Alan R. (Hrsg.), Anthony Burgess and Modernity,
Manchester 2008.

Sheldon, Leslie, »Newspeak and Nadsat: The Disintegration of
Language in 1984 and A Clockwork Orange«, in: Studies in
Contemporary Satire 6 (1979) S. 7–13.

Stoll, Bettina, »Die Russizismen der ›Nadsat‹-Sprache in A Clock-

work Orange«, in: *Literatur in Wissenschaft und Unterricht* 20
(1987) S. 364–373.

Stumm, Reinhardt, »Eine Dampfwalze an Vitalität: Porträt des
Schriftstellers Anthony Burgess«, in: *Die Zeit*, 24. Oktober 1980,
S. 60 f.

Tilton, John W., »*A Clockwork Orange*: Awareness is All«,
in: J.W.T., *Cosmic Satire in the Contemporary Novel*, Lewisburg
(Pa.) 1977, S. 21–42.

www.anthonyburgess.org

Zeittafel zu Leben und Werk von Anthony Burgess

1917 Am 25. Februar in Manchester geboren und auf den Namen John Burgess Wilson getauft. Anthony ist der Konfirmationsname.

1940 Abgang von der Universität Manchester mit dem Grad des Bachelor of Arts in Englischer Literatur.

1940–46 Dienst in der britischen Armee.

1942 Eheschließung mit Llewela Isherwood Jones am 28. Januar.

1943 Burgess' Ehefrau wird in London von amerikanischen Deserteuren angegriffen und schwer misshandelt.

1946–54 Verschiedene Lehrtätigkeiten an Schulen und Colleges.

1949 Abfassung des ersten Romans, *Vision of Battlement* (1965 erschienen).

1954–59 Tätigkeit als Erziehungsoffizier in Malaya und Borneo.

1956 Erscheinen von *Time for a Tiger* (Roman) unter dem Namen Anthony Burgess.

1958 *Enemy in the Blanket* (Roman); *English Literature. A Survey for Students.*

1959 *Beds in the East* (Roman). Rückkehr aus Borneo; (falsche) Diagnose eines Gehirntumors; von da an hauptberuflich Schriftsteller.

1960 *The Doctor Is Sick* (Roman); *The Right to an Answer* (Roman).

1961 *Devil of a State* (Roman); *One Hand Clapping* (Roman; erschienen unter dem Pseudonym Joseph Kell); *The Worm and the Ring* (Roman). Beginn einer umfangreichen Tätigkeit als Essayist und Rezensent. Reise nach Leningrad, deren Eindrücke sich in vielerlei Hinsicht in *A Clockwork Orange* niederschlagen.

1962 *The Wanting Seed* (Roman); *A Clockwork Orange* (Roman).

1963 *Honey for the Bears* (Roman); *Inside Mr. Enderby* (Roman; unter dem Pseudonym Joseph Kell veröffentlicht); *The Novel Today* (Literaturkritik).

1964 *The Eve of Saint Venus* (Roman); *Language Made Plain* (linguistisches Werk); *The Malayan Trilogy* (Roman; beinhaltet *Time for a Tiger, Enemy in the Blanket, Beds in the East*; in Amerika 1965 u. d. T. *The Long Day Wanes*); *Nothing Like the Sun. A Story of Shakespeare's Love-life* (Roman). Geburt des Sohnes Andrea, aus einer Beziehung mit Liliana Macellari.

1965 *Here Comes Everybody. An Introduction to James Joyce for the Ordinary Reader; Vision of Battlements* (Roman).

1966 *Tremor of Intent* (Roman).

1967 *The Novel Now* (Literaturkritik).

1968 Am 20. März Tod seiner Frau, möglicherweise im Zusammenhang mit Folgen des Überfalls von 1943. Heirat mit Liliana Macellari im Dezember. Erscheinen von *Enderby Outside* (Roman; in Amerika zusammen mit *Inside Mr. Enderby* u. d. T. *Enderby*) und *Urgent Copy* (Literaturkritik). Umzug nach Malta aus Protest gegen die Steuerpolitik der englischen Regierung.

1969 Beginn gelegentlicher USA-Aufenthalte als Gastdozent an verschiedenen Universitäten.

1970 *Shakespeare* (Biographie).

1971 *MF* (Roman). Verfilmung von *A Clockwork Orange* durch Stanley Kubrick. Umzug nach Rom.

1973 *Joysprick. An Introduction to the Language of James Joyce; Cyrano!* (Musical-Libretto). Burgess beginnt, Fernseh- und Hörspiele zu verfassen.

1974 *Clockwork Testament; Or, Enderby's End* (Roman); *Napoleon Symphony* (Roman).

1975 »Symphony in C« (Komposition, aufgeführt in Iowa City).

1976 *Beard's Roman Women* (Roman); *Moses: A Narrative* (Gedicht); *New York* (Reiseliteratur). Umzug nach Monte Carlo.

1977 *Abba Abba* (Roman).

1978 *Ernest Hemingway and His World* (Biographie); *1985* (Roman).

1979 *Man of Nazareth* (Roman).

Nachwort

Im Jahre 1959 kehrte Anthony Burgess im Alter von zweiundvierzig Jahren von einer fünfjährigen Tätigkeit als Lehrer in Malaya und Borneo nach England zurück. Zu jener Zeit hatte er drei Romane veröffentlicht, die später unter dem Titel *The Malayan Trilogy* (1964; auch u. d. T. *The Long Day Wanes*, 1981) zusammengefasst wurden. Ärztliche Untersuchungen nach der Rückkehr schienen das Vorhandensein eines Gehirntumors zu bestätigen, Burgess verweigerte jedoch eine Operation, und die Ärzte gaben ihm noch ein Jahr. Burgess entschied sich, den Rest seines Lebens als Schriftsteller zu verbringen, und schrieb ab November 1959 in zwölf Monaten fünf Romane, mit denen er die Versorgung seiner Frau nach seinem Ableben sicherzustellen hoffte. Diese Romane erschienen in den folgenden Jahren (teilweise unter dem Pseudonym Joseph Kell), und nachdem sich die ärztliche Diagnose später als falsch erwies, umfasst das Œuvre von Anthony Burgess eine große Zahl von weiteren Romanen, Sachtexten aller Art, Fernsehspielen und musikalischen Kompositionen.[1]

A Clockwork Orange entstand 1961 nach einem Aufenthalt von Burgess in Leningrad. Bei seinem Erscheinen im Jahre 1962 deutete zunächst wenig darauf hin, dass ausgerechnet dieser Roman in der Folgezeit in erster Linie mit dem Autor Anthony Burgess assoziiert werden sollte. Das Buch erhielt in England eher dürftige Kritiken, während es

---

1 Zur Biographie vgl. Paul Boytinck, »Anthony Burgess: Biographical Background«, in: P. B., *Anthony Burgess: An Annotated Bibliography and Reference Guide*, New York 1985, S. VI–XXXV.

in den USA immerhin zu einem Kulterfolg unter College-Studenten wurde. All dies sollte sich jedoch Anfang der siebziger Jahre ändern, als der Regisseur Stanley Kubrick das Buch verfilmte und mit dem Film einen Skandalerfolg erzielte, der heftige Diskussionen auslöste und den Autor der Romanvorlage berühmt machte. Burgess selbst war die Tatsache, dass sein Ruhm auf diesem einen Werk gründen sollte, recht unangenehm, und wiederholt wertete er das Buch als einen bloßen »jeu de spleen«[2] ab, als zu didaktisch und zu exhibitionistisch in seinem Sprachgebrauch.[3] Ebenfalls nicht gefallen konnte es ihm, dass die Leser des Buches in verschiedenen Teilen der Welt unterschiedliche Textfassungen angeboten bekamen. Bereits 1963 hatte sich der amerikanische Verlag geweigert, das letzte Kapitel, welches ihm zu sentimental erschien, in die amerikanische Ausgabe aufzunehmen, eine Vorgehensweise, die 1972 dann auch für eine englische Taschenbuch-Neuauflage übernommen wurde.[4]

»Horror farce? Social prophecy? Penetrating study of human choice between good and evil?« Dies sind die Deutungsmöglichkeiten, die der englische Taschenbuchverlag

2 Zit. nach: Thomas Churchill, »An Interview with Anthony Burgess«, in: *Malahat Review* Nr. 17 (Januar 1971) S. 103–127.

3 Vgl. Anthony Burgess, *1985*, Boston 1978, S. 94.

4 Zur Signifikanz der unterschiedlichen Versionen siehe John Cullinan, »Anthony Burgess' *A Clockwork Orange*: Two Versions«, in: *English Language Notes* 9 (Juni 1972) S. 287–292. – Andrew Biswell weist in seiner Einführung zur *Restored Edition* (S. xxii f.) darauf hin, dass Burgess sich wohl selbst nicht ganz sicher war, welche Version zu bevorzugen sei. Spätere Ausgaben zu seinen Lebzeiten erschienen allerdings immer mit dem letzten Kapitel.

dem Leser auf dem Umschlag anbot.[5] Erstere Einschätzung mag es sein, die Buchhändler gelegentlich veranlasst, das Buch in die Abteilung »Thriller« und damit implizit immer noch in den Bereich der sogenannten Trivialliteratur abzuschieben, eine Einordnung, die dem Roman sicher nicht gerecht wird. Die Verweise auf die gesellschaftliche Komponente des Textes und auf seine philosophische Fragestellung bezeichnen genauer das Spektrum, innerhalb dessen er diskutiert und gedeutet werden kann.

In welche Welt entführt uns Burgess in seinem »Zukunftsroman«[6]? Abgesehen von einem Rückverweis auf die lange zurückliegenden sechziger Jahre (vgl. S. 16) erhalten wir keinen Hinweis auf Zeit und Ort des Geschehens; wir befinden uns in einer nicht benannten Metropole in einer Zeit, die dem Erscheinungsdatum des Romans um vermutlich einige Jahrzehnte vorausgreift. Der technische Fortschritt (Menschen auf dem Mond, weltweites Satellitenfernsehen) ist schon bald Wirklichkeit geworden; es gibt in diesem Bereich kaum etwas, das den Leser überraschen dürfte. Ähnlich wie George Orwell in *Nineteen Eighty-Four*, dessen London mancherlei Züge des London der Jahre des Zweiten Weltkriegs trägt, hat Burgess Gegenwartsphänomene der frühen sechziger Jahre in Form einer satirischen Extrapolation in die Zukunft verlagert, und in vieler Hinsicht mag uns die Welt von *A Clockwork Orange* von brennender Aktualität erscheinen: Die Bevölkerung

5 Vgl. Anthony Burgess, *A Clockwork Orange*, Harmondsworth 1972.
6 Für diese Bezeichnung hat sich Gottfried Hanselmann in seiner Diskussion der Gattungszugehörigkeit des Romans entschieden. Vgl. G. Hanselmann, *Die Zukunftsromane von Anthony Burgess*, Pfaffenweiler 1985, S. XI.

lebt in Mietskasernen und verbringt die Abende vor dem Fernsehschirm, während Jugendbanden die Straßen der entvölkerten Innenstadt unsicher machen; Bibliotheken werden wenig frequentiert und Zeitungen kaum gelesen; Burgess diagnostiziert die Dominanz einer Massenkultur, die deutliche Elemente wachsender Infantilisierung zeigt und in der die Vorliebe des Protagonisten für klassische Musik, die er mit seinem Schöpfer teilt, gar zu einem Objekt der Lächerlichkeit wird.

Wir erfahren nichts über die territoriale Gestalt dieses Staatswesens. Um einen Weltstaat handelt es sich aber trotz der weltweiten Fernsehübertragungen wohl nicht; immerhin rühmt sich die Regierung noch mit außenpolitischen Erfolgen. Eine Straße ist nach Juri Gagarin, dem ersten Mann im Weltraum, benannt, die Filme, die in den Kinos gezeigt werden, gehen dagegen eindeutig auf Hollywood-Vorbilder zurück. Die Tatsache jedoch, dass diese Filme von einer Firma namens »Statefilm« vertrieben werden, weist auf eine Wendung zu sozialistischen Wirtschaftsformen hin. Es herrscht Arbeitspflicht, die Mutter des Protagonisten arbeitet in einem staatlichen Supermarkt, die Gemälde in den Mietskasernen sind im Stil des sozialistischen Realismus gehalten: alles Indizien für einen beträchtlichen Einfluss des Staates auf Wirtschafts- und Privatleben. Das System hat jedoch noch demokratischen Charakter, denn es gibt eine Opposition, die sich Hoffnungen macht, die Regierung bei den kommenden Wahlen ablösen zu können. Diese Regierung jedoch befindet sich an der Schwelle des Übergangs zu totalitären Herrschaftsformen: die Methoden der Konditionierung und Gehirnwäsche sollen bei gewöhnlichen

Kriminellen unter anderem auch eingesetzt werden, um in den Gefängnissen Platz für politische Gegner zu schaffen. Alles in allem scheint es sich bei dem beschriebenen System, ganz im Sinne der in den sechziger Jahren häufig vertretenen Theorie von der Konvergenz der politischen Systeme, um eine Mischung von Erscheinungsformen der westlichen Gesellschaft mit von Burgess bei seinem Besuch in der Sowjetunion beobachteten Elementen des dortigen Gesellschaftssystems zu handeln.

Eine besondere Affinität zum Russischen weist auch die Sprache der Jugendlichen auf, von der der Leser durch die Erzählung des »Helden« Alex einen ausführlichen Eindruck erhält. Es handelt sich hier eindeutig um eine Gruppensprache, die Personen außerhalb der Gruppe nicht automatisch zugänglich ist. So erkundigt sich Dr Brodsky bei seinem Assistenten nach der Herkunft des »dialect of the tribe« und erhält folgende Erklärung: »Odd bits of old rhyming slang [...]. A bit of gypsy talk, too. But most of the roots are Slav« (S. 147). Diese Beschreibung ist jedoch nur teilweise zutreffend. Bisher ist es nicht gelungen, Elemente des Romani nachzuweisen, und obwohl Alex' Redeweise von zahlreichen Slangbegriffen durchsetzt ist, kann von einer Dominanz des Cockney Rhyming Slang nicht gesprochen werden. Insofern allerdings, als der Rhyming Slang eine besonders kreative Form des Sprachgebrauchs darstellt, besteht der Bezug zu Recht, denn auch Alex' Umgang mit der englischen Sprache ist von hoher schöpferischer Kraft. Dies äußert sich in der Neubildung von Worten und Phrasen, der virtuosen Mischung von zeitgenössischen und obsoleten Redeformen, dem spielerischen Umgang mit den Wortarten. Richtig konstatiert von

Dr Branom ist allerdings der Anteil des Slawischen, genauer der russischen Sprache, an dem »nadsat talk« (von der russischen Endung -*nadcat*ı-teenı bzw. ı-zehnı) genannten Jargon. Zahlreiche Wörter, die sich aus dem Kontext nicht leicht erschließen lassen, erklärt der Rückgriff auf die russische Wurzel.[7] Burgess selbst führt verschiedene Gründe für die Einführung dieser Kunstsprache an: Zum einen funktioniert sie als eine Einführung in die Technik der Gehirnwäsche, dem Leser wird durch die Lektüre des Buchs in subtiler Weise der Grundstock eines russischen Vokabulars vermittelt;[8] zum anderen schafft sie eine gewisse Distanz zum andernfalls pornographischen Effekt der Gewaltdarstellung;[9] und letztlich hat eine künstlich entwickelte Teenager-Sprache gegenüber tatsächlichem Slang den Vorteil, nicht durch den permanenten Sprachwandel an Aktualität und Verständlichkeit zu verlieren.[10] Wichtig ist jedoch ein weiterer Effekt. Über die Sprache zieht Alex

---

7 Vgl. hierzu Bettina Stoll, »Die Russizismen der ıNadsatı-Sprache in *A Clockwork Orange*«, in: *Literatur in Wissenschaft und Unterricht* 20 (1987) S. 364–373.

8 Vgl. Anthony Burgess, »Clockwork Marmalade«, in: *The Listener*, 17. Februar 1972, S. 197–199.

9 Vgl. Anthony Burgess, »Introduction«, in A.B., *A Clockwork Orange*, New York 1988, S. X.

10 Vgl. Reinhardt Stumm, »Eine Dampfwalze an Vitalität: Porträt des Schriftstellers Anthony Burgess«, in: *Die Zeit*, 24. Oktober 1980, S. 60 f. Die Verwendung von Kunstsprachen in Zukunftsromanen hat Tradition. Verwiesen sei hier nicht nur erneut auf Orwells *Nineteen Eighty-Four* (1948), sondern auch auf Vladimir Nabokovs *Bend Sinister* (1947). Dass Burgess' Lust am Spiel mit der Sprache nicht zuletzt auch von dem von ihm hochgeschätzten James Joyce beeinflusst ist, braucht kaum betont zu werden.

als Erzähler den Leser in seine Welt. In dem Maße, wie es ihm gelingt, unsere Neugier zu wecken, so dass wir uns auf die Entschlüsselung des Jargons einlassen, gelingt es Alex, uns auf seine Seite zu bringen, und dies ist notwendig, wenn wir im dritten Teil des Romans Mitleid mit ihm in seiner Opferrolle empfinden sollen. Dazu trägt auch die durch die Virtuosität der Sprache erreichte Distanzierung von den Gewaltakten der beiden ersten Teile bei.

Bei aller sprachlichen Virtuosität bleibt Alex jedoch ein Erzähler, der eine Geschichte erzählt, deren Implikationen er nicht begreift. Die einleitende, zu Beginn aller Hauptteile wiederholte Frage »What's it going to be then, eh?« impliziert sowohl eine Wahlmöglichkeit als auch eine Suche und deutet damit den thematischen Rahmen des Buches an. Alex verbringt seine Zeit mit einer wahl- und ziellosen Reihe von Gewaltakten. Er ist sich bewusst, dass er sich damit außerhalb der Gesellschaft stellt, ohne dass er letztlich in der Lage ist, die Gründe für seine Gewalttätigkeit zu analysieren. Die in einem Zeitungsartikel aufgeführten Erklärungsmuster reichen kaum aus: Der Hinweis auf fehlende Disziplinierung durch Eltern und Lehrer bringt Alex nur zum Lachen; die Erklärung jugendlicher Gewalt durch die Unzulänglichkeit der Erwachsenenwelt wird von ihm in ironischer Weise zur eigenen Entlastung aufgegriffen, gerade dadurch aber auch als unzureichend entlarvt, ebenso wie der erhoffte zivilisierende Effekt großer Kunst; bei Alex steigert der Musikgenuss eher die Lust an der Gewalttätigkeit.[11] Alex versteht sich selbst nicht als Kriminellen,

11 Vgl. hierzu Hanselmann, *Die Zukunftsromane von Anthony Burgess*, S. 25–28.

immer wieder betont er, dass er nicht mit den übrigen Gefängnisinsassen auf eine Stufe gestellt werden möchte. Gewalt scheint für ihn eher ein ästhetisches Phänomen als ein moralisches oder gesellschaftliches Problem zu sein. Als der Staat bereit ist, zur Reduzierung der allgemeinen Kriminalität »Ludovico's Technique« (S. 110), eine neue Methode der Gehirnwäsche, einzusetzen, ist Alex angesichts der Aussicht, bald freizukommen, sofort bereit, sich dem Verfahren zu unterziehen, ohne sich seine Auswirkungen vorstellen zu können. Es bleibt dem Gefängnispfarrer vorbehalten, die philosophische Fragestellung und damit die zentrale Thematik des Buches aufzuwerfen: »What does God want? Does God want goodness or the choice of goodness? Is a man who chooses the bad perhaps in some way better than a man who has the good imposed upon him?« (S. 124).

An dieser Stelle ist es sinnvoll, einen Blick auf das hinter dieser Fragestellung stehende Menschenbild des Autors zu werfen. Burgess bezeichnet sich selbst als »Lancashire Catholic [...] unhealthily interested in free will and original sin«,[12] und die Problematik des Zusammenhangs von Willensfreiheit, Erbsünde und dem Verhältnis von Gut und Böse spielt in seinem Gesamtwerk eine zentrale Rolle, vornehmlich in der Auseinandersetzung mit den theologischen Konzepten der Kirchenlehrer Augustinus und Pelagius aus dem 5. Jahrhundert.[13] Beide differieren vor allem in

---

12 Anthony Burgess, »You've Had Your Time«, in: *Malahat Review* Nr. 44 (1977) S. 14 f.

13 Vgl. hierzu Geoffrey Aggeler, »Pelagius and Augustine in the Novels of Anthony Burgess«, in: *English Studies* 55 (1974) S. 43–55.

der Beurteilung der Erbsünde und der Rolle göttlicher Gnade bei der Erlösung des Menschen. Pelagius sieht den Menschen unbelastet von der Erbsünde, d.h. frei von Schuld und damit imstande, unabhängig von göttlicher Gnade aus eigener Anstrengung das Heil zu erreichen. Für Augustinus dagegen ist der Mensch als Folge der Erbsünde schuldig geboren, allein die göttliche Gnade ermöglicht es ihm, das Gute zu erkennen und erlöst zu werden. Die Entscheidung für das Gute muss jedoch auch bei Augustinus auf einer freien Willensentscheidung beruhen, da andernfalls die göttliche Bestrafung des Bösen nicht gerecht wäre. Bis zu diesem Punkt folgt Burgess dem Augustinus, in seiner Beurteilung des Bösen enthält die seinen Romanen zugrunde liegende Philosophie jedoch ein deutliches Element des Manichäismus, insofern als für ihn das Böse nicht einfach die Abwesenheit des Guten ist, sondern völlig unabhängig davon gedacht werden muss. Im Rahmen dieses Dualismus von Gut und Böse existiert der Mensch als eine Mischform, in der beide Elemente präsent sind und einen dauernden Kampf austragen. Martina Ghosh-Schellhorn bringt Burgess' Position folgendermaßen auf den Punkt: »Burgess sees man as being guilty of sin from the moment of his birth onwards and only capable of being saved by God's grace and not through his own efforts. In this fallen state, the only God-given gift left to man is his own free will by which he can choose either salvation or damnation.«[14] Die Kunst spielt in diesem Weltbild eine entschei-

14 Martina Ghosh-Schellhorn, *Anthony Burgess: A Study in Character*, Frankfurt a. M. 1986, S. 46. Zum philosophischen Hintergrund insgesamt vgl. S. 43–48.

dende Rolle, ist sie doch die Kraft, die die Gegensätze des manichäischen Dualismus überwinden und einheitsstiftend wirken kann, womit die künstlerische Tätigkeit ein positiver Wert an sich ist.

Die Antwort auf die oben zitierten Fragen des Gefängnispfarrers gibt der dritte Teil. Wenn Alex vom Täter zum hilflosen Opfer wird, so zeigt sich, dass mit der physischen Abneigung gegen Gewalt mitnichten ein Impuls zum Guten verbunden ist. Alex ist nur noch mitleiderregend, die Wandlung zur »Clockwork Orange« ist vollzogen und er reagiert nur noch mechanisch, wie auf Kommando, auf bestimmte Stimuli.[15] Den menschenunwürdigen Charakter dieser Konditionierung verdeutlicht vor allem ihr Nebenprodukt, der Verlust der Fähigkeit zum Musikgenuss. Musik ist für Burgess »a figure of celestial bliss«, sie nicht mehr genießen zu können, heißt »the gates of heaven are closed to the boy«.[16]

Wichtig in diesem Zusammenhang ist auch, dass Alex im dritten Teil in mehrfachem Sinne ein Opfer von staatlicher Gewalt und Politik im allgemeinen wird. Bereits die ersten beiden Teile hatten in ihrer Darstellung wenig

15 Burgess hat den Titel mehrfach erklärt: »In 1945, back from the army, I heard an 80-year-old Cockney in a London pub say that somebody was ›as queer as a clockwork orange‹. The ›queer‹ did not mean homosexual: it meant mad. The phrase intrigued me with its unlikely tension of demotic and surrealistic. For nearly twenty years I wanted to use it as the title of something. [...] It was a traditional trope, and it asked to entitle a work which combined a concern with tradition and a bizarre technique« (A. Burgess, »Clockwork Marmalade«, S. 197 f.

16 Anthony Burgess, 1985, S. 95.

Vertrauen in einen Staat erkennen lassen, dessen Polizei zur Gewalttätigkeit neigt und dessen Strafvollzug kaum geeignet erscheint, tatsächlich einen Besserungseffekt zu erreichen. Dieser Eindruck verstärkt sich im dritten Teil, wenn sich herausstellt, dass die Brutalität der Polizei letztlich darauf beruht, dass sie sich aus jugendlichen Gewalttätern rekrutiert, die ihr früheres Privatvergnügen nun staatlich sanktioniert betreiben dürfen. Als wenig besser erweisen sich allerdings auch jene, die vorgeben, Alex zu helfen. Bereits der Gefängnispfarrer hatte zwar die angemessenen Fragen angesichts der staatlich eingesetzten Gehirnwäsche aufgeworfen, gleichzeitig ist er aber dem Alkohol zugetan, und seine tatsächlichen Handlungen werden vor allem von Gesichtspunkten der Karriereplanung bestimmt; ebenso erweisen sich die politischen Gegner der Regierung für Alex als falsche Freunde, die zur Erlangung ihrer (macht)politischen Ziele auch seinen Tod bewusst einkalkulieren.

Vor diesem Hintergrund erscheint auch die Antwort des Romans auf den zweiten Teil der Frage des Gefängnispfarrers eindeutig. Betrachtet man den freien Willen als konstitutiven Bestandteil der menschlichen Existenz, so muss man auch die Möglichkeit akzeptieren, dass der Mensch sich für das Böse entscheiden kann; die Fähigkeit zur freien Entscheidung ist höher zu schätzen als das erzwungene Gute, und dies umso mehr, da Staat und Politik nicht zuzutrauen ist, tatsächlich das Gute schaffen zu können. In dem Sinne, dass er seine Entscheidungsfreiheit zurückerhalten hat, kann Alex am Ende des 20. Kapitels tatsächlich als geheilt betrachtet werden, wie er es selbst formuliert. Angesichts seiner scheinbar ungebrochenen Gewaltbereitschaft eine wenig hoffnungsvolle Aussicht, die die pessimistische Weltsicht des Autors zu bestätigen scheint.

Doch zu einer Antwort auf die Ausgangsfrage »What's it going to be then, eh?« gelangt Alex erst im letzten Kapitel. Er hat die Lust an der puren Gewalttätigkeit verloren, was sich auch in einer Veränderung seines musikalischen Geschmacks niederschlägt, und er wird sich auf die Suche nach einem Partner[17] fürs Leben machen und träumt davon, Vater eines Sohnes zu werden. Alex interpretiert seine Situation im Rahmen eines zyklischen Geschichtsverständnisses, welches seine Parallele in der Struktur des Buches findet, einer Struktur, deren Symmetrie und Abrundung durch den Verzicht auf das 21. Kapitel beträchtlich gestört wird. Der dritte Teil hat Alex an die Orte und zu den Personen des ersten Teils zurückgeführt, und der Kreis schließt sich, als er im letzten Kapitel mit seinen neuen Droogs an den Ausgangspunkt der Geschichte zurückgekehrt ist.

Für Alex selbst wird sich die Geschichte nicht wiederholen, wohl aber für seinen Sohn, zu dem er sein Leben in Beziehung setzt. Aus diesem Blickwinkel gewinnt auch die Parallelisierung von Alex mit F. Alexander, dem Bewohner eines Hauses mit dem Namen »Home«, in das Alex als eine Art verlorener Sohn zurückkehrt, an Bedeutung. »Good Bog [...] he is another Alex« (S. 196), denkt sich Alex, als er den Namen seines vermeintlichen Wohltäters entdeckt, doch nicht nur der Name verbindet die beiden. Beide sind

---

17 Frauen tauchen in *A Clockwork Orange* nahezu ausschließlich als Opfer und niemals als Täter auf, was die Frage der Willensentscheidung für oder gegen das Böse als ein ausgesprochen männliches Problem erscheinen lässt.

Autoren eines Buches mit dem Titel *A Clockwork Orange*; die in F. Alexander angelegte Gewalttätigkeit, als ihm zu dämmern beginnt, dass es sich bei Alex um den Vergewaltiger seiner Frau handelt, verdeutlicht, dass auch in ihm der manichäische Dualismus von Gut und Böse präsent ist, und am Ende landet er, genauso wie zuvor Alex, im Gefängnis, ein Opfer staatlicher Gewalt. Die beiden repräsentieren also, ebenso wie Alex' erhoffter Sohn, Aspekte verschiedener Entwicklungsstadien menschlicher Reife.[18]

Die Frage persönlicher Willensfreiheit wird damit um einen zusätzlichen Gesichtspunkt erweitert. Alex erkennt, dass er nicht nur als Opfer staatlicher Konditionierung, sondern auch zuvor als Heranwachsender Züge einer »Clockwork Orange« trug, womit ein Grundstein zur Überwindung dieses Zustands gelegt ist. Die Fähigkeit des Menschen zu individuellem Wachstum blieb für Burgess als Hoffnungsschimmer zwischen den Polen dauernder Gewalt und willensbrechender Konditionierung, mag die Gattung als solche der schuldhaften Belastung durch die Erbsünde auch nicht entkommen können.

Claus Melchior

18 Vgl. hierzu Philip E. Ray, »Alex before and after: A New Approach to Burgess' *A Clockwork Orange*«, in: *Modern Fiction Studies* 27 (Herbst 1981) S. 479–487.

Inhalt